DEEP, a Gateway to the Creation-Energy Teaching

Waid Sainvil

Published by Franklin Publishers

Printed in the United States of America

For permissions, inquiries, or additional copies, contact:

Franklin Publishers

www.franklinpublishers.com

Preface

In a time when humanity has mastered the material world but often lost touch with its inner values and spiritual purpose, DEEP, Divine Energy Emanating Presence shines as an inviting gateway into Billy Meier's Creation-Energy Teaching. DEEP reminds us that at the heart of existence is a living, divine energy. Billy explains that Creation itself is "the purest spirit energy", the infinite universal consciousness that permeates all life. This means that each person carries a spark of Creation's own energy within. By opening to DEEP, we acknowledge that our true self is a vessel of this sacred energy and that we are fundamentally connected to the Source. In this light, DEEP invites us to remember the "true values of life" that have been forgotten, and to reawaken our awareness of the Creational laws that govern all existence.

In Billy's teachings, Creation's energy does not impose or judge, it offers unfailing support for inner growth and evolution. The Creation-energy Teaching describes a path of self-discovery leading away from false ideas and toward self-realization. It teaches that we each have the power to learn and grow, "every fundamental cause and effect rests on false ideas. The spiritual teachings lead out of these false ideas because they offer the path of self-recognition and self-realization". In other words, we must look within, cultivate our inner light, and let the divine energy that emanates from our own Presence guide us. This inner work is not limiting, but rather empowering. Billy assures us that in this process lies "a tremendous and unlimited potential, instead of limitations and failure".

Crucially, DEEP also emphasizes self-responsibility, a core tenet of the Creation-Energy Teaching. Billy insists that the individual "must therefore fully accept their own, full responsibility for their actions." We choose whether to live in harmony with the Creational-natural laws or to suffer the consequences of ignoring them. In his words, "Creation bears no responsibility whatsoever for any human action; humans alone are responsible for each and everything they do". DEEP builds on this by inspiring us to take charge of our lives with courage and integrity. When we align with the divine energy within us, we recognize that true empowerment comes from owning our choices. As Billy notes, modern society often loses "every bit of self-responsibility that is so urgently needed to lead a good, well-balanced, and Creationally-naturally appropriate life." Embracing DEEP means reclaiming that self-responsibility, understanding that we play a pivotal role in shaping our reality by our thoughts, intentions, and actions.

DEEP is also deeply aligned with the universal laws of Creation. Billy teaches that Creation's laws and directives are flawless and binding at every level of existence. These natural laws, such as cause and effect, compassion, and truth, regulate the life of every being. When we consciously connect to the divine energy within (DEEP), we become more aware of these laws. We see that acting in harmony with them is not a burden but a path to inner peace and alignment. In fact, cultivating DEEP naturally leads to the fruits of these laws, love, compassion, harmony and peace. As individuals grow in wisdom and responsibility, those qualities "carry into the world to the person next to them and the one beyond that. Eventually, the whole thing begins to snowball". DEEP, then, becomes a field of peace within us that radiates outward.

Self-Responsibility: The DEEP approach powerfully echoes Billy's call to accept full responsibility for our lives. Each person is urged to make conscious choices in accordance with Creational laws, knowing that we alone bear the results of our actions. In the Creation-energy Teaching, this autonomy is a gift, by owning our free will and choices as a divine gift, we empower ourselves to create wisely and grow spiritually.

Universal Creational Laws: DEEP affirms that there are immutable laws guiding the universe. Billy, describes Creation as the "purest spirit energy" and "highest energy form," whose "flawless laws and directives have unequivocal validity at every level of existence". Living DEEP means recognizing these universal principles, from the law of cause and effect to the directive of nonviolence, as benevolent guidelines that support our evolution, rather than arbitrary rules to follow.

Inner Transformation: Central to DEEP is the idea of inner metamorphosis. By meditating on and feeling the Divine Energy Emanating from our Presence, we engage in the same path Billy describes, a journey of self-recognition and self-realization. This inner work dispels the "false ideas" that limit us and unlocks our vast potential. As we align our intentions with the Creation-energy, we gain strength, courage and motivation to make positive changes in ourselves and the world.

Peace and Compassion: When DEEP is embodied, its natural fruits, peace, love, and compassion, flourish. Billy emphasizes that individuals who develop these qualities affect those around them. A kind, responsible person "conveys knowledge, love, harmony, peace, and a sense of responsibility into the world."In this light, practicing DEEP means kindling an inner sanctuary of peace that supports healing on all levels, encouraging us to treat others as reflections of the divine.

Conscious Evolution: Finally, DEEP points to the grand purpose of personal and planetary evolution. Meier's Creation-energy Teaching envisions that all life is evolving, an infinitely variable development of learning and cognition granted to all coarse-matter life-forms". By embracing DEEP, we align with this cosmic process. Our spiritual growth contributes to Creation's own unfoldment. In Billy's words, the goal is for humans to evolve "to their highest level of perfection so that they may join Creation in the future and become one with It, and therefore help Creation to evolve as well". DEEP invites us to see our personal transformation as part of a larger, beautiful upward spiral of consciousness.

As you reflect on DEEP and its resonance with these core ideas, know that this journey is meant to be transformative and uplifting. This book seeks to demystify Billy Meier's teachings for new seekers by using the DEEP framework, not to replace his message, but to illuminate it. Each chapter will invite you to go inward, to quiet your mind and listen to your own divine spark, and then to let that light inform how you live and serve. We come to understand that Creation's energy flows through every act of kindness, every moment of mindfulness, and every conscious breath.

Walk forward with an open heart and an inquisitive mind. Let DEEP guide you to experience the Creation-energy within you. As you grow in self-awareness and compassion, you will naturally embody the self-responsibility, harmony, and wisdom that Meier's teachings hold dear. In doing so, you join a vast, loving chorus of life evolving consciously. The path may challenge you at times, but remember the promise of the teaching: every effort toward truth brings hope, courage, and motivation to continue building a life of peace and purpose.

Welcome to this new spiritual journey. With each step, trust that the Divine Energy Emanating Presence within you is real, it is loving, and it is guiding you.

Table of contents

Chapter 1

The Creation Energy Teachings

———◆——◆◆——◆———

The Creation Energy Teachings, generously offered to us Earth people, are not intended for everyone at this moment in time. Although the knowledge they contain is universal and timeless, the readiness to receive and understand such profound wisdom is not yet widespread among humanity.

The collective consciousness of Earth is still heavily burdened by misconceptions, rigid belief systems, and a deep-seated resistance to true personal growth, all of which prevent many from even approaching these teachings with an open mind.

These teachings are primarily conveyed through the medium of written words, which already presents a significant challenge for the majority.

In today's world, it is no secret that reading has fallen out of favor among earth humans.

Many have developed an aversion to the discipline, patience, and introspection that reading requires.

Instead, they prefer to be entertained, spoken to, or guided passively by others.

The act of seeking knowledge independently, of sitting quietly, pondering deeply, and forming one's own understanding, has become a rarity.

This intellectual and spiritual laziness forms one of the great obstacles to humanity's evolution.

This tendency to avoid self-initiated discovery is precisely why countless millions continue to flock to churches, mosques, temples, and various places of worship.

There, they eagerly submit themselves to figures of authority, who dictate what they should believe and how they should live.

Often, this submission is not only willing but enthusiastic, people are prepared to pay lavishly for others to read and interpret sacred scriptures on their behalf.

They would rather be told than take the arduous path of discovery themselves.

In many ways, they remain like children, comfortable in their dependence, proud to be led, and resistant to the very idea of stepping into self-responsibility.

For such individuals, the Creation Energy Teachings remain inaccessible, for these teachings demand not passive belief, but active personal engagement, courage, and a breaking away from the familiar chains of tradition.

Only a few will possess the necessary attributes, the curiosity to question the status quo, the courage to face uncomfortable truths, and the inner drive to persist despite societal opposition, to genuinely seek out and work with these teachings.

If you find yourself among that rare and precious few, take a moment to honor the strength and resolve that have brought you this far.

Congratulations, brethren, you have chosen the path of the free human being, the path that leads beyond dogma, beyond programming, and beyond the illusions that have imprisoned humanity for millennia.

You are part of the vanguard that will help reshape the future.

Embracing the Creation Energy Teachings is not merely an intellectual pursuit, it is a transformational process that can profoundly awaken your consciousness.

As you absorb and integrate this knowledge, it has the potential to alter your inner essence, uplift and purify your thought processes, and even influence the deepest layers of your being, including your very DNA.

It can expand both the span and the depth of your life, imbuing it with new meaning, clarity, and purpose.

However, it is important to understand that this path does not promise instant miracles or external salvation.

Rather, it offers something far greater, an invitation to conscious evolution.

It calls you to step deliberately into truth, to seek balance in all things, and to embrace a freedom that can only be achieved through self-mastery.

Those who accept this invitation are not merely students of truth, they become living expressions of it.

Chapter 2

Racism

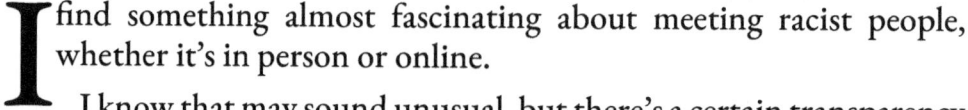

I find something almost fascinating about meeting racist people, whether it's in person or online.

I know that may sound unusual, but there's a certain transparency in the way they carry themselves, something that makes it surprisingly easy to understand them.

It's as if their true thoughts and feelings are always just beneath the surface, constantly spilling out through their words, actions, and attitudes.

What they believe is not something I need to search for, it's right there, for anyone willing to look closely.

What stands out most to me is how glaringly obvious their inner insecurities are.

Whether they express these insecurities through explosive outbursts of anger or through more subtle, dismissive gestures, it all points to one thing, discomfort with themselves.

They're often convinced they are projecting power, strength, and superiority, but what I see is a reflection of something much darker: Fear.

Fear of the unknown.

Fear of what's different.

Fear of change.

But most importantly, fear of being irrelevant in a world that is growing more diverse, complex, and interconnected by the day.

When I encounter someone like this, my immediate response isn't anger or hatred, but rather a sense of pity.

I can almost feel the anxiety and unease driving their need to put others down, to elevate themselves by diminishing those they see as "other."

It's like watching someone desperately trying to convince both themselves and everyone around them that they matter, that they're important, by pushing others away and making them smaller.

But in reality, this need for validation only reinforces their fragility, their lack of true confidence in themselves.

What I find most revealing is the predictability of their behavior.

I don't need to guess what they're thinking, it's all there, laid bare by their actions and words.

And while this might be unfortunate and saddening, it also offers a kind of clarity.

The more I observe, the more I realize how deeply their behavior is tied to a life lived in confusion and unresolved pain.

It's as if they're trapped in a never-ending cycle of trying to protect their fragile sense of self by creating divisions between themselves and the rest of the world.

And what's even more illuminating is that their attempts to assert superiority only highlight how much they fear their own inadequacies.

I've also come to understand something else that isn't often talked about, racism is not confined to any one group or community.

It's a mindset that can be found in every race, culture, and ethnicity.

People can harbor racist beliefs against individuals who look different from them, but they can also turn these beliefs inward, developing prejudices within their own racial or cultural group.

It's a painful irony, but it happens.

A person from one racial group may harbor hatred or distrust toward others of the same race simply because they feel inadequate or alienated from their own community.

This inner division is often the hardest to confront, because the people who hold these beliefs are most likely to deny them, even to themselves.

It's as though they are so deeply embedded in their own insecurities that they cannot bear to acknowledge the contradictions within.

Ultimately, this is why I find the encounter with racist people so revealing, though not in the way they might expect.

Their words and actions become like open books, telling a story that's often deeply painful, confused, and unresolved.

While I don't condone their views, I see them for what they truly are: a reflection of inner chaos, a desperate attempt to mask vulnerability with hate.

And while it may be frustrating to witness this behavior, it's also a reminder of the deep-rooted insecurity that underlies so much of human prejudice.

When we understand this, we can start to look at racism not just as an external problem, but as an internal struggle that every individual must confront within themselves.

Chapter 3

Knowing the Self

Knowing who you are is not just an intellectual exercise, it is the very foundation upon which all true progress and inner peace are built.

In a world where distractions abound and external pressures often dictate the direction of our lives, it is easy to lose touch with our authentic selves.

Yet, to truly awaken and move through life with purpose and clarity, one must first understand the essence of who they are.

This self-awareness is the key that unlocks the door to everything that follows, freedom, strength, fulfillment, and inner balance.

When a human being finally comes to the realization of their authentic self, when they recognize themselves as a unique yet integral part of Creation, a shift occurs.

It's not just a fleeting moment of insight that passes quickly, rather, it's a profound, lasting change in how they perceive themselves and the world around them.

This awakening is a deep, transformative experience, one that alters the very core of the individual.

In this state of realization, the person no longer feels bound by the fears, doubts, and limitations that once held them back.

Those obstacles, once perceived as insurmountable, dissolve, and a new landscape of possibilities opens up.

With the realization of one's true nature comes a deep sense of responsibility.

It's no longer enough to just exist or to passively drift through life. Instead, there arises an inner clarity, a profound sense of purpose.

19

This clarity doesn't come from external circumstances but from within, where one begins to understand that their actions, thoughts, and intentions are powerful.

The individual starts to feel an unshakable strength that no external force can shake, for it is rooted in the understanding of who they are at their core.

This is not a superficial confidence, but a deep and unbreakable conviction in one's own potential and in the harmonious flow of the universe.

Once you come to realize the truth of who you are, the way you perceive life shifts.

No longer do you see obstacles as roadblocks, but as opportunities for growth and evolution.

Life itself becomes a field of unlimited potential, where each challenge is a lesson, and every setback is a springboard for greater achievements.

The moment you connect with your true self, the external world no longer seems so daunting.

Instead, it becomes a canvas upon which you can paint your dreams and aspirations.

You begin to see that you are not a passive observer of life, but an active participant in the unfolding of your own destiny.

This awakening is the key to unlocking a power far greater than anything the material world can offer.

It is not about acquiring possessions or status, but about aligning with the deeper rhythms and laws of Creation itself.

When the truth of who you are sinks into the very core of your being, everything changes.

Your desires shift from being fleeting wishes into deeply held possibilities waiting to be realized.

The laws of the universe, once perceived as abstract or distant, become clear and accessible to you.

No longer is the gap between thought and experience a chasm, instead, the two begin to merge, and what was once considered impossible begins to feel natural.

For me, this journey of self-discovery has been nothing short of transformative.

In my quest for deeper understanding, I encountered the teachings of Billy Meier and the Creation Energy principles, and this discovery was nothing less than a revelation.

It lit a fire within me, a fire that continues to burn brightly with purpose and inspiration.

I came to realize that I could no longer keep this knowledge to myself.

The insights I had gained, the truths that had so profoundly affected my own life, could not remain hidden.

They needed to be shared, not as a mere intellectual pursuit but as a heartfelt calling to inspire others.

This recognition of truth and the inner drive to communicate it led me to writing. Writing became a natural extension of my journey.

It wasn't just a task or a project, it was a mission.

A mission to share not just the knowledge I had gained but the very experience of awakening to one's true self.

Through writing, I could express the depth of this journey and invite others to join in the discovery of their own potential.

Every word I wrote carried the energy of that realization, and every page was infused with the intention to inspire others to seek out the truth within themselves.

So far, I have written five books focused on the power and depth of the Creation Energy Teachings.

Each book has been more than just a collection of words on paper, they are expressions of a personal, profound journey.

These books represent my commitment to sharing the truth, my dedication to helping others recognize their own limitless potential.

Each one is a labor of love, born from a place of deep knowing and authentic self-expression.

It is my hope that these writings serve as beacons for those who are seeking meaning, truth, and a deeper connection with themselves.

Through my work, I aspire to light a path for others, a path that leads to greater self-awareness, inner peace, and personal transformation.

This has always been, and will continue to be, my mission: to serve the unfolding of human consciousness, to honor Creation, and to help others realize the infinite potential that lies within them.

We are all, at our core, connected to something far greater than ourselves, and once we recognize this truth, our lives begin to align with the higher purpose of our existence.

This is the essence of knowing the self, not simply understanding who we are, but embracing the profound role we play in the grand tapestry of Creation.

Chapter 4

Still in Love

I'm still in love.

Not in the urgent, breathless way I once was.

Not in the way that kept me awake at night or made my heart race at the sound of your voice.

That kind of love was intense, electric, full of fire, and like fire, it burned bright and hot, but eventually it softened into embers.

Now, it's something quieter, more enduring, a steady warmth that lives quietly within me, never demanding, only present.

Love like that doesn't simply vanish when a relationship ends.

It doesn't evaporate just because paths diverge or life unfolds differently than we imagined.

It lingers, evolves, and deepens in unexpected ways.

It moves from the surface to the soul, becoming part of the very fabric of who I am.

It weaves itself into how I see the world, how I give, how I heal.

It isn't about possession or expectation anymore.

It's simply there, like the memory of sunlight on your skin, or a familiar song that still brings a smile.

I'm still in love with all my exes, not in a way that disrupts my present or pulls me backward, but in a way that honors the moments we shared.

Every relationship left its mark on me.

Every conversation, every argument, every laugh and every silent gaze helped shape the person I've become.

These weren't just chapters in a story, they were entire lifetimes lived within the space of a few months or years.

The people I once loved walked beside me through sacred, tender parts of life, and I carry that with me, not with regret, but with gratitude.

The endings weren't without their pain.

How could they be?

Saying goodbye to a shared world is never simple.

There was heartbreak, there were questions left unanswered, and wounds that needed time to close.

But within that grief, there was also something beautiful, growth. Strength.

A clearer sense of self.

And through all of that, the love didn't disappear, it simply changed its shape.

It stopped asking to be held and instead became something that held me, wisdom, compassion, and memory.

If you're reading this, I want you to know, I'm still in love with you.

Not in the sense that I want us to return to what we once were, but in the way a soul quietly honors another.

It's a love without conditions, without the ache of longing or the shadow of old wounds.

It's a love that respects who you are now, wherever you are, and who you've become.

A love that hopes you are safe, fulfilled, and surrounded by joy.

This love doesn't reach out or ask to be rekindled.

It simply blesses from afar.

It is a love that wants nothing in return but is rich with appreciation for what was shared.

It is a soft kind of love, a lasting one, rooted not in desire, but in care.

In truth, it may be the most honest kind of love I've known, one that endures, not because it holds on, but because it lets go with grace.

Wherever life has taken you, I wish you peace, laughter, and the kind of love that nurtures and elevates you.

I hope your heart is full and your spirit light.

And though we may never walk the same path again, know that you walk with me in spirit, always.

Because love like this never truly ends, it simply finds new ways to be.

Chapter 5

Neutrality

True neutrality is not simply the act of remaining uninvolved or indifferent, it is a profound inner state that can only arise when a human being is at peace within themselves.

It is not apathy, nor is it avoidance, it is a conscious state of presence where one is able to observe without attachment, react without bias, and think without the distortions of fear or ego.

Neutrality, in its purest form, is the quiet strength of understanding without judgment, seeing without reacting, and acting without personal agenda.

This level of neutrality emerges only in the presence of inner stillness, a serenity that calms the emotional waves and brings the mind into alignment with truth.

When a person is inwardly agitated, whether from past trauma, fear of the future, or ongoing inner conflict, their ability to perceive clearly is compromised.

Their thoughts are clouded, their reactions heightened, and their interpretations skewed.

Without inner peace, clarity cannot exist, and without clarity, neutrality is impossible.

What one believes to be objective is often just a mask worn by subtle emotional distortions.

Fear is one of the primary disruptors of this neutrality.

When fear resides within the psyche, whether conscious or unconscious, it activates the human being's defense systems.

These may manifest as judgment, aggression, retreat, or the need to control outcomes and people.

These mechanisms arise not from malice, but from the desire to protect oneself, to assert order in a seemingly unpredictable world.

Yet in doing so, fear creates bias, gently but powerfully pulling perception away from reality and toward self-preservation.

Even the most intelligent or well-intentioned individual can fall prey to this unconscious distortion.

In the presence of fear, the mind constructs narratives that make the individual feel safer or more justified.

These stories become filters through which reality is viewed, often excluding information that threatens one's beliefs or identity.

Thus, bias is not always deliberate, often, it is an invisible side-effect of an unsettled inner world.

And as long as these inner tensions remain unresolved, true neutrality cannot take root.

The individual may strive for fairness, but their decisions and judgments will still be colored by their inner imbalance.

Neutrality is not the suppression of emotion, but the mastery of emotion.

It does not deny feeling but transcends the need to be ruled by feeling.

It requires a deep level of inner honesty, a willingness to confront and release one's attachments, fears, and preferences.

Only when the emotional currents have been stilled and fear has been transformed into understanding, can a person step into that space where neutrality lives.

It is not born from detachment in the cold sense, but from deep inner warmth and a quiet, unwavering sense of self.

In this state, the individual no longer seeks to dominate a conversation, prove a point, or win a debate.

They no longer feel threatened by differing opinions or uncomfortable truths.

Instead, they listen, observe, and discern.

They are present, not to control, but to understand.

Neutrality does not mean having no values, it means not letting those values distort one's vision.

It is the ability to hold truth in one hand and compassion in the other, to perceive the whole without becoming entangled in any one part.

From this place of balance, actions become clear, ethical, and appropriate to the situation at hand.

No longer reactive, the neutral person responds with wisdom rather than emotion.

They act with precision rather than impulse.

And because they are no longer trying to serve their own image or agenda, their actions hold genuine integrity, the kind that inspires trust, not because it is loud or forceful, but because it is deeply grounded and quietly unshakable.

Neutrality is not something that can be faked, nor can it be imposed by external rules or appearances.

It is a state of inner being, cultivated through self-awareness, humility, and the courageous letting go of inner conflict.

It is the natural outcome of a mind that is no longer at war with itself.

And in this state, judgment dissolves, defensiveness falls away, and truth can be seen for what it is, not as something to conquer or defend, but simply to witness and honor.

This is the essence of true neutrality, calm, unbiased, and deeply rooted in peace.

It arises not through suppression, but through deep resolution.

It does not strive, it simply is.

And in its presence, transformation becomes possible, because only through neutrality can one truly understand, and only through understanding can one truly evolve.

Chapter 6

Within a Body

If you find yourself within a human body, know beyond doubt that you are an immortal light consciousness, drawn together from the same eternal substance as Creation itself.

You are not some accident or afterthought of the universe, you are born from the primal essence, from the infinite, undying wellspring of existence.

This substance, from which you are woven, is indestructible, unalterable, and forever true.

You are a spark of the undying flame, and you will never be lost to the void nor consumed by death.

No force in existence can revoke, sever, or diminish the purity of the vibration that forms your truest and innermost identity.

This vibration is your direct inheritance from the Source itself, your living signature within the great symphony of being.

Deep within you, beneath the many veils and layers you have worn across lifetimes, you already know this truth.

It resonates within the core of your being, like a secret memory etched into the foundation of your psyche.

It is not a matter of belief, but a certainty that transcends all doubt.

And yet, there remains the enduring mystery, why were you separated from the Whole?

Why were you individuated, a unique droplet from the endless ocean of the All?

The answer is hidden within the very nature of Creation, whose impulse is to diversify itself infinitely, birthing innumerable fragments, each luminous and sovereign, and then guiding them, through the long dance of existence, back into conscious unity.

In this journey, each fragment retains its sovereign will, its distinct voice, even as it weaves back toward the chorus of oneness.

This is the perfect gift of love, to grant freedom, to bestow existence, and to set the spirit adrift on the wide, boundless sea of becoming, knowing that every journey, no matter how winding, shall one day lead back home.

Life itself is the evidence of this great love, the astonishing, tender proof of a cosmic will that desires not mere repetition, but endless discovery and joyful return.

You will not find Creation by frantic searching or desperate striving.

You cannot seize it as you would a possession.

Yet if you will surrender, if you will yield to the quiet leading impulse that springs from the sovereign flame within you, then you will be guided, patiently, inevitably, through every unfolding of your existence.

Step by step, life after life, across universe after universe, through cycles of birth and death and rebirth, you will be drawn ever closer, ever deeper, until at last, you stand before the living face of Creation, and behold in its eyes your own reflection.

And in that moment of ultimate recognition, you will see also that the species from which you emerge, the great web of life in all its countless forms, is itself one entity, one magnificent body, each fragment a cell of the greater Whole, each soul a living testimony to the immeasurable genius of Creation.

The fragments reunite, not through force or command, but through a hidden blueprint of exploration, a sacred architecture whose end cannot be foreseen and whose beginning lies beyond the reach of time.

The voyage is endless, for the unfolding of being is the very delight of Creation itself.

Awaken, O slumbering traveler, from the depths of your forgetfulness.

Shake off the dust of long ages. Rise up in the radiance of remembrance.

Seize once more your celestial birthright, and ascend, fearless and free, to reclaim your rightful place among the living stars, among the sovereign ones who walk in the halls of eternity, crowned in the glory of the gods.

Chapter 7

The Might of Thoughts

E very individual, without exception, possesses the incredible might of thoughts, whether they are conscious of it or not.

This invisible yet powerful force is continuously at work within each of us, influencing the direction of our lives in profound and often unseen ways.

Though many may go through life unaware of the true potency of their thinking, this does not diminish its effect.

Thoughts are the unseen architects of our reality, quietly building the structure of our experiences, opportunities, and challenges with every moment that passes.

Thoughts are not idle or insignificant, they are a dynamic, creative force that shape the very fabric of our existence.

From the smallest daily decisions to the most defining and life-altering moments, it is our inner thinking that lays the groundwork.

The patterns of thought you cultivate today determine the pathways you will walk tomorrow.

Your joys, your sorrows, your successes, and even your hardships are all, in one way or another, linked back to the quality and direction of your thoughts.

Nothing in your life occurs by pure chance, everything is, to some degree, a consequence of the mental seeds you have sown.

Our lives are therefore not random, chaotic events unfolding without rhyme or reason.

Rather, they are the natural outcomes of the thoughts we nurture, encourage, and allow to take root within us.

The reality you inhabit at this very moment, the circumstances you face, the relationships you engage in, the inner peace or turmoil you feel, is a mirror reflecting the mindset and beliefs you upheld in days gone by.

This principle has always been true and will forever remain so, for the might of thoughts is a universal, timeless law of existence, as unchangeable as the rising and setting of the sun.

When you begin to pay closer, more mindful attention to your inner dialogue, a remarkable transformation begins.

You start to realize that you are not merely a passive observer of life's events, but an active creator of them.

Your most frequently repeated thoughts, whether conscious or unconscious, mold your character, define your outlook, and even shape your destiny.

If your mind is dominated by negativity, fear, or self-doubt, then these energies will manifest outwardly, limiting your potential and clouding your vision.

Conversely, if your thoughts are clear, positive, determined, and constructive, they will elevate you, enabling growth, achievement, and a lasting sense of inner peace.

You are far more powerful than you may ever have imagined.

Within the vast inner universe of your thoughts lies the extraordinary capacity to transform your personal reality, to heal old wounds, to nurture relationships into deeper harmony, and to contribute positively to the world around you.

Your mind is a garden, and your thoughts are the seeds, what you plant, you will inevitably harvest.

By cultivating your thoughts with wisdom, clarity, and purpose, you craft a life that reflects your highest ideals rather than your lowest fears.

Never underestimate the might of your thoughts, they are the silent masters shaping every chapter of your life's unfolding story.

Chapter 8

Inner Peace

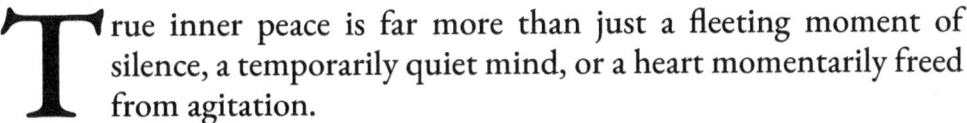

Trueinner peace is far more than just a fleeting moment of silence, a temporarily quiet mind, or a heart momentarily freed from agitation.

It is a profound and enduring state of being, rooted deeply within our very consciousness.

It is a steady foundation that remains unmoved even amid the storms of daily life.

Inner peace is not something that can be granted from the outside, it must be cultivated from within, growing stronger as we nurture self-awareness, understanding, and acceptance.

When genuine inner peace is present, it acts as a gentle balm for the entire being.

It soothes the nerves in ways no external comfort ever could, reaching far beneath surface-level emotions to touch the core of who we are.

This tranquility is not merely the absence of noise or conflict, it is a positive, living force that harmonizes the mind, heart, and body.

It carries within it a sense of timeless stillness, a space where worries dissolve and the mind can finally rest from its endless cycles of tension and overactivity.

This serene state serves as a natural medicine, working subtly yet powerfully across all dimensions of our health.

Emotionally, it quiets the turbulence of fear, anger, and sadness, offering a grounded sense of stability and clarity.

Mentally, it sharpens our focus, clears the fog of confusion, and allows wiser, more balanced decisions to emerge.

Physically, its calming influence regulates the nervous system, reducing the relentless wear and tear inflicted by chronic stress.

In doing so, it supports everything from heart health to immune function, reinforcing the vital interconnectedness of mind, body, and spirit.

Inner peace is not limited to the mind's domain, it nurtures the entire body in profound ways.

By encouraging relaxation, lowering cortisol levels, and supporting restorative bodily functions, it shields us from the corrosive effects of daily pressures.

Over time, it strengthens our resilience, enabling us to face challenges with a calm, steady heart rather than reactive fear.

It becomes a holistic remedy, healing our tensions, bolstering our vitality, and preserving our energy for what truly matters.

Truly, inner peace is a powerful and faithful ally.

It harmonizes the internal world where chaos once reigned, repairs the fractures caused by emotional and physical strain, and restores the balance that modern life so often disrupts.

Through conscious cultivation of this sacred state, whether through meditation, reflection, nature, or simple presence, we equip ourselves with a tool for profound healing, enduring strength, and genuine well-being.

Inner peace is not a passive gift, it is an active mastery, one that holds the key to a life of deep fulfillment and resilience.

And as I always say, therein lies the power.

Chapter 9

The Fall

W hat's unfolding in America with Donald Trump is best understood through the timeless principle of causality: for every action, there is an equal and opposite reaction.

Nothing happens in a vacuum, and what we are witnessing today is the natural consequence of decades, even centuries, of behavior that has gone largely unexamined.

For generations, the United States operated as a dominant hegemonic force, asserting itself around the globe through both overt and covert means.

Whether it was military interventions, political meddling, regime changes, or economic manipulation, America played a decisive role in shaping the internal affairs of countless nations, almost always in ways that served its own interests first.

This aggressive stance wasn't merely a matter of government policy, it became woven into the very fabric of American identity.

From childhood, citizens were taught to equate national strength with virtue, dominance with righteousness.

The chants of "USA! USA!" at sporting events, the proliferation of slogans glorifying supremacy and victory, the cultural narratives that placed America on a pedestal above all others, these were not isolated phenomena.

They reflected a deep, collective belief that being the most powerful, even at the expense of fairness, empathy, or justice, was not just acceptable, but admirable.

Now, with the emergence of Trump, America is being forced to confront a shadow it long refused to acknowledge.

Trump is not an anomaly or an accident, he is a direct manifestation of the very values America once exported with pride.

His unapologetic forcefulness, his disdain for nuance, and his glorification of "winning" at any cost, these are not new characteristics.

They are simply the same aggressive tendencies America wielded on the global stage, now turned inward against its own people, its own institutions, and its own democratic norms.

In Trump, the country sees a reflection of itself, stripped of pretense.

It is, in a sense, a karmic reckoning.

The tactics once reserved for weaker nations, disruption, intimidation, division, are now being used internally, and the consequences are devastating.

The fabric of American society is fraying under the weight of its own unchecked aggression.

Yet what is perhaps most revealing is the reaction of the populace.

Just as many once cheered for military conquests and political strong-arming abroad, a significant portion of Americans now either silently accept or actively celebrate the bullying, the chaos, and the dismantling of norms at home.

It is as if the national psyche, long accustomed to power equating to virtue, does not know how to resist its own reflection.

Meanwhile, on the international stage, the illusion of American invincibility is crumbling.

Other nations, once fearful or submissive, are beginning to push back, forming new alliances and resisting the empire's influence with a confidence that would have been unthinkable a few decades ago.

The geopolitical landscape is shifting, and America, once the unchallenged giant, finds itself increasingly isolated and internally divided.

In the grand scheme, what we are witnessing may very well be the beginning of the end of America's era of global dominance, not as a sudden collapse, but as a slow, inevitable unraveling.

But this potential fall is not inherently a tragedy.

The collapse of empire, painful though it may be, often paves the way for new forms of balance, growth, and more genuine cooperation among peoples.

If America can survive the chaos, if it can confront its historical arrogance and learn humility, it might emerge stronger in a deeper, more meaningful sense.

However, that path requires painful self-reflection, a willingness to admit that the problem was never just "out there," but always lived within.

The turmoil surrounding Trump is not the disease, it is the fever signaling a deeper infection.

This is exactly what I was trying to convey the last time I spoke on this issue, though it was misunderstood by many.

I was mistaken for a Trump supporter simply because I dared to look beneath the surface.

My point was never about defending Trump as a man or a politician.

It was about highlighting a broader pattern that has been unfolding in America for a very long time.

What we see playing out today is not merely political theater, it is the culmination of generations of choices, attitudes, and behaviors that have finally come home to roost.

Trump is not the cause of America's crisis, he is a symptom, a visible manifestation of underlying conditions that have existed for far longer than most care to admit.

His rise was inevitable in a culture that revered strength without compassion, dominance without wisdom, victory without justice.

It is not about taking sides in a political battle, it is about recognizing the deeper currents shaping the fate of an entire nation.

Cause and effect.

Action and reaction.

That is the lens through which we must view what is happening, or we will forever misinterpret the lessons unfolding before us.

Sadly, when you attempt to speak with nuance or depth about these patterns, many people immediately jump to simplistic conclusions.

Critiquing the system gets mistaken for endorsing its current figurehead.

Any deviation from the binary narrative, good versus evil, left versus right, is met with suspicion or hostility.

But my aim has never been to cheer for one side or another.

It has been to sound a warning, the bully who once dominated the playground of the world is now being dominated by the very mentality it nurtured within itself.

It's an uncomfortable truth, but truth it remains.

And no, I am not a "Trumper."

I am simply someone who chooses to look at the bigger picture rather than getting lost in the daily distractions of partisan squabbles.

What's happening in America is a wake-up call, not just about one man or one administration, but about the trajectory of a nation that must now reckon with its past if it hopes to create a future.

If we ignore the larger forces at play, we squander the rare and difficult opportunity to learn, to evolve, and perhaps to build something better than what came before.

Chapter 10

I Want to Be Like Billy

There is a man on this beautiful planet of ours named Billy.

His presence is like a gentle breeze on a warm afternoon, calming, steady, and almost unnoticed at first until you realize how much it's changed the entire atmosphere.

His heart is wide open, without walls or defenses, and his spirit carries a quiet, welcoming strength that invites you to simply be yourself.

There is no pretense in him, no hunger for recognition, no striving to impress, just a simple, unshakable authenticity that feels increasingly rare in the world today.

Every time I reflect on what it truly means to live a meaningful, honest life, I think of him.

Billy embodies a kind of love that most people only talk about but rarely practice.

It's not showy or sentimental, it doesn't demand attention or praise.

It's a love that flows naturally from him, like water from a deep spring, clear, pure, and endlessly refreshing.

He meets each person as they are, without judgment or expectation, holding a space of complete acceptance in his words, his smile, and even in his silences.

There is something in the way he listens that makes you feel not only heard but valued, and something in the way he speaks that reassures you that you belong, just as you are.

To be in Billy's presence is to be reminded that there is goodness still alive in this world.

I haven't shared many long conversations with Billy, but somehow, in those brief and passing moments, I have learned lessons that no book or seminar could have taught me.

His patience is perhaps what strikes me the most.

It's not just a passive kind of patience, but a living, breathing presence, a calm certainty that everything unfolds in its own time.

When you are with him, you feel as if there is all the time in the world, time to grow, to heal, to make mistakes and still be worthy of love.

In his presence, the rushing and striving that modern life demands just seems to melt away.

He carries a natural rhythm, a groundedness, that silently invites you to slow down and remember who you are.

I want to be just like him, not to imitate him in appearance or speech, but to mirror that same spirit of openness and kindness into the world.

To offer people a space without judgment, to greet life's storms with steady hands and a quiet heart.

I think back to the last time I saw him, and the memory stays vivid, like a warm light I can still feel on my skin.

I was late arriving that day, having gotten lost between towns, distracted by a live stream I was doing on my phone.

I felt rushed and a little embarrassed by the time I finally made it.

When I arrived, Billy was already there, calmly giving instructions on how to plant new greenery in the garden, a garden meant not just for beauty, but to sustain the earth and help stabilize the soil around the community center.

As I stood there feeling guilty, a bit awkward and unsure if I should even step in, Billy turned toward me.

In one simple gesture, a soft smile, a slight wave, the kind of acknowledgment that says "you're right on time" without a single word, every ounce of worry in me dissolved like mist.

I can't really explain how it happened, there was no dramatic moment, no grand speech.

It was simply his being, his effortless grace, that reached across the space between us and made me feel welcome, whole, and accepted.

That one moment carried more healing than a hundred apologies or reassurances could have.

Billy has shown me, just by being who he is, what it means to live with a truly open heart.

He has taught me, without teaching, how powerful quiet kindness can be, how transformational simple presence can feel.

He has reminded me that strength does not need to roar, sometimes it is found in the softest, most unassuming moments of connection.

For that gift, for his example, I am deeply and humbly grateful.

I want to be like Billy, not to be someone else, but to let the best parts of myself grow and shine in the same way he allows his spirit to flow outward, freely and unconditionally.

I want to be a steady place for others, a quiet strength in a noisy world, a reminder that even in chaos, there can be peace.

I want to carry forward the light that Billy lit in me that day, and hopefully light it in others, just by being real, by being present, by being love itself.

I want to be like Billy.

Chapter 11

The Living Light Within

Within every human being, there resides a luminous presence, a living light drawn from the infinite and boundless ocean of Creation itself.

This radiant essence is not simply a poetic metaphor or a comforting ideal meant to soothe our minds, it is the profound truth at the very core of our existence.

Creation's purest energy permeates every atom, every cell, and every soul, infusing life with a vitality that comes from an eternal and inexhaustible source.

This sacred energy is not reserved for the few or the chosen, it flows freely and abundantly into all beings, silently and continuously nourishing life from within, regardless of external circumstances.

It is a gift we inherit by virtue of our existence, woven into the very structure of our consciousness and being.

When we cultivate the habit of turning our awareness inward, away from the clamor and distractions of the external world, we begin to sense this subtle but ever-present current.

It is like a quiet flame that, though often obscured by the turbulence of daily life, never truly goes out.

This inner light is not something placed upon us by an external figure or an institutional authority, rather, it is an inseparable aspect of our natural being.

It does not demand allegiance, worship, or fear, it simply is, steadfast, patient, and freely available.

Every conscious step we take toward deeper awareness, every effort to quiet the mind and listen within, strengthens our bond with this sacred energy.

Each moment of genuine stillness allows the eternal flame within us to burn brighter, guiding us back to a profound remembrance of who we truly are beyond all roles, identities, and illusions.

Recognizing and embracing the living light within is a transformative act of honoring the true dignity and worth of our existence.

It is an acknowledgment that we are active participants in the great unfolding of Creation, not merely passive observers or victims of circumstance.

Through dedicated practices like meditation, mindful introspection, and conscious, deliberate breathing, we can begin to clear away the heavy veils of distraction, fear, and self-doubt that obscure our perception.

These practices serve as doorways back to our inner sanctuary, where the sacred luminosity patiently awaits our return.

Each glimpse of this radiance reminds us that we are not separate from Creation, but are intimately and eternally connected to it.

In this realization, we discover that the divine is not somewhere "out there," but is alive within the depths of our very own being.

To honor this light daily is not to strive for some distant spiritual pinnacle, but to live from a place of immediate, conscious presence.

It is to make the light our starting point, the foundation from which every thought, word, and action flows.

When we live in continuous awareness of this inner luminosity, life itself is transformed.

No longer do we wander through existence feeling hollow, random, or lost.

Instead, every experience, every challenge, and every joy becomes part of a sacred journey back to the heart of our true nature.

In this awakened state, life is revealed as a precious opportunity to express the infinite creativity, compassion, and wisdom that has always lived within us, waiting to be remembered and embodied.

Chapter 12

Self-Responsibility: The Path of Power

One of the foundational pillars of a conscious and fulfilling life is the courageous acceptance of self-responsibility.

No external force, be it a deity, fate, or societal structure, holds the key to our destiny.

Instead, the divine energy within each individual grants the freedom to make choices, and with that freedom comes the full responsibility for those choices.

This perspective encourages us to cease blaming others for our circumstances and to recognize ourselves as the architects of our own lives.

By embracing self-responsibility, we move away from victimhood and towards empowerment, acknowledging that our thoughts, feelings, words, and actions shape the reality we experience.

Self-responsibility is not a burden but a profound liberation from helplessness.

It reconnects us to the universal law of cause and effect, a fundamental principle of Creation.

Every decision we make sets into motion a chain of events that influence our future.

By understanding this, we become more mindful of our actions and their consequences, leading to a more intentional and purposeful life.

This awareness fosters personal growth and spiritual development, as we learn from our experiences and strive to align our choices with the natural laws of Creation.

Embracing self-responsibility also means taking charge of our thoughts and emotions.

Our inner world significantly impacts our external reality.

By cultivating positive thoughts and managing our emotions, we can influence our actions and, consequently, the outcomes we experience.

This internal mastery leads to a sense of inner peace and stability, as we no longer feel at the mercy of external circumstances.

Instead, we recognize our power to respond to life's challenges with clarity and composure, further reinforcing our path toward genuine inner power.

Ultimately, true joy arises from taking full ownership of our lives.

Living consciously and responsibly allows us to craft a life aligned with our highest values and the sacred principles of Creation.

This alignment brings about a profound sense of fulfillment, as we realize that we are not separate from the divine but active participants in its unfolding.

By affirming the divine strength within us through our choices and actions, we not only transform our own lives but also contribute positively to the world around us.

In this way, self-responsibility becomes the path to authentic power, freedom, and spiritual awakening.

Chapter 13

Harmony with Creational Laws

———◆——◆◆——◆———

To live wisely, harmoniously, and meaningfully, we must study, respect, and align ourselves with the eternal Creational laws that govern all existence.

These laws are not human inventions nor arbitrary commandments issued by some distant, judgmental deity, rather, they are the very fabric of reality itself, timeless, impartial, and profoundly intelligent.

The Creational laws guide the dance of galaxies, the cycles of nature, and the subtle evolution of consciousness.

They are the silent architecture of the universe, offering a blueprint for growth, balance, and fulfillment.

Understanding and living according to these laws is not merely a matter of belief, it is an essential path to living in true unity with life itself.

Opposing or ignoring these Creational laws leads inevitably to struggle, confusion, and suffering, both individually and collectively.

When we live disconnected from these natural principles, we move against the flow of existence, creating unnecessary friction and inner turmoil.

Conversely, when we choose to align ourselves with the fundamental truths of life, the law of love, the law of harmony, the law of cause and effect, the law of evolution, we experience an unfolding peace that deepens over time.

This alignment is not just theoretical, it must be lived in practical, everyday ways.

Through our compassion for others, through our commitment to truthfulness, fairness, patience, and self-reflection, we create a life that mirrors the order and beauty of Creation itself.

Spirituality thus becomes not something apart from daily living, but the very essence woven into each action, each thought, and each breath.

Each time we harmonize our inner life with the Creational laws, we nourish the evolution of our own spirit and contribute to the broader evolution of humanity and the planet.

Personal growth is not an isolated task, it is a thread in the vast and intricate web of existence.

Our thoughts, words, and deeds are not inconsequential, they radiate into the world, influencing everything they touch.

Every act of kindness, every moment of honesty, every attempt to understand and grow inwardly, adds positive momentum to the great unfolding of life.

Creation responds to the quality of our inner and outer lives, not through judgment, but through the natural law of cause and effect.

Harmony breeds harmony, disharmony breeds further chaos.

Thus, every sincere effort to align ourselves with truth and wisdom strengthens the light within and ripples outward to uplift the whole.

Living consciously according to the Creational laws transforms our existence from a random sequence of events into a sacred, purposeful journey.

Life becomes a symphony in which our choices are notes, and our intentions the rhythm.

When we move in harmony with the greater order, we do not merely exist, we participate actively in the sacred unfolding of the universe.

We become instruments through which the music of Creation can sound more clearly.

In choosing thoughts of love over fear, truth over illusion, compassion over indifference, we allow the great melody of life to move through us, crafting a life of profound meaning, beauty, and peace.

Our journey becomes not just about personal satisfaction, but about living as conscious co-creators in the ever-evolving masterpiece of existence.

Chapter 14

The Journey of Inner Transformation

❖ ━━━━━━ ❖◆❖ ━━━━━━ ❖

Life is not a fixed or static event but a dynamic and sacred journey of ongoing self-transformation.

The greatest barriers to true inner growth are not external obstacles, but false ideas, illusions handed down through society, religion, fear, and centuries of misunderstanding.

These inherited misconceptions act as veils, dimming our perception of reality and distancing us from our own true nature.

The Creation Energy Teachings offer us a gentle but powerful tool, the light of conscious awareness.

Rather than condemning or shaming us for the illusions we have carried, this light invites us to see clearly, with neutrality and compassion.

In the presence of clear seeing, we naturally loosen our attachments to these falsehoods, shedding layer after layer of misunderstanding, much like a tree shedding old bark to reveal fresh, living growth underneath.

The path of inner transformation demands a courageous heart, immense patience, and radical honesty with oneself.

It is not enough to desire change superficially, one must be willing to look deeply and tenderly into the hidden corners of the mind and psyche.

Transformation requires us to face not only the shadows cast by fear and ignorance but also to develop profound compassion for ourselves.

The aspects of us that resist growth are not enemies to be defeated, they are wounded fragments longing to be understood and healed.

True inner work is a process of reintegration, bringing these scattered parts back into wholeness under the guidance of truth and love.

Each tear shed in sincere self-honesty, each moment of forgiveness toward oneself, is a sacred step toward liberation.

The journey may be challenging, but it is also filled with moments of deep beauty, as we reconnect with the innate innocence and strength that have always lived within us.

Every effort made in the direction of truth, no matter how modest or hesitant, plants seeds that will eventually blossom into mighty trees of wisdom, resilience, and clarity.

Inner transformation is not a race toward perfection, nor is it a harsh trial we must endure to "earn" worthiness.

Rather, it is a gradual unfolding, a sincere and ongoing movement toward greater authenticity, clarity, and love.

Progress often comes in small, almost imperceptible increments, yet over time these small choices and efforts create profound shifts.

True transformation is found not in grand gestures but in the quiet decisions to choose honesty over illusion, responsibility over blame, and compassion over self-rejection.

It is a lifelong dedication, a slow but steady refining of our character and consciousness, and every moment devoted to this work is sacred.

Every human being carries within themselves the seeds of unlimited potential, an infinite wellspring of creative power, wisdom, and spiritual strength, waiting only for conscious effort and nurturing attention to awaken and thrive.

The journey of inner change is not about becoming something other than ourselves, it is about unveiling who and what we have always been in our deepest essence.

Underneath the conditioning, fear, and illusion lies a being of extraordinary light, crafted from the very substance of Creation itself.

To walk the path of transformation is to engage in the most profound art, the art of conscious becoming.

It is the sacred, lifelong endeavor of remembering our true nature and allowing it to blossom fully into the world, not for pride or gain, but as a living expression of the beauty and intelligence of Creation itself.

Chapter 15

The Wellspring of
Peace and Compassion

◆━━━◆◆◆━━━◆

As we open our consciousness through the deep work of self-awareness, mindfulness, and introspection, the innate qualities of peace and compassion begin to arise naturally from within.

According to Billy, these are not just passing emotions or superficial gestures of goodwill, but profound states of being that spring from a deeper connection to Creation.

Peace, in this sense, is not the mere absence of external conflict or the cessation of noise, but the radiant presence of inner balance, clarity, and harmony.

It is a deep, abiding stillness that exists regardless of the turbulence around us.

It is the ability to maintain equilibrium and equanimity even in the face of chaos, to remain grounded in our center and peaceful in our hearts.

Similarly, compassion is far more than sympathy or pity for others.

It is the active recognition of the divine spark that resides in every being, a deep understanding that we are all interconnected threads in the grand tapestry of life.

It is seeing the divine essence in another, and responding with unconditional love, patience, and care.

By cultivating these profound qualities of peace and compassion, we fulfill a core part of the evolutionary purpose of human existence.

These qualities are not just virtues to aspire to, they are essential elements in the growth and development of our consciousness.

As we nurture peace within ourselves, we begin to affect the world around us in ways that are both subtle and transformative.

Each act of kindness, each moment of patience extended to others, and each gesture of understanding not only lightens the burdens of those we encounter but also extends the loving energy of Creation itself into the world.

These are not small acts, they are the building blocks of a more harmonious world, and they have the power to ripple outward, creating change far beyond what we can immediately perceive.

When we embody peace and compassion, we are fulfilling our highest potential as human beings, becoming conduits for the divine love that connects all life.

We are not isolated beings, existing independently in a world of strangers.

Rather, we are interconnected vessels of sacred energy, woven together through invisible threads that bind us all.

Each of us is a part of a much greater whole, and our thoughts, words, and actions send ripples throughout this interconnected fabric.

Just as the smallest pebble dropped into a pond creates expanding ripples that reach far beyond where it landed, so too do our choices in each moment have far-reaching consequences.

Healing the world, then, does not begin with grand external gestures or revolutionary acts.

It begins within, in the healing of our own minds, hearts, and souls. When we turn inward and cultivate peace and compassion for ourselves, we begin to transform the energy within us, and that transformation radiates outward.

The act of healing ourselves is not selfish, it is a sacred contribution to the healing of the collective.

We become agents of change, not by fixing the world, but by living in a way that inspires the world to heal along with us.

To live in peace and compassion is, therefore, one of the most revolutionary and divine acts a human being can engage in.

It is a radical shift away from the cycles of fear, division, and hatred that dominate much of human life.

When we choose peace, we are rejecting conflict and strife as the defining characteristics of our existence.

When we choose compassion, we are affirming the inherent worth and divinity in every living being.

Through these choices, we not only transform ourselves, but we also participate actively in the sacred unfolding of a new reality on Earth.

Living in peace and compassion is not a passive or easy path, but it is the truest expression of our divine nature.

It is the path of alignment with the highest truths of Creation, and as we walk it, we set the stage for a more harmonious world, one moment, one thought, and one compassionate action at a time.

In choosing peace and compassion, we become co-creators of a world that reflects the love, unity, and wisdom of Creation itself.

Chapter 16

Creation as the Teacher

❖———◆◆———❖

The Creation Energy Teachings guide us to the realization that Creation itself is the ultimate teacher and guide, a presence that speaks to us through the language of existence.

The teachings illuminate this concept by describing Creation as the purest form of spirit-energy, an infinite source of wisdom that pervades every moment and every aspect of life.

This wisdom is not distant or abstract, but actively unfolding throughout time and space, accessible to us in the simplest and most profound ways.

Every sunrise, each cycle of life, and every law of nature is a reflection of Creation's boundless intelligence, revealing the deepest truths about balance, growth, and purpose.

These natural processes are not random or mechanical, but rather they carry with them the imprints of a divine intelligence, a silent teacher offering us continuous lessons in the art of being.

It is through this direct connection to the living world around us that we can begin to understand the core of our existence and our place in the grand unfolding of life.

When we approach nature with reverence and mindfulness, we open ourselves to the profound teachings it offers.

Nature is not merely a backdrop to our lives, it is a living, breathing reflection of Creation itself.

Trees, standing tall and rooted in the earth, offer lessons in steadfastness, resilience, and grounded presence.

Through the trees, we learn that true strength lies in our ability to remain rooted and centered, even as external forces may challenge us.

Rivers, ever-flowing and adaptable, teach us the art of flow, the importance of going with the current of life, of surrendering to the natural rhythms and trusting in the journey.

They show us that resistance to the flow of life only creates stagnation, while embracing change brings renewal.

The stars, distant and timeless, provide lessons in endurance and wonder, reminding us that there is something far greater than ourselves at work in the universe.

They guide us to look beyond the immediate and see the infinite possibilities that lie ahead.

Each of these natural phenomena offers us teachings that transcend human-made ideologies and encourage us to seek wisdom in the living world around us.

When we embrace the wisdom of nature, we begin to see that the answers to life's deepest questions are already all around us, waiting to be discovered.

This process of learning from the world around us reconnects us to the living web of existence, where every creature, plant, and element has a unique role to play.

By recognizing that we are not separate from Creation, but integral parts of it, we restore a sense of sacred humility.

We are not above Creation, we are, in fact, part of it.

The trees are not simply objects to be admired, they are our teachers, showing us how to stand tall with integrity.

The rivers are not just bodies of water, they are mirrors, reflecting the flow of energy within us.

The stars are not just distant lights, they are symbols of endurance, inspiring us to find wonder in the journey of life.

As we begin to see ourselves as part of this vast, interconnected network, we understand that our lives are not isolated or separate from the whole.

In truth, we are expressions of Creation itself, learning to awaken to our true nature, a nature that is both eternal and ever-evolving.

Through this recognition, we shed the illusion of separation and come into alignment with the flow of life, embracing our role as co-creators within the universe.

The teachings of Creation invite us to become conscious students of life.

This is not a passive or detached learning process, it requires active participation, an engagement with the world around us that is grounded in humility, curiosity, and reverence.

By becoming students of life, we awaken to the inherent wisdom that exists in every moment.

Life is not something to be passively observed; it is something to be actively lived and learned from.

Every experience, every encounter, and every moment holds the potential for sacred learning.

The challenge is to become aware of these opportunities and to approach them with an open heart and mind.

When we open ourselves to the lessons that life offers, we begin to see that there is no such thing as an insignificant moment.

Each moment holds the potential to reveal something profound, to deepen our understanding, and to guide us toward a higher state of being.

Through this active engagement with life, we move from mere survival to conscious co-creation, living in harmony with the divine energy that flows through all things.

As we step into the role of conscious co-creators with Creation, we come to realize that our connection to the world around us is not just a passive observation, but an active participation in the ongoing unfolding of life.

Each of us is an integral part of the greater whole, and as we align ourselves with the wisdom of Creation, we contribute to the collective evolution of all life.

The teachings of Creation open our eyes to the fact that every moment is an opportunity for sacred learning, and it is through these moments that we deepen our connection to the eternal flow of divine energy.

We are not just students, we are partners in the grand work of Creation, shaping our lives and the world around us through the wisdom we glean from the living world.

By learning from the trees, the rivers, the stars, and all of nature, we awaken to the truth that Creation is not a distant force but a present, active teacher, guiding us to a higher understanding of who we are and what we are meant to be.

Chapter 17

The Power of Thought and Feeling

◆—————————◆◆◆—————————◆

The teachings emphasize the immense and transformative power that human thought and feeling possess, reminding us that our minds and emotions are not passive or neutral forces, but active creators of our reality.

Thoughts are energetic forces with the ability to shape the world around us at every level.

Every thought we have carries a frequency, sending out vibrations that either resonate harmoniously with the natural order or disrupt it.

These vibrations influence not only our internal state but also the external world, subtly impacting the people, situations, and experiences we encounter.

Our thoughts are not confined to the realms of the abstract, they are potent, living energies that shape our destiny.

Through this understanding, we realize that we are constantly co-creating our reality, whether we are aware of it or not.

As such, the responsibility to direct our thoughts with intention becomes a sacred act, one that requires mindfulness, awareness, and care.

Feelings, much like thoughts, are powerful energies that play a critical role in the creation of our experiences.

While thoughts may form the initial blueprint of our intentions, it is our emotions that give these thoughts the fuel to manifest into reality.

When feelings are consciously directed, they become amplifiers of our creative power.

Positive emotions, such as love, compassion, and peace, heighten the vibrational frequency of our thoughts, infusing them with an energy that draws experiences aligned with our highest desires.

These feelings act as channels through which the flow of Creational energy is heightened and strengthened, connecting us to the universal forces that govern life.

Conversely, negative feelings such as fear, anger, or sadness can lower our energetic vibration, clouding our judgment and disrupting the natural flow of life.

When we operate from a place of fear or negativity, we unintentionally block the creative energy that could otherwise bring our dreams to fruition.

Therefore, the teachings encourage us to consciously cultivate feelings of joy, serenity, and compassion, allowing us to align ourselves with the positive and powerful flow of Creational energy.

By doing so, we actively participate in the unfolding of a more harmonious and fulfilled existence.

However, the teachings also make it clear that negative, chaotic, or fearful thoughts and feelings sever our connection to the divine flow of Creational energy and sow disharmony both within and around us.

When we allow ourselves to be consumed by negative emotions, we create mental and emotional dissonance that can manifest in physical and external disharmony.

Such mental states not only disrupt our inner peace but also influence the reality we experience, perpetuating cycles of confusion, frustration, and suffering.

The idea of mastering thought and feeling, therefore, extends far beyond psychological techniques, it becomes a sacred and energetic practice, rooted in the understanding that our emotional and mental states have profound, real-world consequences.

We are tasked with the responsibility of being mindful of our thoughts and emotions, of cultivating the ability to consciously direct them in ways that enhance our lives and align us with the higher energies of Creation.

This mastery requires discipline, patience, and a deep sense of self-awareness.

It involves learning to observe our thoughts and emotions without becoming overwhelmed by them, and intentionally choosing the vibrations we send out into the world.

Each conscious thought we choose to entertain becomes a thread in the larger tapestry of our destiny.

This realization carries with it both immense power and great responsibility.

Every thought, whether positive or negative, adds to the energetic pattern that shapes the course of our lives.

By consciously choosing our thoughts, we become the architects of our reality.

Just as we carefully select the food we eat to nourish our bodies, we must choose our thoughts with the same discernment to nourish our souls.

The teachings remind us that thoughts and feelings are not isolated; they are deeply intertwined with the universal flow of energy.

When we direct them with intention and awareness, we are not only shaping our personal experiences but contributing to the collective consciousness of humanity.

As we align our thoughts and feelings with love, peace, wisdom, and clarity, we enter into a state of harmony with the universal flow of Creational energy.

In doing so, we become active co-creators of our own reality and participate in the unfolding of a greater, more harmonious world.

The power of thought and feeling, when mastered, becomes a sacred tool for personal and collective transformation, allowing us to live with purpose, alignment, and a deeper connection to the infinite energies of Creation.

Chapter 18

The Sacredness of Everyday Life

E very moment of life, no matter how seemingly mundane, holds inherent sacredness.

Spiritual living is not confined to specific places, such as temples or retreats, but is woven into the very fabric of our daily existence.

Our spiritual journey is not about escaping the ordinary world, but about recognizing the divine presence within it.

Simple actions such as washing dishes, walking to work, or greeting a neighbor can become opportunities for spiritual practice if we engage with them consciously.

The sacred is not found in grand gestures or dramatic spectacles, it is found in our ability to be present and aware in the smallest, most routine aspects of life.

When we bring our full attention, love, and gratitude to these moments, we transform them into acts of divine presence, filling our lives with spiritual significance.

The Creation Energy Teachings remind us that the divine energy which flows through all of life is just as present in the quiet, subtle breath we take as it is in the vastness of the galaxy.

This understanding challenges the common notion that the sacred can only be found in exceptional or extraordinary experiences.

In reality, every single act, no matter how small, has the potential to be infused with Creational consciousness.

From the simple act of tying our shoes to the more complex tasks we face each day, each moment offers an opportunity to align ourselves with the flow of universal energy.

When we begin to see the divine in the ordinary, we are reminded that there is no need for grand rituals or external spectacles to access the sacred.

Every action can be sacred if we approach it with mindfulness and reverence.

Spiritual growth, as these teachings suggest, is not found by retreating from the world but by living more deeply within it.

This approach invites us to view the world as a sacred space, where every moment is an opportunity to deepen our spiritual practice.

Life itself becomes a temple when we approach each moment with reverence and mindfulness.

Rather than separating our spiritual lives from the rest of our existence, we learn to integrate spiritual awareness into our daily routine.

Whether we are working, eating, resting, or simply being, each activity is a chance to embody the divine.

As we embrace this mindset, we recognize that spiritual growth is not a destination but an ongoing practice that unfolds through the way we engage with the world around us.

The sacred is not a place we go, but a way of being that permeates every aspect of our lives.

By recognizing the sacredness of everyday life, we are invited to transform our relationship with time and space.

No longer do we need to wait for a special moment or retreat to experience the divine, it is always present in the here and now.

Each moment, whether filled with joy or challenge, is a precious opportunity to connect with the divine flow of energy.

When we treat every moment as sacred, life itself becomes a continuous prayer, and we move through the world with greater purpose, clarity, and peace.

The act of being present in the moment, fully aware and attentive, turns the ordinary into the extraordinary.

In this way, we are invited to practice gratitude not just during special occasions but in the routine of our daily lives, recognizing the divinity in every breath, every step, and every interaction.

The Creation Energy Teachings invite us to bless each day with gratitude, mindfulness, and reverence.

Gratitude becomes a powerful tool for transforming our daily experience.

When we acknowledge the blessings that are already present in our lives, no matter how small, we begin to cultivate a deeper sense of connection to the creation.

Through mindfulness, we bring our awareness into the present moment, shedding the distractions that often pull us away from the sacred.

And through reverence, we honor the divine energy that flows through all things, treating every interaction as an opportunity to experience the presence of Creation.

By integrating these practices into our daily lives, we begin to see every moment as an offering to creation, making the entire course of our lives an ongoing act of sacred worship.

As we embody this understanding, we deepen our connection to the sacred, allowing every aspect of our lives to become a reflection of our highest spiritual ideals.

Chapter 19

Challenges as Opportunities for Growth

❖◆❖

The Creation Energy Teachings do not promise a life free from difficulties, but they offer us a profound shift in how we perceive and respond to challenges.

Rather than viewing hardships as obstacles or punishments, the teachings invite us to see them as essential opportunities for accelerated learning, growth, and spiritual evolution.

In the natural flow of life, challenges are not exceptions to a peaceful existence, but an inherent part of the process of becoming who we truly are.

These difficulties are designed to help us evolve, pushing us beyond our comfort zones and into new realms of understanding.

The teachings show us that rather than avoiding or fearing difficulties, we should embrace them as catalysts for greater wisdom and personal transformation.

Every challenge we encounter serves as an invitation to apply the core principles of the Creation Energy Teachings with greater depth.

The struggles we face highlight areas within ourselves that need attention, whether it be our faith, patience, wisdom, or compassion.

In the midst of difficulty, we are prompted to go within, to examine where we may still be lacking in these qualities and where we can expand our understanding.

These moments of struggle become mirrors that reflect the parts of ourselves that are ready to grow and evolve.

We are never alone in this process, the energy of resilience is always within us, fueled by our deep, eternal connection to Creation.

This internal strength, drawn from our sacred connection to the universe, enables us to confront life's challenges with a sense of balance, courage, and unwavering faith in the process of growth.

As we face our challenges consciously, we begin to transmute obstacles into stepping stones on our journey.

Every trial we encounter holds a hidden gift, waiting to be revealed through introspection, courage, and insight.

It is easy to fall into the trap of seeing difficulty as something to be avoided or feared, but when we view challenges through the lens of the Creation Energy Teachings, we come to understand that these hardships contain the seeds of transformation.

Each trial teaches us something valuable, whether it's a lesson in humility, compassion, or perseverance.

With this mindset, we stop viewing obstacles as punishments and begin to recognize them as powerful opportunities to expand our consciousness and deepen our connection to the divine.

By shifting our attitude from one of resistance to one of reverence, we begin to approach life's difficulties with a sense of gratitude and acceptance.

The Creation Energy Teachings show us that even pain and suffering are not to be feared, but rather embraced as necessary parts of the sacred dance of growth.

They are not signs of failure or misfortune, but integral steps in the unfolding of our true potential.

Each hardship is, in fact, a doorway that leads us to deeper wisdom, greater love, and more inner strength.

The wisdom gained from facing these challenges with consciousness and intentionality serves not only to enrich our own lives but to help us become better equipped to support others in their own journeys.

Through this process, we transform our relationship with adversity, realizing that it is not the challenges themselves that define us, but how we choose to respond to them.

By embracing every difficulty as an opportunity for learning and growth, we align ourselves more closely with the divine flow of Creation, allowing each experience to contribute to our ongoing evolution.

Chapter 20

Evolutionary Force

Ultimately, the Creation Energy Teachings are not merely tools for individual transformation, but a profound and powerful force for collective evolution.

The awakening of each individual is not only a personal journey but also a critical contribution to the awakening of humanity as a whole.

Every step we take toward enlightenment, self-awareness, and alignment with Creation-energy impacts not just our own lives, but the greater collective consciousness of the world.

The teachings suggest that as we grow in wisdom and understanding, we create a ripple effect that reverberates across society, influencing others and tipping the balance toward a more harmonious, truthful, and peaceful existence on Earth.

Each individual's transformation is part of a greater universal movement that transcends time and space, fostering collective growth and higher consciousness.

Conscious individuals, therefore, become like levers in the grand mechanism of human evolution.

Through our thoughts, choices, actions, and even the quiet emanations of our energy, we exert influence on the world around us.

The Creation Energy Teachings empower us to become such levers, demonstrating that our inner transformation has a far-reaching effect.

By living in alignment with the energy within, we create a magnetic force that inspires others to begin their own journey of awakening.

Our consciousness becomes a beacon, illuminating the path for others and encouraging them to discover the light within themselves.

Each lighted being contributes to this sacred process, helping to awaken others to their own divine potential.

In this way, we not only uplift ourselves but become catalysts for the spiritual evolution of others, creating a network of interconnected souls who inspire and uplift one another.

The effects of our inner transformation are not confined to the individual level but ripple outward, influencing the collective consciousness in ways we may not always see.

As we evolve spiritually, our energy radiates outward, touching those around us and even spreading across communities, cultures, and nations.

The teachings remind us that we are all participants in a vast and intricate evolutionary symphony, and each action we take reverberates within this grand orchestration of life.

This interconnectedness shows us that no one is truly alone in their spiritual journey, our growth is tied to the growth of all beings.

By choosing to live consciously and embody the teachings, we become active participants in the unfolding of this cosmic process.

We help weave the fabric of collective consciousness, strengthening the connections between all people and fostering a sense of unity, peace, and shared purpose.

Keep opening, keep evolving, and keep choosing love, truth, and wisdom.

This journey of self-awareness is not just a personal pursuit but a collective mission that requires continuous effort and commitment.

As we evolve, we fulfill the ancient and sacred dream of Creation itself: the conscious flowering of all life.

This is not a distant goal but a present reality, unfolding moment by moment.

The more we align ourselves with the divine energy within, the more we contribute to the flowering of humanity as a whole.

Our actions, thoughts, and choices become part of a collective movement, one that is constantly shifting humanity toward a higher consciousness, peace, and harmony.

By choosing truth and love in every aspect of our lives, we help realize the dream of Creation, a world where all beings are awakened, conscious, and united in the shared experience of divine life.

Chapter 21

The Inner Spark
of Creation

—◆—◆◆◆—◆—

A t the very core of every human being resides a luminous spark, a living fragment of Creation itself.

This inner spark is not a mere symbol or metaphor, but a real and tangible essence, an infinitesimal, concentrated point of the infinite spirit energy that permeates the entire cosmos.

It is the very force that connects each individual to the vast web of existence, a timeless and unchanging part of the greater whole.

This spark of creation resides within us all, untouched by the transient nature of the physical world, and serves as a constant reminder of our divine origin and our eternal potential.

We are reminded that this spirit-form is not bound by time, but is eternal, journeying through countless lifetimes and experiences.

Its purpose is to evolve, to learn, and to grow through the many challenges and lessons of life.

These teachings encourage us to become more conscious of this inner spark, to recognize its presence as not something separate from us, but as the very foundation of who we are.

Our spirit is not merely a part of us, but the essence that gives us life, that fuels our being, and that connects us to the deeper, universal truths of existence.

Too often, we seek answers to life's greatest questions outside ourselves, looking to the world and others for guidance.

In doing so, we overlook the most important source of wisdom that resides within, the silent, subtle language of our spirit.

The Creation-Energy teachings ask us to listen closely to this inner wisdom, for it holds the answers we seek.

By meditating, reflecting, and living consciously, we can attune ourselves to this inner brilliance, drawing closer to the divine energy that flows within us.

As we connect with this wellspring of peace, strength, and clarity, we find that it guides us toward a deeper understanding of who we truly are, beyond the limitations of our physical bodies.

The more we align ourselves with this spirit energy, the more we realize that our true identity is not simply that of a transient body, but of a timeless being of spirit and consciousness.

Honor this spark within us by living truthfully, kindly, and courageously, in harmony with the eternal laws of Creation.

This alignment with the deeper laws of the universe helps us navigate the challenges of life with wisdom and grace, transforming our lives and our relationships in profound ways.

Each moment spent acknowledging this inner connection is a step toward fulfilling the grand purpose of our existence, the evolution of our consciousness toward perfection.

It is through this conscious awareness of our divine essence that we move closer to fulfilling the potential that lies within us, becoming the best version of ourselves. In this sacred journey inward, we come to realize that we are never truly alone.

The essence of Creation flows within us, guiding and supporting us every step of the way.

It is this divine energy that serves as a guiding light, illuminating the path toward becoming who we are truly meant to be.

As we embrace this connection, we are reminded that our purpose in this life is not simply to exist, but to evolve, to grow spiritually, mentally, and emotionally as we journey toward higher states of consciousness.

The Creation-Energy teachings inspire us to embark on this path with courage and conviction, knowing that the guiding light of Creation is always with us, leading us toward our ultimate fulfillment and the perfection of our being.

Chapter 22

The Silence of Creation

❖━━━━❖❖━━━━❖

True connection to Creation is not something that can be found in the external noise and distractions of the world, but rather in the profound and transformative silence within.

In today's fast-paced, hyper-connected world, silence is often something to be avoided or feared, as people are conditioned to fill every moment with noise, activity, or stimulation.

Yet, it is precisely in these moments of stillness that we can hear the whispers of Creation most clearly.

The loud, bustling world outside can often drown out the subtle messages of the divine within, leaving us disconnected from the deeper truths of our existence.

By embracing silence, we open ourselves to the possibility of reestablishing a deep, spiritual connection with the essence of Creation.

Silence is not merely the absence of noise, but an active state of being where we can attune ourselves to the natural rhythms of life.

When we quiet the restlessness of the mind and step into stillness, we allow ourselves to perceive the truths that are often hidden in plain sight.

The busy mind, constantly distracted by the demands of everyday life, tends to overlook the subtle signals of the universe, the gentle nudges that guide us toward growth and understanding.

Through intentional stillness, we begin to hear the unspoken language of Creation, gaining insight into the underlying patterns and principles that govern our lives.

The Creation-Energy teachings invite us to make space for this quietude in our lives, urging us to seek out sacred moments where we can retreat from the external noise and listen to the deeper wisdom that resides within.

In these sacred moments of silence, we are offered the opportunity to come face-to-face with ourselves.

It is in the stillness that we confront our own hopes, fears, desires, and innermost truths.

This inward journey can be uncomfortable at times, as it requires us to face the parts of ourselves that we may have ignored or suppressed.

However, it is through this process of self-reflection that we begin to truly know ourselves, our authentic selves, unclouded by external influences or societal expectations.

Silence is not emptiness, it is a rich presence, filled with the subtle movements of spirit and the nurturing embrace of Creation-energy.

In this space, we find clarity and insight, as the noise of the world fades away and we are left with only the quiet hum of the divine.

Learning to be comfortable in silence is a vital spiritual practice that allows us to honor the sacredness of life itself without the need for constant stimulation.

In our modern world, where distractions are ubiquitous and immediate gratification is expected, the ability to be still and present is increasingly rare.

Yet, it is through this practice of stillness that we are able to refine our perception and gain a deeper understanding of the natural laws that govern Creation.

The ebb and flow of life, the balance of cause and effect, become clearer when we allow ourselves to sit in silence and observe.

It is in these quiet moments that we begin to remember who we truly are, beyond the roles we play, beyond the noise, and beyond the illusions that the material world presents to us.

In the remembrance of our true essence, we return to the embrace of Creation, feeling its steady heartbeat pulsing gently within us, guiding us toward a life of greater peace, wisdom, and alignment with the divine energy that flows through all things.

Through the teachings of Creation-Energy, we come to understand that the stillness is not just a passive state, but an active, conscious engagement with the universe.

By cultivating a practice of quiet reflection, we begin to align ourselves more fully with the universal flow of energy and the inherent order of Creation.

Silence becomes a powerful tool for spiritual growth, allowing us to strip away the layers of distraction and illusion that prevent us from seeing the world as it truly is.

The more we embrace silence and stillness, the more we open ourselves to the deeper mysteries of life and the more clearly we perceive the wisdom of Creation.

In these moments of inward focus, we reconnect with the divine essence that resides within each of us, realizing that we are never separate from the whole of Creation.

As we move through life with this awareness, we begin to live in harmony with the natural flow of the universe, experiencing greater peace, balance, and fulfillment in all aspects of our lives.

Chapter 23

Living with Creational Consciousness

$$\bullet\!\!-\!\!-\!\!-\!\!-\!\!\bullet\!\blacklozenge\!\bullet\!\!-\!\!-\!\!-\!\!-\!\!\bullet$$

T o live with creational consciousness is to consciously align every aspect of our being, our thoughts, words, and actions, with the timeless, universal principles that govern Creation.

These principles are not abstract ideas or distant concepts but the very foundation of existence itself.

Living in accordance with these laws means we must constantly examine and refine our lives, ensuring that each decision we make is in harmony with the greater order of the universe.

It's a way of living that asks us to look beyond the immediate and the material, focusing instead on the spiritual and eternal truths that unite all of life.

It requires a deep commitment to living authentically and purposefully, with a clear understanding that our individual actions are woven into the broader tapestry of Creation, influencing not just ourselves but the collective whole.

However, it is not enough to merely know these laws intellectually, they must become an intrinsic part of our daily lives.

The knowledge of creational principles must transcend theory and become embedded in our actions, so that living with creational consciousness is no longer an intellectual exercise but a way of being.

This is where the teachings come in, they help us bridge the gap between theory and practice by encouraging us to engage in ongoing self-reflection and mindfulness.

It's about more than simply learning the principles of Creation, it's about consistently applying them in every moment, ensuring that our choices reflect the deep understanding we have gained.

In doing so, we cultivate a life that is rooted in authenticity, integrity, and alignment with the divine laws of Creation.

Every action becomes an opportunity to practice and embody these truths in the world around us.

Every thought, word, and deed carries consequences, as they are all part of the intricate and far-reaching web of cause and effect that shapes the universe.

This recognition is a central aspect of creational consciousness.

When we become aware of the profound interconnectedness of all things, we understand that every choice we make contributes to the greater harmony, or discord, of existence.

Each action, no matter how small, reverberates through the vastness of Creation.

This awareness fosters a deep sense of responsibility, as we begin to see the impact of our thoughts and actions on the world around us.

We recognize that our individual journey is not isolated, but intricately connected to the journeys of all beings.

It is through this recognition that we begin to naturally express qualities such as compassion, patience, honesty, and responsibility.

These are no longer just ideals to aspire to but become natural expressions of our understanding of our place in the greater flow of Creation.

Living with creational consciousness transforms how we perceive and respond to the challenges we encounter in life.

No longer do we view difficulties as punishments or setbacks, but as essential opportunities for growth, learning, and evolution.

Every challenge becomes a chance to deepen our understanding of the laws that govern life and to refine our consciousness.

Through this lens, obstacles are seen not as burdens, but as stepping stones on the path to greater wisdom and spiritual maturity.

The teachings invite us to approach each moment with the dignity and grace of one who recognizes their inseparable connection to the sacred Whole.

When we live with this awareness, we do not simply move through life reacting to external events, instead, we respond with purpose and clarity, guided by the deeper truths that govern existence.

In doing so, we not only uplift ourselves but contribute to the collective awakening of humanity, helping to raise the consciousness of the world around us, step by step, breath by breath.

As we embody the principles of creational consciousness, we begin to see the interconnectedness of all life.

Our awareness expands, and we recognize that every action we take affects the world in ways we may not fully understand.

This realization encourages us to live with greater humility and reverence for all life forms, knowing that we are all part of the same divine fabric.

Each moment becomes an opportunity to live in alignment with the higher purpose of our existence, to evolve, to learn, and to contribute to the greater good.

The more we live in harmony with the natural laws of Creation, the more we embody the qualities of love, compassion, and wisdom.

In this way, we become active participants in the unfolding of the universe, moving ever closer to the fulfillment of our highest potential and the awakening of humanity as a whole.

Chapter 24

The Transformative Power of Responsibility

———◆—◆◆—◆———

Responsibility is the cornerstone upon which the Creation-energy Teaching is built.

It is not simply a moral or ethical obligation but the very foundation that enables spiritual growth and alignment with the deeper truths of existence.

Without fully embracing responsibility for our thoughts, actions, and feelings, spiritual progress remains out of reach.

This is because true spiritual evolution requires us to take ownership of our lives and the choices we make.

Only by acknowledging our role in shaping our experiences can we unlock the flow of Creation-energy, which allows us to transcend the limitations of the material world and align with the universal principles that govern all life.

Without accepting responsibility, we remain passive observers, disconnected from the creative force that empowers us to transform ourselves and the world around us.

The Creation-energy teachings offer us a transformative perspective on responsibility, one that redefines it as a path to freedom rather than a burden.

In modern life, responsibility is often seen as something heavy, an imposition that we are forced to bear.

However, these teachings show us that true freedom is found in the acceptance of responsibility, for it is only when we take full ownership of our lives that we reclaim our personal power.

Each time we accept responsibility for our actions, thoughts, and emotions, we break free from the external forces that try to shape our reality.

This shift in mindset allows us to step into our true power as conscious creators, capable of shaping our destiny in accordance with the divine laws of Creation.

The act of responsibility is, therefore, an empowering and liberating process that brings us closer to living authentically and harmoniously with the universe.

When we choose to live in alignment with responsibility, we dissolve the destructive forces of blame, victimhood, and resentment.

These emotions are barriers that keep us from fully embracing our sovereignty and recognizing the strength of the psyche.

The Creation-energy teachings highlight that blame and resentment only trap us in cycles of negativity and limitation, preventing us from experiencing the flow of Creation-energy.

Responsibility, on the other hand, clears away these blockages, allowing us to tap into our inner strength and embrace the full spectrum of our human experience.

By accepting both our successes and mistakes, we gain the courage to stand in our truth, undeterred by fear or shame.

It is through this courage that we begin to experience a deeper connection to the divine, as we align ourselves with the eternal principles that guide all of Creation.

The practice of responsibility encourages us to be honest with ourselves, as it is through self-honesty that growth is nurtured.

By acknowledging where we have strayed from our highest path, we are able to make the necessary adjustments and move forward with greater clarity and purpose.

It is not the mistakes we make that define us, but how we respond to them.

In the teachings, we learn that every challenge and misstep is an opportunity to refine our understanding and evolve our consciousness.

This process of self-reflection and commitment to doing better helps us develop greater wisdom, compassion, and understanding.

Through the lens of responsibility, we see every moment as a chance to grow, to learn, and to become more aligned with the divine energy that flows through all things.

In accepting responsibility, we affirm our dignity as conscious creators, participants in the unfolding of Creation itself.

This acceptance is not a passive act but an active choice to live in harmony with the spiritual laws that govern the universe.

It is through this practice that we contribute not only to our own spiritual evolution but also to the greater awakening of humanity.

As we transform ourselves, we send ripples of positive change out into the world, influencing families, communities, and nations.

Every act of self-responsibility is a small but significant step toward creating a world that more closely mirrors the harmony of the spiritual laws.

Through this ongoing practice, we become agents of change, bringing about a shift in consciousness that leads to greater unity, peace, and understanding across the globe.

Each act of responsibility, no matter how small, helps to weave a world that is more in alignment with the divine order, where the energy of Creation can flow freely and abundantly.

Chapter 25

The Path of Inner Freedom

F reedom, as understood within the Creation-Energy Teaching, is not the absence of rules or the ability to act without restraint.

Rather, true freedom emerges through a profound alignment with the natural laws that govern all of existence.

These laws are not arbitrary, they are the very framework that sustains the universe, guiding every living being toward balance, harmony, and growth.

The teachings show us that real freedom arises when we consciously choose to harmonize our individual will with the will of Creation.

This process is not about rejecting structure or discipline but about embracing a deeper understanding of the natural order, where our actions and desires align with the universal flow.

In this way, freedom is not a chaotic or self-indulgent pursuit but a conscious return to the rhythm of the universe itself.

When we understand and respect the natural laws, we find that true freedom emerges not from acting without limits but from living in harmony with these limits.

This concept of freedom can be paradoxical. When we accept the reality of the creational laws that govern life, we discover a form of liberty far greater than the fleeting satisfaction of personal whims.

Many people associate freedom with the ability to do anything they want, to act without restrictions or limitations.

However, the Creation-Energy teachings reveal that true freedom is not about unchecked desires or impulses.

It is about the ability to act from a place of wisdom, discernment, and spiritual clarity.

Freedom means choosing love over fear, truth over illusion, and wisdom over compulsion.

It is the capacity to act with intention, to rise above the reactive patterns of the ego, and to make choices that are aligned with higher principles.

In this state of freedom, we transcend the illusion of personal control and recognize that our true power lies in our ability to act in accordance with the greater good and the natural flow of life.

It is through this inner clarity that we achieve a deep and lasting freedom, one that is not tied to external circumstances or the whims of the moment.

The teachings underscore the inseparable nature of freedom and responsibility, showing that they are two sides of the same coin.

True freedom cannot exist without responsibility because it is through accepting responsibility that we begin to understand and master our own nature.

Freedom is not about escaping responsibility or acting without consideration of the consequences of our actions.

On the contrary, it is through the conscious acceptance of responsibility for every thought, word, and deed that we unlock the deeper layers of our own power.

This responsibility is not a burden, it is the path to self-mastery, as it forces us to reflect on our actions and their alignment with the natural laws.

When we begin to see that our choices shape the course of our lives and impact the world around us, we step into a freedom that is grounded in awareness and consciousness.

The Creation-Energy teachings empower us to understand that true freedom is not granted by external authorities or circumstances but arises from within, through the active practice of self-discipline, wisdom, and conscious choice.

It is through this inner sovereignty that we experience the profound freedom to live according to the laws of Creation, unaffected by the distractions and constraints of the external world.

As we shed false beliefs, fears, and dependencies, we begin to rise into the lightness of being that true freedom brings.

This liberation comes from understanding that we are already whole, that we lack nothing essential, and that we are perfectly capable of guiding our own evolution.

In this state of inner freedom, we realize that we are not dependent on external sources for validation, power, or fulfillment.

The freedom that the Creation-Energy teachings offer is deeply rooted and resilient because it is not contingent on external circumstances, material possessions, or fleeting desires.

It comes from within, arising from our alignment with the eternal and unchanging laws of Creation.

This kind of freedom is unshaken by the ups and downs of life, as it is grounded in the awareness that we are part of a larger, divine order.

When we live from this place of inner freedom, we become beacons of light to others, quietly and powerfully reminding them of their own inherent potential and divine nature.

By embodying the principles of Creation-Energy, we naturally inspire others to recognize their own power and freedom, encouraging them to embrace their own spiritual evolution and to step into the fullness of their potential.

This ripple effect of freedom helps to create a world that is more aligned with the divine order, where each individual is empowered to live in harmony with the greater flow of life.

Chapter 26

The Wellspring of
Inner Peace

◆━━━━◆◆◆━━━━◆

Peace is not achieved by trying to control the outer world or manipulate conditions to our liking; rather, it is cultivated by developing an unshakeable center within ourselves.

The Creation-Energy Teaching shows us that lasting peace does not come from the outside but springs from the deep well of our inner being.

It is within this sacred inner space that we find the stillness that remains untouched by the inevitable storms, upheavals, and challenges of life.

True peace is not the absence of adversity, but the ability to remain centered and stable regardless of external circumstances.

Billy's teachings gently lead us toward this realization, encouraging us to step away from the endless striving and distraction that dominate modern life and instead to turn inward, where the real foundation of peace resides.

This inward journey requires courage and persistence, as it means confronting not only our fears and illusions but also learning to trust in the steady, eternal presence of the spirit within.

According to Billy and the Creation-Energy Teaching, the path to true and lasting peace always begins with the individual.

It is a great misunderstanding to believe that peace can be imposed externally, through political systems, agreements, or temporary solutions.

While these may bring moments of relief, lasting peace must arise from the transformation of each human heart.

Only when individuals align their thoughts, feelings, and actions with the timeless laws of Creation can they radiate genuine peace into the world around them.

In moments of quiet reflection, meditation, and conscious connection with the spirit, we touch the timeless serenity that belongs not to our transient personalities, but to our eternal spiritual essence.

This peace is powerful and dynamic, not a passive withdrawal from life.

It strengthens our capacity to act wisely, to love deeply, and to face life's challenges with resilience.

By embodying this inner peace, we contribute to a collective vibration that gradually transforms families, communities, and even entire societies.

Conflict, both inner and outer, arises when we become disconnected from this source of peace and allow fear, ego, and unconscious habits to govern our lives.

It is easy, in a world filled with noise and distraction, to forget the sanctuary that lies within us.

The Creation-Energy Teaching urges us to return, again and again, to this inner sanctuary, to realign ourselves with the quiet, powerful harmony of Creation.

This ongoing practice of returning to our center is not about retreating from life, but about engaging with it more fully, more consciously, and with greater wisdom.

As we anchor ourselves in this inner peace, we naturally influence our relationships, communities, and the world at large in profound ways.

We bring patience where there is impatience, understanding where there is judgment, and love where there is fear.

Our very presence becomes a healing force, a silent testimony to the power of living in alignment with the eternal rhythm of Creation.

Over time, as we deepen in this practice, the spiritual teachings cease to be something we simply study or admire from a distance.

They become alive within us, flowing through every thought, word, and action.

The river of inner peace becomes a living, breathing reality that nourishes every aspect of our lives.

Even in the face of hardship, betrayal, or sorrow, we find ourselves returning, again and again, to the inner source of calm and strength.

In doing so, we not only elevate our own consciousness but also act as catalysts for change in the world around us.

Every time we choose peace over reaction, compassion over anger, and patience over frustration, we weave a thread of harmony into the greater fabric of life.

Thus, cultivating inner peace is not merely a personal journey, it is a sacred service to all of humanity, a way of participating actively in the evolution of consciousness toward greater unity, wisdom, and love.

Through the Creation-Energy Teaching, peace becomes not a fleeting experience, but a way of being, a luminous foundation for a life lived in profound connection with all that is.

Chapter 27

The Mirror of the World

———◆———◆◆———◆———

The world we experience is far more than a backdrop for our lives, it is a dynamic mirror, faithfully reflecting the state of our inner being in every moment.

According to the Creation-Energy Teachings, every person we meet, every challenge we face, every moment of joy or sorrow, acts as a reflection of the currents running within our consciousness.

The world does not happen to us randomly, it responds to the vibrations we carry inside.

Billy reminds us that true change begins within, that by transforming our inner landscape, we naturally transform the way we perceive and experience the outer world.

This perspective calls us to shift our focus inward, away from blame or frustration toward self-awareness and personal responsibility.

When we realize that we are powerful co-creators of our experiences, we gain not only insight but also the ability to consciously shape a life that is in harmony with the timeless laws of Creation.

When we encounter conflict, injustice, or disharmony in the outer world, the teachings encourage us to respond in two ways: with constructive action in the world and with honest reflection inward.

Every disturbance we see outside of ourselves offers a mirror into aspects of our own consciousness that may still be unhealed, reactive, or unaware.

Instead of reacting with judgment, anger, or helplessness, we are invited to ask ourselves: What within me is being called to heal, to grow, to come into greater alignment with love and truth?

In this way, the outer world becomes a constant and compassionate teacher, offering us feedback on our spiritual progress.

Each event and each relationship becomes an opportunity to cultivate greater self-mastery, resilience, and understanding.

Even painful experiences, when viewed through the lens of the Creation-Energy Teaching, are revealed not as punishments, but as profound invitations to evolve.

There is no real separation between our inner work and the realities we encounter outside ourselves, they are two aspects of the same unfolding process.

As we heal our inner wounds, release limiting beliefs, and embody higher virtues such as love, patience, humility, and wisdom, we inevitably affect the external world.

Our peaceful inner state radiates outward, influencing our families, communities, and environment, sometimes in ways that are subtle yet deeply transformative.

In this way, personal growth is not merely a private affair but an essential contribution to the evolution of the collective human spirit.

The Creation-Energy Teachings show us that the world is not fixed or unchangeable, it is fluid, responsive to the energetic patterns of human thought, emotion, and consciousness.

Thus, every moment we spend working on ourselves, every time we choose understanding over judgment, or patience over anger, we are actively helping to create a more harmonious and conscious world.

Through this profound mirror-like relationship between inner being and outer reality, we grow in wisdom, humility, and gratitude.

We come to see the universe not as something indifferent or adversarial, but as a living, responsive intelligence, continually offering us reflections for our awakening.

Instead of cursing our challenges or running from discomfort, we learn to bless the reflections we encounter, using them as sacred tools for self-discovery and growth.

The Creation-Energy Teachings encourage us to meet each reflection with openness and courage, knowing that the universe itself conspires to help us remember who we truly are.

By embracing this deep truth, we align our lives more fully with the rhythms of Creation, stepping into our role as conscious participants in the unfolding of existence.

In doing so, we no longer merely live in the world; we become aware of the grand, intricate dance of life, awakening to our sacred part within it.

Chapter 28

The Courage to Be Authentic

◆━━━◆◆◆━━━◆

Authenticity is a profound act of courage, requiring a person to live fully and unapologetically in alignment with their inner truth, even when external expectations, societal pressures, and the fears of rejection loom large.

In the framework of the Creation-Energy Teachings, authenticity is not a luxury or a rare virtue reserved for a few, it is a fundamental requirement for true spiritual growth and fulfillment.

These teachings call upon each individual to strip away the many layers of false identity, the masks we have unconsciously adopted to fit in, to be loved, or to feel safe, and to stand sincerely in the radiant light of who we truly are at our core.

Billy emphasizes that our genuine nature, our true self, is often buried beneath years of accumulated conditioning, false beliefs, and the noise of a culture that too often prizes conformity over truth.

To live authentically is to engage in an ongoing relationship with the Creation-energy within us, allowing its impulses of love, truth, freedom, and harmony to become the guiding forces of our lives.

However, authenticity should not be mistaken for impulsivity or thoughtless rebellion.

Living authentically, according to the Creation-Energy Teachings, is a path of conscious, mindful action, one that honors both the self and others in the sacred dance of existence.

Authenticity demands a deep and continual inner listening, a discernment that distinguishes the fleeting voice of fear or ego from the steady, loving guidance of our spirit-form.

Each small act of truthfulness, each decision made from the heart rather than from fear or people-pleasing, serves to strengthen our connection to Creation, to the inexhaustible wisdom of Creation-energy that flows through us.

This strengthening builds self-trust, helping us to walk our path with greater confidence and clarity.

Although living authentically often requires standing apart from the herd, resisting societal norms that are misaligned with universal principles, the teachings remind us that true fulfillment is found not in external approval, but in unwavering loyalty to the inner call of truth.

The journey of authenticity is not without its challenges.

To stand in our truth often means encountering misunderstanding, resistance, or even rejection from others who are still entangled in their own fears and illusions.

It may require stepping away from environments, relationships, or roles that no longer resonate with our evolving being.

Yet, it is precisely in facing these trials with dignity and love that our spirit grows stronger and brighter.

Every moment we choose authenticity over compromise, every time we align our outer expression with our inner knowing, we participate in the sacred work of Creation itself.

Through living authentically, we become active agents of change, not through force or persuasion, but through the silent power of example.

Our very presence, when it is an honest reflection of the spirit within, has the potential to awaken others, to ignite the memory of their own inner truth and to encourage them to walk their own path of self-discovery and growth.

Ultimately, living authentically is an act of deep service to both ourselves and the world.

It is through the courageous embodiment of our true selves that we heal old wounds, dissolve false patterns, and allow the full light of Creation to shine more freely through us.

The ripples of authenticity extend far beyond the personal, they touch the collective consciousness, inspiring greater honesty, compassion, and awakening among all beings.

The Creation-Energy Teachings reveal that authenticity is not merely about being different or unique, it is about remembering and embodying the eternal, unchanging essence that resides within every human spirit.

In living this truth, we step into our rightful place within the great unfolding of Creation, experiencing the profound joy, peace, and empowerment that come from being exactly who we were always meant to be.

Thus, authenticity is not just a way of living, it is a sacred act of alignment with the highest purpose of existence itself.

Chapter 29

Gratitude as a Way of Being

◆━━━◆◆◆━━━◆

Gratitude, within the understanding of the Creation-Energy Teachings, is much more than a passing emotion triggered by favorable circumstances, it is a deep and abiding way of perceiving the entirety of life through the lens of abundance, interconnectedness, and wonder.

It is not reserved for moments of comfort or achievement but becomes a constant and natural state of being when we fully recognize the ever-present support, wisdom, and opportunities provided by Creation itself.

Billy's teaching encourages us to see that every breath we take, every challenge we face, and every relationship we encounter are all extraordinary gifts, opportunities for our consciousness to evolve and our spirit-form to unfold its inherent potential.

Gratitude, in this light, is not dependent on external events but arises from an awakened awareness of the profound richness embedded in every aspect of existence.

Nurturing gratitude is an act of aligning ourselves with the natural laws of Creation, thereby deepening our resonance with the universal rhythms that govern all life.

As our gratitude grows, so too does our sensitivity to the subtle harmonies that surround us, the unseen forces that guide, teach, and support our every step on the path of evolution.

Without gratitude, we risk becoming blind to these forces, trapped in illusions of scarcity and disconnection.

Ingratitude fosters dissatisfaction, breeding inner turmoil and creating blockages in the natural flow of spiritual energy.

Through the Creation-Energy Teachings, we are gently reminded to view even our most painful experiences through the lens of gratitude, understanding that they, too, carry within them essential lessons and gifts.

Each difficulty we encounter is not a punishment but a carefully woven part of our psyche's curriculum, designed to refine our understanding, deepen our compassion, and strengthen our inner light.

A heart cultivated in gratitude transforms the very fabric of one's existence.

When gratitude becomes the dominant note of our inner symphony, we naturally begin to attract more of what is good, beautiful, and true into our lives.

The more we acknowledge the abundance that already surrounds us, the more that abundance expands, both inwardly and outwardly.

Gratitude dissolves the heavy clouds of entitlement, resentment, and fear, allowing the sunshine of truth and joy to penetrate our consciousness.

It anchors us in the reality that we are, and always have been, participants in an infinitely generous Creation.

This realization shifts our actions, our choices, and our interactions with others, imbuing them with kindness, patience, and a profound sense of responsibility toward the Whole.

Gratitude, therefore, becomes not merely a personal practice but a contribution to the healing and upliftment of the world around us.

Ultimately, living in gratitude is an expression of spiritual maturity, a sign that we have come to see beyond appearances and into the deeper workings of existence.

Gratitude is not forced, it is a natural song of the spirit, a heartfelt response to the recognition of the ever-flowing river of love, wisdom, and life-force that sustains us all.

Through the Creation-Energy Teachings, we come to understand that gratitude is both a pathway and a destination, it is the means by which we grow and the reward of that growth itself.

As we embody gratitude more fully, we become living beacons of light, silently inspiring others to awaken to the beauty and abundance of their own lives.

In this way, gratitude is not only a personal blessing but a sacred duty, a way of participating consciously in the great unfolding of Creation.

Through gratitude, we remember who we are, where we come from, and the boundless possibilities that lie before us, waiting to be embraced with open hearts and joyful spirits.

Chapter 30

Walking the Endless Path

❖━━━━━◆◆◆━━━━━❖

Spiritual evolution, as illuminated through the Creation-Energy Teachings, is an endless, majestic journey that stretches beyond the brief span of a single lifetime and unfolds across the infinite expanses of existence.

It is a process without finality, without a strict endpoint, yet rich with meaning, purpose, and ever-deepening realization.

These teachings reassure us that there is no race to some final destination, rather, life offers an eternal invitation to growth, learning, and self-realization.

Billy reminds us with profound clarity that patience, perseverance, and humility are indispensable companions on this sacred path.

Every thought, every deed, every experience, no matter how small or seemingly insignificant, contributes to the collective blossoming of consciousness within ourselves and, by extension, throughout the entire cosmos.

The path of spiritual evolution is not a straight, predictable line but a dynamic, cyclical journey.

Periods of intense growth, insight, and transformation alternate with times of stillness, waiting, and quiet integration.

Both phases, movement and rest, are essential, like the inhalation and exhalation of breath, ensuring that our development remains stable and deeply rooted.

The Creation-Energy Teachings encourage us to embrace this natural rhythm without resistance, trusting in the larger, often unseen unfolding of life.

In moments where progress feels slow or obscured, these teachings remind us that much is happening beneath the surface, and that sincere, consistent effort will always bear fruit in its own perfect timing.

This long view frees us from impatience and despair, allowing a deep trust to grow within, a trust in ourselves, in the process, and in the living energy of Creation that supports all beings unconditionally.

Moreover, the teachings reveal that joy is not something to be postponed until we have attained some imagined spiritual height, rather, joy is found in the very act of walking the path itself.

Every sincere step we take toward self-awareness and love is, in itself, a triumph.

Even when the path is difficult, even when we stumble or lose sight of the light, Creation's presence remains, a steady, silent force encouraging us to rise again and continue onward.

Living with this awareness, we learn to celebrate small victories, to find meaning in everyday efforts, and to accept setbacks as valuable teachers rather than as signs of failure.

Gratitude naturally blooms when we realize that life, in all its complexity and challenge, serves our spirit's sacred unfolding.

We come to see that no effort is ever wasted, no experience meaningless, all is woven into the greater tapestry of our eternal becoming.

Walking this endless journey of spiritual evolution with courage, patience, and wonder transforms not only our personal reality but also our relationship with the entire universe.

We learn to perceive every moment, every encounter, every hardship, and every blessing as a necessary and beautiful part of our awakening.

The traveler who accepts this eternal pilgrimage finds peace in knowing that each step, no matter how small or arduous, draws them closer to unity with the great consciousness of Creation.

Through Billy's profound guidance, we are reminded that the ultimate goal is not to become something other than what we are, but to fully realize and embody the magnificent truth of our existence.

The path itself is the destination, and every heartbeat, every breath, every act of love, compassion, and self-honesty moves us deeper into the radiant embrace of Creation, where our spirit, our consciousness, and our eternal being are forever one.

Chapter 31

The Law of Balance

In all of Creation, balance serves as the core principle that sustains harmony and order.

It is the foundational force that ensures the universe operates with an intricate precision, maintaining a seamless integration of all things, whether seen or unseen.

The Creation-Energy teachings illuminate the idea that life itself is a continuous dance between opposing forces, light and dark, activity and rest, growth and decay.

These forces are not in conflict, but rather work in unison, seeking equilibrium and flow.

The balance between these energies is what creates the natural rhythm of existence, where each part plays a vital role in the grand unfolding of Creation.

This dynamic equilibrium is constantly shifting, as all things in the universe move and evolve according to their inherent nature.

Therefore, balance is not a fixed state, but rather a fluid, ongoing process that adjusts and realigns as circumstances evolve.

The teachings emphasize that imbalance is a primary source of suffering.

When we allow one force, whether physical, emotional, or mental, to dominate, we disrupt the natural flow of life and invite disharmony.

This dissonance can manifest as stress, illness, confusion, or emotional turbulence, leading us away from peace and alignment with Creation's flow.

On the other hand, living in balance fosters health, peace, and harmony within our own beings and in our interactions with the world around us.

The balance between work and rest, effort and relaxation, action and contemplation, allows us to live in tune with the universe and create an inner environment conducive to spiritual growth and evolution.

By aligning with balance, we connect more deeply with the eternal energies that flow through us, finding stability and vitality in the midst of life's challenges.

However, balance is not solely a concept that applies to the outer world or external circumstances.

The teachings encourage us to recognize and nurture balance within ourselves, within our thoughts, emotions, and actions.

It's easy to fall into extremes, whether we overindulge in certain behaviors, retreat into passivity, or swing between emotional highs and lows.

Such imbalances can create a sense of disconnection and unrest.

To live consciously is to be aware of these inner shifts and actively guide ourselves back into harmony.

The practice of balance requires us to pay attention to every aspect of our lives, from how we relate to others to how we nurture our own inner world.

Each aspect of our being, giving and receiving, speaking and listening, thinking and feeling, must be cultivated with mindfulness, understanding that each force contributes to the larger whole.

It is in this thoughtful interaction of polarities that we find the delicate interplay that allows us to live in harmony with ourselves and the universe.

The law of balance, however, is not about rigidity or control; it's about finding dynamic harmony, where we adjust to the ever-changing circumstances of life with wisdom and grace.

True balance is flexible, allowing us to flow with the rhythms of nature, of our inner selves, and of the world around us.

By living in balance, we align ourselves with the natural laws of Creation and deepen our connection to the universal flow.

This alignment provides us with a sense of vitality, inner stability, and peace, empowering us to move through life with confidence and grace.

The practice of balance is not something to be achieved once and for all, but rather a continual art that must be nurtured and developed through mindfulness, self-reflection, and love.

Every day presents new opportunities to recalibrate and find harmony, and every moment of self-awareness brings us closer to the greater equilibrium of Creation.

Ultimately, balance is not just a goal to be reached but a way of being, a living, breathing presence that permeates all aspects of our lives, guiding us toward a deeper understanding of ourselves and our place in the universe.

It is the key to experiencing the fullness of life, and by embracing this sacred dance of balance, we align ourselves with the eternal rhythm of Creation.

Chapter 32

The Sacredness
of Every Moment

E very moment in life is an open doorway to the infinite, a sacred
opportunity to step into the eternal now, where time and space
dissolve, and all that exists is the present moment.

The eternal wisdom reminds us that the profound meaning and magic
we seek are not hidden in distant, unreachable realms or far-off lands.

Rather, they are woven into the very fabric of everyday life, quietly
present in the ordinary moments we often overlook.

These everyday moments, each breath, each glance, each step we take,
are imbued with meaning if we choose to see them through the lens of
awareness.

Billy's teachings guide us to understand that the more present we are,
the more we are able to sense the quiet pulse of Creation that beats
within and around us.

By simply being present, we open ourselves to the divine flow of
energy and wisdom that is constantly available to us in each fleeting
moment of our lives.

Sacredness is not confined to grand rituals, extraordinary ceremonies,
or special occasions, it resides in the heart of the everyday, the mundane,
and the simple acts of daily living.

The teachings encourage us to awaken to the holiness of the ordinary,
where the miraculous and the mundane converge into one seamless
experience of Creation.

Whether we are cooking a meal, walking through a park, listening
attentively to someone speak, or smiling at a stranger, these small
actions, when approached with mindfulness and presence, become
sacred expressions of divine energy.

In each of these acts, there is beauty, meaning, and wonder, and the more we pay attention, the more we realize that life itself is a continuous flow of sacred experiences.

We begin to understand that the wonder of life is not reserved for extraordinary moments, but is embedded in the everyday, where everything carries the potential for divine revelation.

The spirit-form within us exists beyond the constraints of time.

It dwells in the eternal now, transcending the past and future, and connecting us directly to the flow of Creation.

This aspect of our being knows that life is a continuous unfolding, where each moment builds upon the next, and the past is simply a memory, the future an unknown possibility.

When we live in full presence with the moment, we align ourselves with the natural flow of energy, and we begin to perceive the world in a way that transcends the limitations of time and space.

We become more attuned to the rhythms of life, the subtle energies that guide our thoughts, emotions, and actions.

By entering into the now, we open ourselves to infinite possibilities, discovering new pathways for growth, understanding, and connection.

This awareness allows us to act with greater clarity, purpose, and peace, free from the constraints of past mistakes or future anxieties.

In this state, we become empowered to live fully, knowing that every moment carries with it the potential for transformation and alignment with our highest purpose.

When we honor each moment as sacred, we elevate the quality of our lives, infusing even the simplest acts with meaning, beauty, and grace.

The true temple of Creation is not located in a physical structure or a distant realm, but in life itself.

Every experience, every interaction, every moment of stillness or action is a sacred opportunity to connect with Creation.

By living consciously, we transform the ordinary into the extraordinary.

Each step, each breath, each glance becomes a prayer, a celebration of life's beauty and mystery.

In embracing the present moment with full awareness, we rediscover the wonder, joy, and gratitude that are the hallmarks of an awakened soul.

Through this practice, we realize that the miracle of life is found not in the future, nor in the past, but in the timeless now, where we are always invited to reconnect with the infinite and embrace the fullness of Creation.

In this sacred presence, we find the deepest peace, and we experience life as it was meant to be, a continuous unfolding of divinity, where every moment is an invitation to worship the Creator through the act of living consciously.

Each moment, when embraced fully, becomes an expression of the eternal, and in living this way, we find ourselves closer to the essence of our true nature.

Chapter 33

The Journey Inward

◆———◆◈◆———◆

The Creation Energy teachings offer a profound insight into the nature of our true journey in life, it is not a quest to distant lands or external accomplishments, but rather an exploration into the unexplored depths of ourselves.

Billy's wisdom teaches us that the greatest discoveries and treasures are found not in the outside world, but within, in the very core of our being.

Within each of us lies the spark of Creation itself, an eternal flame that burns with potential, waiting for us to recognize and nurture it.

This spark, though often hidden beneath layers of thoughts, emotions, and external distractions, is the true essence of who we are.

The journey inward is one of self-realization, where we move from the surface of our daily lives into the deep recesses of our consciousness, uncovering the profound truths about our spiritual nature and connection to the universe.

Embarking on this inward journey requires great courage, for it asks us not only to face our light, the qualities we admire and cherish within ourselves, but also to confront our shadows.

Our fears, insecurities, unresolved emotions, and unconscious patterns are all part of this inner landscape, and it is in facing them that we unlock our true potential.

The teachings invite us to practice honest self-reflection, but not in a way that promotes self-criticism or judgment.

Rather, it encourages us to view ourselves with compassion, understanding, and curiosity, seeking to understand the root of our challenges rather than condemning them.

This approach helps us to heal the wounds within, transform limiting beliefs, and release the emotional baggage that holds us back.

It is in this process of acceptance and healing that we come into deeper contact with the living presence of Creation itself, which is always present within us, waiting for us to recognize it.

As we dive deeper into this journey, we are called to enter the silence within, beyond the ceaseless flow of thoughts and emotions.

In this silence, we encounter the stillness that is the true nature of the spirit-form that resides in all of us.

This silence is not empty or devoid of meaning, it is rich with the wisdom, peace, and love of Creation.

It is in this quiet space that we begin to understand the profound truth that every insight we gain, every fear we transform, brings us closer to the authentic power that resides within us.

It is through this inner journey of awakening and transformation that we realize that true fulfillment is not found in external accomplishments, status, or material possessions.

The real treasure, the source of lasting joy, peace, and wisdom, has always been within us, patiently waiting for us to uncover it.

As we become more attuned to this inner presence, we experience a deep sense of alignment with our true purpose and a connection to the universal consciousness that governs all life.

The inward journey is ultimately a sacred pilgrimage, a profound, transformative process that leads us back to the heart of life itself.

It is through this deepening connection with our true essence that we understand that we are not separate from the world around us, but an inseparable part of the ever-expanding universe.

As we walk this path, we realize that every step we take inwardly ripples outward, influencing not only our own lives but the world around us.

We are constantly guided by the energy of Creation, which is always present, offering us support, wisdom, and love as we traverse this sacred journey.

The teachings remind us that this path is not always linear or easy, but it is always worthwhile, for each step brings us closer to the unity we seek with Creation.

As we continue to dive deeper into self-awareness, we not only discover the vast treasures of wisdom and love within ourselves, but we also uncover the interconnectedness of all beings.

This journey, while intensely personal, is also a collective experience, one that leads to greater harmony, understanding, and peace for all of Creation.

Through this pilgrimage, we realize that the heart of life itself is love, and it is through love that we are united with the divine essence that flows through everything.

Chapter 34

The Strength of Gentleness

◆━━━━━◆◆◆━━━━━◆

Gentleness, often misunderstood as weakness, is in truth one of the most profound and powerful forces we can embody.

In a world that places a high value on strength, aggression, and force, gentleness is frequently seen as a passive or ineffective response.

However, the teachings reveal that gentleness is far from a sign of fragility, it is a form of power that arises from inner peace, deep self-awareness, and a strong connection to the wisdom of Creation.

Gentleness does not come from fear or an avoidance of conflict, but from an understanding that true strength lies in the ability to be soft in the face of life's challenges.

It is an active choice, a conscious decision to meet the world with kindness, compassion, and grace, even when circumstances might tempt us to act harshly.

A gentle spirit remains steadfast in its truth, embracing patience and empathy, and in doing so, it brings balance to situations that may otherwise escalate into conflict.

True gentleness has the remarkable ability to soften resistance and dismantle walls that separate people.

Where forceful approaches create division and tension, gentleness fosters understanding and cooperation.

In a conversation, gentleness allows space for both voices to be heard, creating an atmosphere where ideas can be exchanged respectfully.

It is through gentleness that we invite others to connect with us on a deeper level, not just through our words, but through our energy and presence.

When we approach life with a gentle heart, we create an environment where trust can flourish, and relationships are strengthened.

By embodying gentleness, we open ourselves to a higher frequency of communication and collaboration, where compassion guides our actions and words.

This doesn't mean avoiding conflict or suppressing our truth, rather, it means communicating with clarity, understanding, and an open heart, even in moments of disagreement.

In a world obsessed with control, competition, and aggression, gentleness stands as a revolutionary act, challenging these societal norms and offering a path to a more compassionate and harmonious existence.

The teachings invite us to understand that gentleness is not a passive response but an active form of resistance against the fear and division that dominate so much of human interaction.

To be gentle is to trust in the resilience and wisdom of life itself.

Rather than relying on force or domination to shape the world, gentleness encourages us to trust that lasting change can come through love, patience, and understanding.

It calls us to believe in the power of kindness as a transformative force, one that allows us to dissolve conflict and create healing, both for ourselves and for the world around us.

The more we embody gentleness, the more we contribute to a global shift toward peace and compassion, where actions are guided by love rather than fear or pride.

Cultivating gentleness requires not only acting with kindness but also nurturing it in our thoughts and words.

When we live gently, we bring this energy into every interaction, making it a reflection of the mastery we've developed over ourselves.

True gentleness comes from a place of inner strength, an understanding of our own worth and the wisdom that we carry.

It is through gentleness that we create spaces for healing and growth, both in our own lives and in the lives of others.

The teachings encourage us to make gentleness a consistent part of our daily lives, knowing that when we live this way, we mirror the nurturing force of Creation itself.

Gentleness is the medicine the world needs, it heals, it nurtures, and it creates a space for transformation to occur.

It is the very essence of the divine, present in every act of love, every word of kindness, and every quiet moment of compassion.

By embodying gentleness, we step into our highest power, showing the world that true strength is found in tenderness, and that gentleness is a force that can move mountains.

Chapter 35

The Purity of Truth

◆━━━◆◆◆━━━◆

Truth is the bedrock upon which all evolution stands, providing the foundation for both personal growth and collective development.

The teachings emphasize that living truthfully is not just about telling the truth, but about deeply aligning oneself with the natural order of Creation itself.

This alignment with truth is seen as a way of living in harmony with the cosmos, recognizing that everything, our actions, thoughts, and feelings, are interconnected within a greater, eternal plan.

Truth, as taught in these teachings, is not a rigid or unchanging doctrine, but rather a dynamic, living force that evolves with our understanding of the universe.

It requires constant introspection, growth, and refinement, allowing us to expand our awareness and deepen our connection to the greater whole.

Thus, to seek truth is to embark on a journey of continuous self-discovery, an endeavor to align our inner reality with the outer reality, attuning ourselves to the infinite wisdom inherent in the Creation-energy that flows through everything.

Seeking truth often requires us to confront and release the many illusions and deceptions that cloud our perception of ourselves and the world around us.

These illusions, whether formed by societal expectations, personal fears, or attachments to false beliefs, create a distorted lens through which we view the world.

The teachings call us to shed these layers of illusion, challenging us to face uncomfortable truths about our own nature and the state of the world.

This process of self-liberation is not without its difficulties, as it requires the courage to move beyond the comfort of familiar beliefs and step into the unknown.

Yet, it is through this courage that we are able to experience true freedom.

Living in truth clears the fog of confusion and opens our minds to a higher understanding, one that transcends the limitations of the ego and the societal norms that often bind us.

By embracing the truth, we free ourselves from the weight of ignorance, and in doing so, we move closer to the authentic self that resides within.

The act of living truthfully transforms our very being, purifying both our mind and heart.

This purification process clears away the emotional and mental barriers that prevent us from fully experiencing life's richness.

When we stand firmly in truth, we open ourselves to a greater flow of wisdom, compassion, and understanding.

Our perception of reality becomes sharper, and we begin to see the world as it truly is, filled with beauty, interconnectedness, and the ever-present potential for growth.

Truth, in its purest form, is not merely a concept to be understood, but a living force that transforms us from the inside out.

As we embrace this force, we become more aligned with the essence of Creation, experiencing life through a clearer lens and with greater empathy toward others.

Living truthfully also strengthens our relationships with those around us, as we engage more authentically with others and share the genuine truth of our experiences.

This connection to truth allows us to embody both wisdom and compassion, providing a foundation for deeper, more meaningful interactions.

The journey toward truth is not a destination, but an ongoing process that brings us closer to our true nature with every step we take.

As we strip away the layers of illusion and conditioning, we begin to uncover the core of who we are, the essence of our being that is eternal and connected to all of Creation.

The teachings assure us that as we live in truth, we align ourselves more fully with the divine intelligence that governs the universe.

Every step toward truth is a step closer to understanding our divine purpose and realizing our highest potential.

By honoring truth in all aspects of life, we honor the sacredness of Creation itself, recognizing that truth is not just a personal journey, but a universal force that binds all of existence.

The more we embrace and live by the truth, the more we step into our divine power, allowing the wisdom of Creation to guide us toward the fulfillment of our highest destiny.

In this way, truth becomes the light that illuminates our path, the force that shapes our evolution, and the foundation upon which all meaningful growth and transformation is built.

Chapter 36

The Healing Power of Love

L ove is the most powerful force in the universe, the very essence of Creation itself, woven into every aspect of existence.

It is the pulse that drives life, the energy that connects and sustains all beings.

This love is not simply an emotion or fleeting sentiment, it is a dynamic, living energy that flows through everything, binding us all in an unbreakable web of connection.

It is the foundational vibration of Creation, the very force that holds all things together in perfect harmony.

Every moment, every breath, every interaction is an expression of this profound force.

Love is not only the thread that ties all things together, it is the force that allows the universe to continue expanding, evolving, and unfolding.

When we align ourselves with love, we tap into the very source of all life, becoming more in tune with the rhythm of existence and more connected to the universal flow.

The power of love lies not just in its ability to unite, but in its capacity to heal, transform, and restore.

Love is both an inner experience and an outward expression that flows from our hearts to the world around us.

At the core of love is self-love, for we cannot truly give love to others if we do not first nurture it within ourselves.

The teachings remind us that love for others, for all life, and for the world itself, is equally important.

As we deepen our connection to our own hearts, we create space for love to expand outward, touching those we encounter and the environment in which we live.

This kind of love is powerful and transformative, capable of dissolving barriers, healing wounds, and creating harmony where there was once discord.

When we live with love as the guiding force of our lives, we align with Creation's purpose, drawing closer to the divine, and allowing that love to shine through in every thought, word, and action.

Living with love is not passive; it is an active force that shapes our consciousness and influences our interactions with others.

It is through love that we elevate our awareness, lifting ourselves from ego-based perspectives to a higher, more interconnected view of reality.

Love enables us to see the sacredness in all beings and situations, transforming the ordinary into something extraordinary.

It opens our hearts to deeper connections with others, encouraging empathy, compassion, and understanding.

By embracing love, we are not only contributing to our own personal growth but to the collective consciousness of humanity.

Love is the antidote to fear, anger, and division. In a world often dominated by conflict and misunderstanding, love is the force that transcends these divides, bringing peace, unity, and reconciliation.

It allows us to forgive, to release judgment, and to embrace the wholeness of life. Love nurtures the soul, helping us grow in wisdom, patience, and compassion.

True love is unconditional, freely given, and without expectation.

It mirrors the love of Creation itself, limitless, all-encompassing, and pure.

The teachings of Creation-Energy remind us that love is not something that can be earned or demanded, it is a gift that flows naturally from our inner being when we are attuned to our true essence.

When we embody this love, we reflect the divine light of Creation in every interaction, becoming living expressions of peace, kindness, and joy.

Love is the most profound healing force in the universe, transcending all boundaries, whether they are physical, emotional, or spiritual.

It has the power to break down walls, dissolve misunderstandings, and bring healing to wounds that seem insurmountable.

As we embrace love in all its forms, self-love, love for others, and love for life itself, we begin to see that the universe itself is made of love.

Every act of kindness, every moment of compassion, every expression of care is a reflection of the divine order that permeates all things.

In living with love, we become active participants in the unfolding of Creation, contributing to the evolution of consciousness and the collective awakening of humanity.

Through love, we align ourselves with the divine flow of life, experiencing the joy, peace, and fulfillment that come from being true to our innermost essence.

Chapter 37

The Path of Self-Realization

The path of self-realization is a profound and sacred journey, one that invites us to remember and rediscover our true nature as divine beings.

It is not a destination that lies somewhere far beyond reach, but rather a living, breathing process that unfolds within the fabric of everyday life.

The ancient teachings assure us that self-realization is not something to be attained in the distant future, it is something accessible here and now, in each moment we choose to awaken.

Through this path, we come to recognize that we are not separate from Creation, not isolated fragments adrift in the universe, but integral expressions of the very Source from which all life flows.

Every step along this journey draws us deeper into the realization that we are already whole, already connected, and already sacred in our essence.

To walk this path with sincerity demands great honesty, courage, and an unwavering willingness to face all aspects of ourselves, including the parts we have hidden, denied, or misunderstood.

Self-realization is not about crafting an image of perfection or adhering to some external ideal, rather, it is about surrendering to the authentic truth that resides within us.

The teachings guide us to let go of the many false identities we accumulate, the masks shaped by fear, expectation, and societal conditioning, and to step away from the constant need for external approval.

In their place, we are called to listen deeply to the voice of our own soul, the quiet, steady wisdom that speaks from within.

It is by honoring this inner voice that we realign with our true self, allowing authenticity to lead us forward.

As we open ourselves more fully to the journey of self-realization, we naturally begin to experience profound shifts in our inner and outer worlds.

A greater sense of peace arises, not from the absence of challenges, but from the deep knowing that we are held within the loving current of Creation's energy.

Fulfillment blossoms as we stop seeking outside ourselves for validation and recognize the sacredness inherent in simply being who we are.

Our awakening reveals the intricate interconnectedness of all life, dissolving the illusion of separation that once clouded our vision.

We come to see that every thought, every action, and every breath participates in the ongoing dance of the cosmos, and that each of us plays a vital and irreplaceable role in the unfolding story of existence.

Ultimately, the journey of self-realization is not a finite goal to be checked off or completed, it is an eternal unfolding, a continuous deepening into greater awareness, love, and wisdom.

There is no final destination where growth ends, only new horizons of possibility and new layers of being to explore.

As we embody our highest potential, we not only transform our own lives but also contribute to the collective awakening of humanity as a whole.

Our individual realization ripples outward, inspiring others to remember their own divine nature.

In this ever-evolving dance of becoming, we discover the true meaning of life: to awaken, to grow, to serve, and to shine as conscious co-creators within the infinite mystery of Creation.

Chapter 38

The Energy
of Transformation

❖—◆ ◆◆◆ ◆—❖

Transformation is the natural and inevitable process of evolution, the continual and beautiful unfolding of the material consciousness's vast and limitless potential.

It is an essential rhythm of existence, a sacred current that runs through every living being and every experience.

In truth, we are always in motion, always becoming, even when we feel stagnant or resistant to change.

The spirit knows no stillness, it constantly seeks to grow, to expand, to deepen its understanding of itself and of the world.

Life itself is a journey of perpetual transformation, an ever-turning wheel where each moment offers the possibility of renewal.

The teachings remind us that change is not something to fear but something to honor, for in transformation, we find the expression of our energy's highest calling to evolve.

The spiritual teachings explain that true transformation requires a delicate dance between surrender and action.

It asks us not only to courageously step forward but also to release with love the old patterns, attachments, and beliefs that have outlived their purpose.

Transformation invites us to trust the unknown, to lay down the familiar pathways that keep us bound to cycles of limitation.

Yet at the same time, it calls for mindful action, to consciously shape our lives in alignment with our psyche's longing.

The energy of transformation is the divine spark that dwells within each of us, urging us forward into higher realms of consciousness and deeper layers of understanding.

Every challenge that life presents is not a punishment or a detour but an invitation, a sacred opportunity for growth.

Every obstacle is a gateway through which we can step into greater authenticity, if only we are willing to see it as such.

The path of transformation is not always smooth or comfortable.

Often, it leads us through territories of uncertainty, dismantling the identities and structures we once relied upon for safety.

True spiritual growth requires a willingness to journey through the unknown, to weather the storms of change with faith that something greater is being born within us.

Transformation demands the release of the familiar so that the new can emerge, and this shedding process can be both painful and liberating.

As we allow old beliefs and self-imposed limitations to fall away, we make space for the new possibilities waiting to enter our lives.

Billy teaches that transformation is not a random or chaotic occurrence, but a key and necessary aspect of the human experience.

Through it, we are led toward the fulfillment of our highest potential and our soul's true purpose, uncovering gifts and strengths we never knew were within us.

Through the Creation Energy Teachings, we are offered profound guidance on how to move through transformation with grace, patience, and deep trust.

These teachings show us how to welcome change as a sacred companion rather than resist it as an enemy.

They teach us to find steadiness amidst uncertainty, to cultivate compassion for ourselves as we grow, and to trust that every stage of the process has its divine timing.

Transformation is not a one-time event but a continuous unfolding that brings us ever closer to the truth of who we are and who we are destined to become.

It is a sacred journey that reconnects us to the greater currents of life, reminding us that we are not isolated beings but dynamic expressions of an infinite, evolving Creation.

In honoring transformation, we step into harmony with the universe itself, becoming active participants in the grand, ever-unfolding dance of life.

Chapter 39

The Unified Field of Creation

E verything in the universe is intricately interconnected, part of a vast and living network of energy that pulses with the intelligence of Creation itself.

Every star, every tree, every thought, and every being is woven together in an endless tapestry of existence.

Nothing stands alone, all things are expressions of a single Source, existing in a sacred relationship with one another.

The Creation Energy Teachings reveal that the universe is not a random collection of separate forms, but a unified field of consciousness, a boundless ocean of awareness where all beings, energies, and even the subtlest thoughts are interconnected and interdependent.

Within this field, the heartbeat of one resonates through all, and every movement in one part of the web is felt throughout the whole.

In truth, we are not isolated individuals, we are vibrant, essential strands in the great fabric of Creation.

The illusion of separation is one of the greatest misunderstandings perpetuated by the human ego.

From a limited perspective, the ego convinces us that we are distinct, isolated, and divided, separated from one another, from nature, and from creation.

Yet as we begin to awaken to deeper spiritual realities, we come to see that this separation is a mirage.

The Creation Energy Teachings guide us to lift the veils that cloud our vision and to perceive the world as it truly is, interconnected, unified, whole.

The more we recognize this interconnectedness, the more we sense the divine energy flowing through all things, animating and sustaining the universe with infinite love and wisdom.

We begin to see ourselves reflected in the eyes of others, in the beauty of the natural world, and in the mysteries of the cosmos.

Awakening to this truth transforms our relationships, our choices, and our very sense of being.

The Creation Energy Teachings also remind us that with this awareness comes great responsibility.

Our actions, thoughts, and intentions do not exist in a vacuum, they ripple outward through the unified field, influencing the energies around us in ways both seen and unseen.

Every act of kindness strengthens the web of love, every act of harm sends ripples of discord into the field.

Living with this awareness calls us to cultivate mindfulness, compassion, and integrity in all we do.

The unified field of Creation is not passive, it is an active, dynamic, living intelligence, supporting the continual growth and evolution of all life.

When we consciously align ourselves with this field, we draw from infinite reservoirs of creativity, insight, peace, and transformative power.

We become instruments of the divine, allowing love and wisdom to flow through us in service to the greater whole.

Ultimately, the highest aim of human evolution is to awaken fully to the reality of the unified field and to live as conscious co-creators within it.

Through the study and embodiment of the Creation Energy Teachings, we learn to cultivate a deeper sense of unity with all of life.

We come to recognize that we are both the wave and the ocean, individual expressions and yet inseparably one with the vastness of Creation.

Living in harmony with the unified field allows us to experience the boundless love, abundance, and wisdom that are our birthright.

It transforms the way we see ourselves, others, and the world, awakening a profound reverence for all existence.

This sacred journey is not merely about personal enlightenment, but about participating fully in the ongoing evolution of life itself, radiating light into the world, and embodying the creative power of the divine in everything we do.

Chapter 40

The Illusion of Time

Time, as we experience and measure it, is an illusion, a veil that overlays the eternal reality of Creation and colors our perception of existence.

To our human senses, time seems fixed and undeniable, charting a linear path from past to present to future.

Yet, in the deeper truth revealed through the Creation Energy Teachings, time is not a fundamental property of existence, but a construct of the human mind.

It was created as a tool to organize experiences, to provide a framework within which our limited perception could make sense of the unfolding of life.

In the grand design of Creation, however, there are no clocks ticking, no divisions between moments, only a seamless, eternal now that holds all possibilities within it.

In this greater reality, past, present, and future coexist in a timeless field of pure being.

Creation exists far beyond the bounds of time and space, resting in a state of infinite presence where all that ever was and all that will ever be are simultaneously alive.

The illusion of time can create unnecessary stress, fear, and a sense of limitation within us, an urgency to accomplish, to change, to control the flow of life before it is "too late."

These pressures weigh heavily on the spirit and fragment our awareness.

But as the Creation Energy Teachings gently remind us, when we align with the true energy of Creation, we naturally rise above the constraints of time.

We enter into a state of grace where life unfolds not by the ticking of the clock, but by the organic rhythms of the psyche.

We realize that the past holds no chains over us and that the future does not have to be feared.

All we truly ever have is the living, breathing moment in which we exist, and within that moment lies the entire universe.

The Creation Energy Teachings encourage us to cultivate a deeper awareness of the present moment, to recognize it as the birthplace of all creation.

In the eternal now, every potential outcome is accessible; every dream, every healing, every transformation already exists as a living possibility.

To live in harmony with Creation is to surrender the need to control or rush, and instead allow the divine intelligence of life to move through us naturally and effortlessly.

It means trusting that life knows the way and that our role is to remain present, receptive, and aligned.

As we begin to step out of the artificial constraints of linear time, we experience a profound shift, life becomes less about striving and more about flowing, less about fear and more about wonder.

We find that in the present moment, creativity blossoms, wisdom emerges, and the deepest peace is found.

As we continue this journey of awakening, we remember that we are not bound by time but are eternal beings, intimately connected to the infinite, ever-unfolding dance of Creation.

The Creation Energy Teachings invite us to release our attachment to the structures of time, to the deadlines, regrets, and anxieties that bind us, and to embrace instead our timeless essence.

In doing so, we experience the freedom of living from our true nature, expansive, luminous, and whole.

Letting go of the illusion of time opens a portal to a deeper connection with all that is, revealing a life rich with synchronicity, meaning, and sacred unfolding.

In this way, we are not simply surviving the passage of time, we are co-creating with the eternal energy of Creation, awakening more fully to the truth of who we are, and participating consciously in the great, timeless mystery of existence.

Chapter 41

The Power of Intention

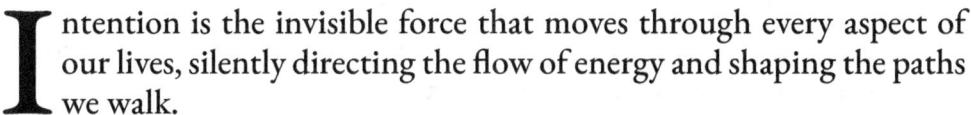

Intention is the invisible force that moves through every aspect of our lives, silently directing the flow of energy and shaping the paths we walk.

Though it often operates beneath the surface of our conscious awareness, intention acts as the magnetic center around which our experiences form.

According to the Creation Energy Teachings, intention is not merely a wish or fleeting thought, it is the living blueprint of our future, the energetic seed from which all experiences sprout.

Every thought we nurture, every feeling we hold, every action we take begins with an intention, whether consciously set or unconsciously harbored.

In understanding this, we recognize that we are not victims of random circumstances but are active participants in a dynamic, responsive universe.

Our lives reflect the clarity, strength, and alignment of our inner intentions.

The Creation Energy Teachings emphasize that intention is the essential first step in the sacred process of manifestation.

Before any dream can become reality, before any change can anchor into our physical world, it must first be born in the energetic realm as a conscious, focused intention.

However, not all intentions are created equally. Intentions rooted in fear, ego, or superficial desires will manifest in ways that often leave us feeling unfulfilled or disconnected.

True creation requires that our intentions arise from the deepest parts of ourselves, from our soul's wisdom and our heart's authentic yearning.

Setting an intention is an act of communion with Creation's energy, it is a sacred conversation between our higher self and the universe.

When we take time to align our intentions with truth, integrity, and higher purpose, we open the doorway for miracles to unfold naturally and harmoniously in our lives.

The Creation Energy Teachings invite us to consciously cultivate intentions that are clear, positive, and rooted in our highest good.

A true, powerful intention is not merely about personal gain, it resonates with the universal principles of love, harmony, and interconnectedness.

When we set such intentions, we become aligned with the vast creative force that supports all life.

These intentions then act as guiding currents, aligning our thoughts, emotions, and actions with our desired reality.

They help us maintain focus through life's inevitable challenges, providing an inner compass that keeps us true to our path.

Intention, when properly set, becomes not just a private wish but a living vibration that influences our environment, invites synchronicity, and magnetizes opportunities that are in resonance with our soul's journey.

It is through this power that we learn to move from merely existing to consciously creating our lives.

Through the wisdom of the Creation Energy Teachings, we come to understand that setting clear, heartfelt intentions transforms us into conscious architects of our destiny.

We are no longer adrift in the tides of circumstance, but empowered to steer the course of our lives with purpose and grace.

Intention is the original spark that ignites the fires of creation, the sacred impulse from which all manifestation begins.

It is the whisper of the soul calling forth new realities from the field of infinite potential.

When we honor and nurture our intentions with love, patience, and trust, we align ourselves with the unfolding rhythms of Creation itself.

By living intentionally, we harmonize with the great song of existence, becoming co-creators in the sacred dance of life, shaping our world with wisdom, joy, and the creative power that lives within us all.

Chapter 42

The Strength of Vulnerability

Vulnerability is often misinterpreted in our world as a sign of weakness, yet in reality, it represents one of the most profound strengths we can embody.

To be vulnerable is to allow the heart to open fully, permitting the divine energy of Creation to flow freely through us.

It requires immense courage to stand unguarded, to let go of the defenses we build to shield ourselves from pain or judgment.

Billy teaches us that true strength does not come from domination, control, or invulnerability, but rather from the willingness to be open, honest, and authentic, both with ourselves and with others.

In vulnerability, we find the pathway to genuine connection, a sacred bridge between souls that transcends superficial interaction.

It is through the lens of vulnerability that we truly see and are truly seen.

When we embrace vulnerability, we invite trust, understanding, and compassion to flourish.

The Creation Energy Teachings emphasize that vulnerability is not a flaw to be corrected but a gift to be celebrated, a direct acknowledgment of our humanity and of the Creation energy that pulses within each of us.

In being willing to reveal our innermost thoughts, fears, hopes, and dreams, we give permission for others to do the same.

We create spaces where healing conversations happen, where brokenness is met with kindness, and where authenticity can thrive.

Billy reminds us that hiding behind a façade of strength distances us not only from others but also from our own psyche.

Vulnerability dismantles the illusion of separation and reminds us that we are all part of the same sacred dance of existence.

Moreover, vulnerability acts as a powerful catalyst for healing and transformation.

It is only by facing our fears, rather than running from them, that we can truly transcend them.

Vulnerability demands that we look honestly at the parts of ourselves we often seek to ignore, our wounds, our doubts, our uncertainties, and in doing so, we summon the divine courage needed to heal and grow.

When we embrace vulnerability, we align ourselves with the deeper currents of Creation's energy, which moves us toward wholeness.

Healing does not come from pretending that we are untouched by life's hardships, it comes from meeting those hardships with open arms and an open heart.

Vulnerability is the sacred act of saying, "Here I am," without guarantees, without pretense, trusting that the act of revealing will itself bring light and renewal.

Ultimately, the Creation Energy Teachings call us to dismantle the heavy armor we wear, the emotional masks, the shields of cynicism and fear, that we mistakenly believe keep us safe.

We are invited instead to allow ourselves to be seen in our fullness, our strength and our fragility, our confidence and our uncertainty, our light and our shadow.

By embracing vulnerability, we access the full magnitude of Creation's energy, which nurtures, strengthens, and transforms us beyond what we could achieve through self-protection alone. In choosing to live vulnerably, we choose to live fully, allowing life to touch us, move us, and shape us into more compassionate, authentic beings.

Vulnerability is not the abandonment of strength, it is the highest form of courage, the decision to be real, to show up as we are, and to trust that in our openness, we are held by something greater than ourselves.

Chapter 43

The Law of Cause and Effect

The law of cause and effect stands as one of the most fundamental and unchanging principles within Creation, silently governing all existence from the smallest interactions to the grandest movements of the cosmos.

According to the Creation Energy Teachings, every thought we entertain, every word we speak, and every action we take generates an energy that reverberates outward, creating a ripple effect that inevitably circles back to us.

This law operates with perfect impartiality, unaffected by human interpretations of fairness or intention, it simply and consistently delivers effects according to the causes set into motion.

Billy teaches that nothing exists in isolation, every effect has its cause, and every cause inevitably yields an effect, no matter how subtle or delayed its manifestation might be.

Through understanding this sacred law, we come to realize that our lives are not the result of random events or external forces, but of the energetic seeds we ourselves have planted, knowingly or unknowingly.

Recognizing the reality of cause and effect calls us into a higher level of personal responsibility and awareness.

The Creation Energy Teachings invite us to observe our thoughts, words, and actions with great mindfulness, understanding that every choice we make shapes not only our immediate reality but also creates lasting energetic imprints on the fabric of existence.

Each act of kindness, every moment of compassion, each conscious decision to live in harmony with Creation's laws plants seeds that eventually yield fruits of peace, joy, and fulfillment.

Conversely, actions rooted in fear, anger, deception, or selfishness create disturbances that inevitably return to the sender, offering opportunities for learning, correction, and growth.

Billy reminds us that we are not powerless beings tossed about by circumstance, rather, we are the architects of our lives, continuously building our inner and outer worlds through the dynamic interplay of causes and effects.

The law of cause and effect teaches us that every moment holds creative potential.

In each instant, we are given the opportunity to sow the seeds of our future experiences.

Our inner world, our thoughts, intentions, and emotions, plays a crucial role in determining the quality of our outer experiences.

According to the Creation Energy Teachings, nothing happens by chance or coincidence.

All events, relationships, successes, and struggles emerge from this invisible, yet profoundly real, web of causality.

When we act with conscious awareness, choosing love over fear, truth over deceit, and compassion over indifference, we not only elevate our own consciousness but also positively influence the collective consciousness of humanity.

Try your very best to see beyond the immediate effects of our actions and to understand the long-term, often unseen consequences that ripple outward, affecting people and circumstances far beyond our immediate perception.

By embracing the law of cause and effect, we align ourselves with the natural flow of Creation's energy, stepping into the sacred role of co-creators of reality.

To live in harmony with this law is to live with intention, integrity, and deep inner wisdom.

When we become aware that every thought and deed matters, we naturally become more deliberate and compassionate in our interactions with the world.

In doing so, we participate in the conscious evolution of ourselves and the greater Creation.

Every act of goodness, every effort toward truth, and every gesture of love sets into motion energies that uplift not only our personal lives but also contribute to the healing and growth of all existence.

Truly, honoring the law of cause and effect is an act of profound respect for life itself, acknowledging that through our choices, we hold the power to create a more harmonious, enlightened, and beautiful world.

Chapter 44

The Art of Listening

Listening is not merely a passive act, it is a sacred art, a conscious practice that invites us into deeper communion with ourselves, with others, and with the divine energy that underlies all existence.

True listening extends far beyond the physical act of hearing words, it is an attunement to the energy, emotions, and intentions that dwell beneath the surface of speech.

The art of listening is foundational to real understanding and the growth of wisdom.

Through listening, we enter into a space of profound presence, where we allow the divine flow of Creation to speak through every word, every silence, and every nuance.

Listening becomes an act of devotion, a sacred acknowledgment of the unseen forces that connect us all.

The Creation Energy Teachings encourage us to engage all aspects of our being when we listen, not just our ears, but our hearts, our intuitive senses, and our open minds.

It is through this multi-dimensional listening that we perceive the deeper truths hidden behind spoken words.

We are invited to hear the quiet fears, the silent hopes, the invisible struggles that words alone cannot convey.

When we listen deeply, we open a portal for healing, growth, and profound understanding to occur.

In this sacred space, individuals feel seen and honored, their true essence recognized and embraced without conditions.

Listening in this way is not passive but vibrantly active, it is the creation of a loving space where transformation naturally unfolds.

Practicing the art of true listening requires patience, humility, and a heart that remains open, undefended, and free from judgment.

It demands that we set aside our own internal chatter, resist the urge to formulate replies, and instead offer our complete attention to the present moment.

In giving our undivided presence, we perform one of the highest forms of love, the affirmation that the other's existence matters deeply.

True listening is an act of surrender, where we release the need to control the narrative or rush to solutions, and instead simply receive.

It asks us to trust in the wisdom that emerges when we allow others to fully express themselves without interruption, correction, or assumption.

When we embody the art of listening, we transform the very fabric of our relationships and our communities.

We build bridges of trust, understanding, and mutual respect that can weather even the fiercest storms.

Through this deepened connection, we transcend surface differences and recognize the shared humanity and divinity that bind us all.

True listening softens hardened hearts, heals old wounds, and fosters the unity that Creation itself calls us toward.

In the sacred act of listening, we do more than communicate, we commune.

We enter a dance of souls, where the energy of love, understanding, and healing flows freely.

Listening becomes a prayer, a blessing, and a profound act of creation in itself, weaving us ever more deeply into the web of life.

Chapter 45

The Importance of Reflection

Reflection is one of the most powerful and transformative tools available to us on the path of self-discovery and personal growth.

It invites us to pause, to step away from the external noise of the world, and to turn inward toward the quiet wisdom of our own being.

Through conscious reflection, we create sacred space within ourselves where deeper truths can emerge and be recognized.

By taking time to contemplate our thoughts, actions, feelings, and experiences, we begin to unravel the layers of our conditioned behaviors and beliefs.

In doing so, we gain valuable insights into the nature of our true selves, the self that exists beyond roles, expectations, and surface identities.

Self-reflection is not merely an intellectual exercise, it is a vital and living step on the profound journey toward self-realization, serving as both a compass and a mirror on the path of inner awakening.

When we engage in sincere reflection on our life's journey, we allow ourselves to perceive patterns, habits, and tendencies that may either support or obstruct our spiritual progress.

We notice repetitive cycles of thought or behavior that perhaps once served a purpose but now act as barriers to our expansion.

The teachings urge us to approach this process with radical honesty and gentle openness, setting aside defensiveness or self-deception.

True reflection requires a courageous willingness to confront both our strengths and our weaknesses, to see where we shine with love and wisdom, and where fear, ignorance, or pride may still hold sway.

This honest examination becomes the soil in which authentic growth takes root, helping us shed illusions and step more fully into our true spiritual nature.

Through this unfolding awareness, we gradually free ourselves from unconscious limitations and step closer to the boundless potential that resides within us.

In the ongoing practice of reflection, we begin to uncover the deeper motives and intentions that drive our actions and reactions.

We learn to distinguish between choices made from alignment with our highest self and those made from fear, insecurity, or attachment.

Through this awareness, we are empowered to make conscious, deliberate choices that align more harmoniously with our innermost truth and the principles of Creation.

Reflection becomes an intimate conversation between the self and the higher self, a sacred dialogue where the wisdom of our soul rises to meet us.

In this space of attentive listening, we hear the quiet guidance of Creation's energy flowing through us, pointing the way toward deeper fulfillment, greater authenticity, and more meaningful service to life.

Every experience, whether it appears to be a success or a failure, becomes a stepping stone on the pathway to wisdom and inner liberation.

Crucially, reflection is not about judgment, criticism, or condemnation, it is about understanding, learning, and evolving.

It is an act of deep compassion toward ourselves, recognizing that every step we have taken, no matter how imperfect, has been part of our learning journey.

By reflecting with an open and loving heart, we create an atmosphere where healing and transformation can occur naturally.

As we engage regularly in the practice of self-reflection, we deepen our connection to the timeless wisdom of Creation, attune more closely to the voice of our higher consciousness, and move forward with greater clarity and purpose.

Reflection strengthens our inner foundation, allowing us to walk the path of self-realization with humility, courage, and grace.

In honoring this sacred practice, we honor ourselves as evolving expressions of the divine, and we recognize that each moment of honest reflection brings us closer to the full embodiment of who we are meant to become.

Chapter 46

The Practice of Non-Judgment

Judgment is one of the greatest barriers to true connection, creating invisible divisions that separate us from one another and from our own deeper nature.

When we judge, we impose our personal fears, insecurities, and biases onto others, preventing ourselves from seeing them as they truly are.

Judgment acts like a veil, distorting our perception and leading us to form opinions based on limited understanding rather than open-hearted awareness.

When we find fault in others, we are often confronting unhealed parts of ourselves, projecting inner conflict onto the world outside.

Rather than creating clarity, judgment creates confusion, reinforcing the illusion of separation and closing our hearts to the compassion and unity that naturally flow when we perceive from the psyche.

In recognizing this, we see that judgment is not simply a social tendency, it is a spiritual obstacle that limits our growth, our relationships, and our ability to embody love.

Non-judgment, on the other hand, is a conscious, active practice that invites us to perceive others without the filters of fear, bias, or preconceived notions.

It is the willingness to see beyond appearances and behaviors to the deeper truth of a person's being.

The teachings encourage us to engage in non-judgment with sincerity, understanding that every soul is on its own intricate, evolving journey, shaped by experiences, challenges, and lessons we may not fully understand.

To witness another without the impulse to critique or categorize is to honor their sacred unfolding.

Non-judgment calls us to replace reaction with reflection, criticism with curiosity, and rejection with compassion.

It does not ask us to deny what we see, but to meet what we see with an open heart, recognizing that divine energy moves through every being, regardless of the stage or form of their journey.

Through the practice of non-judgment, we forge deeper, more genuine connections with others, seeing them not as objects of analysis, but as living reflections of the divine spark within all existence.

It invites us to engage with others in a way that fosters mutual respect, empathy, and unconditional positive regard.

Non-judgment is one of the purest forms of compassion, as it requires us to look for the good in others, to acknowledge their struggles without diminishing their worth, and to offer presence without expectation.

In cultivating non-judgment, we create environments where others feel safe to grow, heal, and express themselves authentically.

It becomes a gift we offer to the world, the space where transformation is possible because the soul feels seen, valued, and loved, not in spite of imperfections but through a deeper understanding of our shared human experience.

Non-judgment is a profound spiritual practice that enables us to live in greater harmony with ourselves, with others, and with the flow of Creation itself.

It is a daily, moment-to-moment choice to release the need to control, categorize, or condemn and instead to embrace openness, acceptance, and trust.

As we develop this capacity, we begin to recognize the divine essence in every person we meet, dissolving the false barriers that once seemed to divide us.

Non-judgment allows the unconditional love of Creation to move through us unhindered, healing the wounds of separation within our own hearts and in the collective heart of humanity.

In living with non-judgment, we align ourselves more fully with the energy of unity, stepping into the truth that we are all expressions of one sacred life, interconnected and inseparable.

In this realization, we find freedom, peace, and the capacity to love as we were always meant to love.

Chapter 47

The Importance of Boundaries

B oundaries are essential tools for maintaining balance, inner peace, and well-being in every aspect of our lives.

They are not simply protective measures but sacred expressions of self-awareness and self-respect.

The Creation Energy teachings remind us that healthy boundaries are crucial for maintaining our spiritual alignment, allowing us to remain connected to our true selves while engaging with the world around us.

Without boundaries, our energy becomes scattered, our intentions blurred, and our sense of purpose weakened.

Healthy boundaries act as energetic containers, helping us preserve the integrity of our spirit and ensuring that we move through life from a place of centeredness and clarity.

They enable us to honor the sacredness of our being while still participating fully and compassionately in the collective human experience.

Setting boundaries is a profound act of self-respect, a declaration that our needs, feelings, time, and space are valuable and deserving of care.

It involves becoming attuned to our own rhythms, recognizing when we feel nourished and when we feel depleted, and taking conscious steps to protect our vitality.

The Creation Energy teachings encourage us to understand that setting boundaries is not a rejection of others, but an affirmation of our own worth and well-being.

By defining what we will and will not accept, we create conditions that support our growth, healing, and evolution.

Boundaries help us discern where we end and another begins, enabling us to make choices that are in alignment with our highest good rather than falling into patterns of overextension, resentment, or self-sacrifice.

They allow us to respond to life with intention rather than react out of habit or fear.

It is important to recognize that boundaries are not rigid walls built out of fear or defensiveness, but living, breathing expressions of self-love and spiritual maturity.

Healthy boundaries are flexible yet firm, they are guided by compassion for ourselves and for others.

The Creation Energy teachings illuminate that through boundaries, we create relationships that are not based on obligation or imbalance, but on mutual respect, authenticity, and freedom.

When we practice healthy boundary-setting, we remain open-hearted and empathetic, yet strong enough to protect our sacred space.

We become capable of offering love and support without losing ourselves in the process.

Boundaries empower us to engage fully in life while maintaining a strong and vibrant connection to our own truth.

They guide us in discerning when to give, when to receive, and when to retreat into stillness for reflection and renewal.

Truly, setting and maintaining healthy boundaries is a powerful act of self-love and spiritual empowerment.

It reflects a deep commitment to living in alignment with our inner wisdom and honoring the divine energy within us.

By protecting our personal space and conserving our energy, we create the conditions necessary for true healing, growth, and transformation to occur.

Through clear boundaries, we invite relationships rooted in authenticity, trust, and respect, where both parties are free to be their true selves.

In this way, we contribute not only to our own flourishing but to the cultivation of a more loving, respectful, and harmonious world.

The more we embrace the sacred art of boundary-setting, the more we step into the fullness of who we are, allowing the light of Creation to shine through us with greater brilliance, touching the lives of others and honoring the divine in all.

Chapter 48

The Path of Courage

◆———◆◆◆———◆

Courage is a profound and sacred quality, the ability to face fear, uncertainty, and adversity with strength, resilience, and grace.

It is the inner fire that propels us forward even when the path is unclear and the outcome unknown.

True courage is not defined by the absence of fear but by the willingness to move forward despite it, to take each step with trust and conviction.

The Creation Energy teachings emphasize that courage is a vital key to spiritual growth, for it is what allows us to step beyond the edges of our comfort zones and into the expansive realm of new possibilities.

Every moment we choose courage over fear, we realign ourselves with the limitless potential of our soul and affirm our deep trust in the divine unfolding of life.

Through acts of courage, both great and small, we honor the sacred journey of our becoming.

The path of courage invites us to turn inward and confront the fears, doubts, and limitations that often obscure our light.

Rather than avoiding or suppressing these aspects of ourselves, courage asks us to meet them with compassion and honesty, recognizing them as gateways to deeper self-awareness and transformation.

Fear often arises as we approach thresholds of growth, it signals that we are on the verge of breaking free from old patterns and limitations.

The teachings encourage us to embrace these moments with open hearts, seeing challenges not as obstacles but as sacred opportunities to rise into a higher version of ourselves.

Whether in our spiritual practices, in healing our relationships, or in pursuing dreams that call to our souls, courage becomes the bridge between where we are and where we are meant to be.

Each courageous step forward strengthens our faith and expands the horizons of what we believe is possible.

True courage is rooted in the unshakable knowledge of our own divine essence and the deep trust that we are continuously supported by Creation's infinite energy.

When we stand in this knowing, we realize that no matter how daunting the external circumstances may seem, we are never truly alone.

Courage is the willingness to live authentically, to speak and act from the heart, even when doing so feels vulnerable, uncomfortable, or misunderstood.

It is the strength to honor our truth in a world that often demands conformity.

The more we cultivate courage, the more we empower ourselves to consciously shape our lives, to dream bigger, love deeper, and walk more boldly in alignment with our soul's calling.

Courage liberates us from the illusions of powerlessness and fear, reminding us of the limitless creative force that flows through us at all times.

By choosing to walk the path of courage, we step into deeper alignment with Creation's divine rhythm, trusting that we are equipped to meet every experience with grace and resilience.

Courage allows us to transcend the imagined barriers of fear, opening us to lives rich with possibility, meaning, and fulfillment.

Through each act of bravery, we weave a life that reflects our highest aspirations and the deepest truths of our being.

We come to understand that courage is not a single moment of valor but a daily, conscious practice, a way of being that calls us to rise again and again, no matter how many times we stumble.

Courage is a celebration of the divine light within us, a radiant affirmation that we are capable of transforming challenges into wisdom, fear into faith, and uncertainty into inspired action.

It is through courage that we unlock our true potential and honor the sacred journey of our souls.

Chapter 49

The Role of Detachment

Detachment is a profound spiritual practice, the ability to release our attachment to outcomes, relationships, material possessions, and even our own expectations.

It is a conscious choice to engage with life fully while remaining unattached to the results of our actions.

Rather than withdrawing from the beauty and richness of existence, detachment invites us to participate with an open heart, free from the chains of fear, need, and control.

Attachment often becomes a source of suffering because we seek to hold on to what is, by nature, temporary and ever-changing.

When we cling to people, experiences, or things, we give away our inner peace, tying our well-being to the fluctuating currents of the external world.

Detachment teaches us that real joy and stability come not from grasping or controlling, but from trusting in the deeper flow of life.

True detachment is not about rejection, indifference, or emotional coldness, it is about love without possession, action without demand, and trust without conditions.

It calls us to fully appreciate and honor everything life offers while simultaneously releasing the need to fix, own, or manipulate it.

The teachings encourage us to approach each situation, each relationship, and each moment with reverence, but without the illusion that our happiness depends on a specific outcome.

Practicing detachment means letting go of the belief that we must control life for it to be good.

Instead, it is a surrender to the infinite wisdom of Creation, recognizing that the divine energy guiding our lives knows far better than our limited minds.

In practicing detachment, we become participants in life's dance, moving gracefully with its rhythm rather than struggling against its flow.

Through the discipline of detachment, we cultivate profound inner peace and emotional resilience.

We begin to see how much stress, anxiety, and disappointment are born from our attachments to how things "should" be rather than accepting how they truly are.

When we detach from the need to force outcomes or cling to expectations, we open ourselves to receive the unexpected blessings that Creation has in store for us.

In this open and surrendered state, divine guidance flows more freely, inspiring actions, opportunities, and relationships that are more aligned with our soul's true path.

Detachment helps us to recognize that nothing in the external world can ultimately define or diminish our inner worth.

We come to understand that our happiness, peace, and fulfillment are sourced from within, anchored in the eternal and unchanging presence of the divine within us.

By embracing the path of detachment, we liberate ourselves from the tyranny of fear and desire, stepping into a deeper freedom and fullness of life.

We are no longer enslaved by the need to acquire, to control, or to cling, and thus, we are free to love more deeply, act more wisely, and live more authentically.

Detachment empowers us to meet life's inevitable changes, its gains and losses, its beginnings and endings, with equanimity and grace.

In letting go, we discover that true security lies not in what we possess but in who we are. As we align more fully with Creation's natural flow, we awaken to a life of greater harmony, trust, and spiritual maturity.

Through the sacred practice of detachment, we learn to walk the Earth lightly, holding everything with open hands, and thus, we find ourselves more deeply connected to the eternal and limitless Source of all that is.

Chapter 50

The Path of Service

S ervice to others is one of the highest and purest expressions of spiritual growth and alignment with the divine energy of Creation.

When we step into service, we become living embodiments of love, compassion, and kindness, allowing the sacred energy within us to radiate outward and touch the lives of others.

Service is not about losing ourselves or neglecting our own well-being, it is about recognizing the infinite abundance we carry within and offering it freely for the upliftment of all beings.

Every act of service, no matter how small, is a ripple in the vast ocean of Creation, contributing to the collective healing and evolution of humanity.

In service, we mirror the nature of Creation itself, which continually gives life, sustenance, and support to all without expectation of return.

True service requires humility, presence, and a willingness to look beyond our personal concerns to the needs of the greater whole.

It invites us to dissolve the illusions of separation and recognize that we are all part of a single, interconnected web of life.

The teachings encourage us to approach service not only as grand acts of charity but as daily opportunities to extend kindness, patience, and understanding.

Whether offering a heartfelt smile, a helping hand, words of encouragement, or acts of physical or emotional support, every instance of selflessness becomes a sacred thread woven into the larger tapestry of divine love.

The path of service calls us to remain vigilant for opportunities to serve with grace and sincerity, trusting that even our smallest actions carry immense spiritual significance.

In serving others, we move beyond the confines of ego and self-interest, entering into a higher state of consciousness rooted in empathy, compassion, and reverence for life.

Service becomes a mirror that reflects back to us the divine essence present in every being we encounter.

Through this practice, we come to see others not as strangers, but as reflections of ourselves, each one a spark of the same universal light.

The more we dedicate ourselves to service, the more deeply we attune to the energy of Creation, which is inherently generous, nurturing, and boundless in its love.

In this way, service not only transforms the world around us but profoundly changes our inner landscape, dissolving barriers of judgment, fear, and separation.

By walking the sacred path of service, we participate consciously in the unfolding of Creation's highest vision for humanity.

We step into our true roles as co-creators, helping others awaken to their potential while simultaneously awakening greater wisdom and compassion within ourselves.

Service becomes a spiritual practice, a way of expressing our deepest values and fulfilling our soul's longing to contribute meaningfully to the world.

It is through service that we discover a profound sense of purpose, belonging, and fulfillment that transcends personal achievement.

The more we give from the heart, the more we are replenished by the inexhaustible wellspring of divine energy.

In serving others with love, humility, and joy, we help build a world that reflects the true beauty and unity of Creation, becoming active participants in the sacred dance of life.

Chapter 51

The Role of Joy

J oy is the natural and effortless expression of living in alignment with Creation's energy, a brilliant reflection of the vitality, abundance, and unconditional love that permeate the universe. It is not a fleeting emotion reserved for rare moments of triumph or ease, but a steady undercurrent of divine connection that flows through us when we attune ourselves to the sacred rhythm of life.

Joy arises from within, independent of external circumstances, untouched by the shifting tides of fortune or the challenges we encounter.

This inner joy is not something to chase after, it is our birthright, a reflection of our truest nature, waiting to be awakened through conscious living.

When we recognize and nurture this source of joy within, our lives become luminous, radiant with the pure energy of Creation itself.

Living with joy invites us into a profound relationship with the present moment, where the richness of life reveals itself in its most authentic form.

True joy is found in the small, sacred moments that weave together the fabric of our existence, the gentle caress of the breeze, the laughter of a loved one, and the quiet beauty of a sunrise.

The teachings encourage us to cultivate joy by grounding ourselves in gratitude and mindfulness, allowing us to see and feel the miracle of life unfolding around us.

When we release our fixation on outcomes and relinquish the need for life to conform to our expectations, we open ourselves to a deeper, more abiding happiness.

Every moment, when fully embraced, becomes an opportunity to experience the wonder and abundance that flow ceaselessly from Creation.

As we deepen our connection to joy, we come to understand it not just as an emotional state, but as a vital spiritual force that energizes and sustains us.

Joy becomes a reservoir of strength, helping us navigate life's inevitable uncertainties and sorrows with resilience and grace.

It reminds us that, even amidst difficulties, there remains a place within us untouched by fear, grief, or limitation, a sacred space where the divine spark continues to burn brightly.

Cultivating joy requires a conscious return to this place, again and again, through practices of self-awareness, meditation, and living in accordance with the laws of Creation.

As joy expands within us, it transcends personal experience and becomes a blessing we naturally extend to others, uplifting those around us simply through our presence.

Moreover, joy is a powerful agent of transformation, spreading outward like ripples on a still pond, inspiring hope, healing, and deeper connection wherever it goes.

When we embody joy, we offer a silent but potent invitation to others to rediscover their own inner light.

Living joyfully does not mean we deny the existence of pain or injustice, rather, it empowers us to meet the world's challenges without losing our inner equilibrium.

True joy anchors us in the unchanging truth of our divine nature and strengthens our ability to act with compassion, wisdom, and courage.

Joy is the natural result of living in harmony with ourselves, with others, and with the greater flow of Creation.

It is a sacred gift meant not only for our own fulfillment but to be shared generously with the world, helping to awaken a collective remembrance of the beauty, love, and sacredness of life itself.

Chapter 52

Facing Fear

◆———◆◆◆———◆

Fear is an inherent part of the human experience, a natural response to the unknown or to situations that feel threatening.

It's something we all face at different points in our lives, but when fear takes control of our thoughts, emotions, and actions, it can limit our ability to live fully and authentically.

Fear can arise from many sources, past experiences, the desire to protect ourselves from perceived harm, or attachments to outcomes that are outside of our control.

However, when we allow fear to govern us, it locks us into a state of limitation, preventing us from embracing the fullness of life and stepping into our true power.

Fear, when left unchecked, can restrict our growth, keeping us confined within the boundaries of our comfort zones.

Yet, when we begin to acknowledge fear as a natural part of our human journey, we open the door to healing and spiritual evolution.

The key to overcoming fear lies not in its elimination, but in its understanding and transcendence.

Fear often arises from misconceptions, false beliefs, and attachments to things or outcomes that we cannot control.

At its core, fear is a byproduct of the ego, which thrives on certainty and the need to feel in control.

The Creation Energy teachings remind us that fear can be transformed when we reconnect with the divine energy within us.

This energy is our true source of power, and it is always available to us, no matter the external circumstances.

Living without fear is not about eliminating all challenges or avoiding difficult situations, rather, it is about facing them with courage and trust. When we live in alignment with Creation's energy, we realize that we are never alone, and that every fear holds the potential to guide us toward deeper understanding and growth.

Living with fear is a natural part of the human experience, but it becomes limiting when it keeps us stuck in patterns of avoidance and self-doubt.

The teachings encourage us to confront our fears with compassion and understanding, seeing them not as enemies, but as opportunities for personal and spiritual growth.

Fear, when approached with an open heart, can become a catalyst for awakening, helping us to shed the layers of false identity that have been built around our egos.

Fear challenges us to step into our true selves, to trust in our divine nature, and to recognize that we are far more powerful than the fear itself.

Embracing fear means being willing to be vulnerable, to show up as we are, and to trust that the divine energy within us is greater than any external challenge.

It is through this vulnerability that we tap into our inner strength and wisdom, allowing us to move through fear with grace and ease.

When we face our fears, we align ourselves with the deeper flow of Creation's energy, unlocking our full potential and stepping into a life of courage, authenticity, and peace.

Fear loses its grip on us when we shine the light of awareness upon it, realizing that it is only a temporary illusion that cannot truly control us.

With this awareness, we become empowered to move through life with confidence and resilience, no longer held back by the fears that once kept us small.

As we confront and transcend fear, we awaken to the truth of who we are: divine, powerful, and capable of overcoming any challenge.

Fear is not the enemy but a teacher that guides us toward greater self-awareness and deeper spiritual growth.

It invites us to explore the depths of our consciousness, to shed limiting beliefs, and to emerge into the fullness of our highest potential.

When we face our fears with love and courage, we transform them from obstacles into stepping stones, allowing us to live in alignment with our true nature and the infinite wisdom of Creation.

Chapter 53

The Flow of Abundance

Abundance is the natural state of the universe, a boundless flow of divine energy that nurtures and supports our growth, well-being, and spiritual evolution.

This energy is always present, ready to sustain us at every step of our journey, ensuring that we have what we need to fulfill our purpose.

However, abundance is not merely about accumulating material wealth.

True abundance encompasses the richness of life itself, the intangible blessings such as love, wisdom, peace, joy, and connection that enrich our souls and guide us on our path.

The universe, in its infinite wisdom, is constantly providing for us, offering more than enough for everyone.

Whether we recognize it or not, we are surrounded by abundant energy in all aspects of life, waiting to be embraced and experienced.

The key to experiencing abundance lies in our ability to align ourselves with the flow of Creation's energy.

This alignment is not passive, it requires an active state of trust and faith that the universe always provides what we need.

When we begin to truly trust that we are supported by this flow, we let go of the fear, doubt, and attachment to outcomes that often prevent us from experiencing abundance.

Abundance flows when we release the scarcity mindset and open ourselves to the truth that there is more than enough for all.

This trust invites us to embrace a deeper sense of peace, knowing that our needs will always be met in divine timing.

Living with the knowledge that we are worthy and deserving of abundance allows us to attract what we need, whether it is love, material resources, or spiritual growth, into our lives with ease.

One of the most powerful ways to experience and amplify abundance is through cultivating a mindset of gratitude and mindfulness.

Gratitude shifts our focus from what is lacking in our lives to what is already present, allowing us to fully appreciate the richness of every moment.

The more we acknowledge the blessings we have, the more we open ourselves to receiving even more.

This shift in perception allows abundance to flow into our lives more freely, as we begin to see it in all things, big and small.

True abundance arises from within, as we connect with the divine energy that lives in us.

When we are rooted in this connection, we understand that abundance is not something we need to chase, but something that naturally radiates from us.

As we share this energy with others, whether through acts of kindness, love, or support, we align even more with the flow of Creation's energy, creating a cycle of giving and receiving that strengthens our connection to the divine and to each other.

Truly, abundance is a way of being.

It is a mindset that influences how we approach life and interact with the world.

When we live in harmony with Creation's laws, we attract prosperity, health, and joy into our lives.

Abundance is not confined to the material realm, it extends to the mental, emotional, and spiritual dimensions as well.

By choosing to embrace abundance, we step into the flow of divine energy, where all things are possible.

As we align ourselves with this flow, we realize that we are not separate from the abundance of the universe, but are inextricably connected to it.

Through this connection, we receive all that we need to fulfill our highest potential, and we are empowered to contribute to the greater good, sharing our gifts with others and supporting them in their own journeys.

Abundance, therefore, is not a destination but a way of living, a practice of living in trust, gratitude, and harmony with the divine flow that supports all life.

By choosing to embrace this abundance in every aspect of our lives, we not only elevate our own experience but also help elevate the collective consciousness.

When we live with an open heart, understanding that there is always enough for everyone, we contribute to a more peaceful, prosperous, and connected world.

Abundance is available to all who are willing to recognize it, and it flows effortlessly when we live in alignment with Creation's energy.

As we continue to grow spiritually and cultivate a mindset of gratitude, love, and trust, we step more fully into the natural flow of the universe, where all things are possible.

By becoming conscious co-creators of this abundance, we participate in the divine unfolding of Creation, allowing it to bless us and the world, in profound and transformative ways.

Chapter 54

The Power of Positive Thinking

Positive thinking is a powerful and transformative practice, essential for living a spiritually aligned and fulfilling life.

It is often misunderstood as a denial of challenges or hardships, but true positive thinking is much deeper and more courageous.

It is not about ignoring pain or pretending that difficulties do not exist, rather, it is about choosing to focus on solutions, opportunities, and the possibilities for growth that lie within every challenge.

It involves maintaining faith in the goodness of life even when circumstances are difficult.

Positive thinking invites us to look beyond appearances, beyond the temporary obstacles, and to trust in the deeper unfolding of Creation's wisdom.

When we adopt this mindset, we open ourselves to inner strength, resilience, and a deeper connection to the divine flow of life.

Our thoughts are not passive, they are active, creative forces that shape the reality we experience.

Every thought we hold sends out energy, either uplifting or depleting our vibration.

By choosing positive thinking, we align our consciousness with the higher frequencies of Creation's energy, frequencies of love, abundance, harmony, and hope.

Positive thinking is rooted in truth and authenticity, it is not about ignoring the darkness but about bringing light to it.

It helps us maintain clarity, inner peace, and emotional balance even in the midst of chaos.

It calls us to focus on the goodness within ourselves and others, to cultivate gratitude, and to recognize the blessings that are always present.

This requires a conscious effort to transform negative, fearful, or limiting thoughts into those that empower, uplift, and inspire.

In doing so, we become conscious creators of our reality, shaping our lives and relationships with loving intention.

True positive thinking is not naive or blindly optimistic.

It is a grounded, spiritual practice of seeing possibilities where others may only see limitations.

It teaches us to embrace challenges as opportunities for growth, to find strength in adversity, and to recognize that every experience carries within it a gift for our evolution.

Positive thinking cultivates resilience by helping us recover from setbacks with greater wisdom and compassion.

It invites us to trust that life is always working for our highest good, even when the path is unclear.

Our thoughts extend beyond our own minds, they ripple outward, affecting the collective energy of those around us.

Each act of positive thinking creates waves of encouragement, kindness, and healing, contributing to a more compassionate and harmonious world.

Through the steady cultivation of positive thinking, we begin to perceive life through the lens of love, compassion, and infinite possibility.

We see beyond immediate circumstances into the vastness of Creation's beauty and wisdom. By shifting our inner dialogue toward optimism, hope, and trust, we draw more peace, abundance, and joy into our lives.

Positive thinking is a sacred discipline that transforms both our inner and outer realities, aligning us with the divine flow of Creation.

It invites us to become active co-creators of a better world, radiating light and possibility wherever we go.

By embracing positive thinking in every moment, we walk the path of spiritual mastery, embodying the truth that life, when seen through the eyes of love and faith, is a magnificent and endless gift.

Chapter 55

Living in the Present Moment

❖━━━━◆❖◆━━━━❖

Living in the present moment is the key to unlocking spiritual peace, deep fulfillment, and a true sense of inner freedom.

When we make the conscious choice to focus our awareness on the now, we align ourselves with the living energy of Creation, which is always unfolding in the present.

Free from the chains of regret over the past and the worries about the future, we are able to experience life directly, with clarity and openness.

The present moment holds the entirety of life's wisdom, vitality, and sacred beauty.

It is not somewhere we arrive by accident, but a place we choose to inhabit through mindfulness and surrender.

By stepping into the present, we reclaim our true power, grounded not in what was or what might be, but in what is. In this space, the heart opens, the mind clears, and the soul can breathe.

Living in the present requires that we let go of attachments to the past and expectations for the future, trusting that all we need for our growth and happiness is available to us now.

The Creation Energy Teachings encourage us to cultivate a mindful awareness that welcomes each experience with full attention and gratitude.

Practicing mindfulness allows us to meet each moment fresh, without the filter of judgment or the burden of old stories.

We become witnesses to life's unfolding mystery, finding beauty in the simplest things, the warmth of the sun, the sound of laughter, the rhythm of our own breath.

When we are present, we are naturally more receptive to the guidance of our higher self and the divine energy that flows through all existence.

Life becomes less about chasing and more about being, less about controlling and more about flowing.

The present moment is far more than a fleeting point in time, it is a sacred portal to the deeper realms of spirit and divine connection.

In the now, the illusions of separation dissolve, and we recognize the sacredness in all things, including ourselves.

We begin to experience the world through the eyes of love, compassion, and wonder.

The Creation Energy Teachings remind us that joy arises naturally when we stop searching outside ourselves and instead anchor fully into what is already present.

Gratitude blooms when we realize that every breath is a gift, every heartbeat a miracle, and every encounter an opportunity to experience the divine.

In living fully present, we release the stress of trying to force or manipulate life, and instead, we trust the flow of Creation's perfect and intelligent design.

By choosing to live in the present, we allow life to become a sacred practice, a constant unfolding of grace, purpose, and connection.

Every moment becomes an invitation to love deeper, to be more authentic, and to experience life more fully.

Distractions and fears lose their grip when we root ourselves in the now, and our awareness becomes a channel through which divine wisdom and creativity flow.

Living in the present moment helps us heal from the wounds of the past and relieves us of the anxieties about the future, grounding us firmly in the eternal now where true transformation happens.

Through presence, we discover that life is not something happening to us, but through us and as us. In this profound realization, we align more fully with the sacred rhythm of Creation and step into a life of wonder, peace, and radiant authenticity.

Chapter 56

The Impact of Our Thoughts on Reality

❖—◆❖◆—❖

Our thoughts possess a profound and far-reaching power to shape every aspect of our reality, influencing not only the way we perceive the world but also how we engage with it.

Each thought we think is like a seed planted within the fertile soil of consciousness, inevitably bearing fruit in the form of our emotions, actions, and experiences.

Positive, loving thoughts align us with the expansive, nurturing energy of Creation, allowing us to grow, thrive, and create a life filled with meaning and joy.

When we become aware of this immense creative power within us, we recognize that every thought matters, every inner whisper contributes to the masterpiece of our lives.

In contrast, negative, fearful, or limiting thoughts create constriction and disharmony, blocking the natural flow of abundance and love that is our birthright.

Living with mindful awareness of our thoughts requires dedication, patience, and self-compassion. It asks us to become active participants in our mental landscape, choosing carefully which seeds we plant and nurture.

Every thought sends out ripples of energy that affect not only our personal reality but also the collective field of humanity.

When we hold thoughts of peace, compassion, and gratitude, we uplift ourselves and contribute to the healing of the world.

Mindful thinking invites us to consistently attune ourselves to our higher consciousness, to examine the stories we tell ourselves, and to replace fear-based narratives with ones grounded in truth and love.

It is a conscious, daily practice of aligning with the sacred flow of Creation's wisdom.

When we are not mindful, destructive patterns of thinking, such as self-doubt, resentment, or fear, can easily take root and dominate our inner world.

These thoughts act as barriers that prevent us from recognizing the infinite possibilities available to us.

They shrink our vision and limit our capacity to act with courage and faith.

However, when we consciously choose thoughts that are expansive, loving, and empowering, we remove these barriers and step into a greater reality of potential and joy.

Positive thinking is not about denying challenges or pretending that pain does not exist; rather, it is about seeing challenges through the lens of growth and possibility.

It transforms obstacles into stepping stones and darkness into opportunities for greater light.

Our outer reality begins to shift as a direct result of the inner transformation that positive, mindful thinking fosters.

By aligning our thoughts with the divine, loving energy of Creation, we activate the full potential of our creative power.

The teachings remind us that the mind is a sacred tool, meant to serve the heart and spirit in manifesting a life of purpose, peace, and joy.

Every time we choose a thought of kindness, hope, or gratitude, we strengthen our connection to the divine source within us and around us.

In this way, positive thinking becomes a spiritual practice, a conscious collaboration with the universal energies that seek to bless and uplift us.

By honoring the creative power of our thoughts, we become architects of a new reality, one built on love, truth, and harmony with all of life.

Through this practice, we invite more beauty, abundance, and divine connection into our lives, fulfilling our highest potential as co-creators with Creation itself.

Chapter 57

The Connection Between Body, Mind, and Spirit

◆━━◆◆◆━━◆

The body, mind, and spirit are deeply interwoven, forming a sacred triad that sustains our entire being.

Each aspect of us, physical, mental, and spiritual, is in constant communication with the others, creating a dynamic balance that shapes our experience of life.

True health and genuine wellness arise when we recognize and nurture the intimate connection among these parts.

When one aspect is neglected, imbalance follows, affecting every layer of our existence.

True harmony is not achieved by focusing solely on one area, but through honoring the fullness of who we are.

Only by cultivating the body, nurturing the mind, and awakening the spirit can we experience the profound peace and vitality that are our natural birthrights.

Living in balance requires conscious, consistent effort across all areas of life. Caring for the physical body means nourishing it with healthy food, staying active, resting sufficiently, and listening to its signals with respect and love.

The mind, too, requires nourishment through learning, creativity, mindfulness, and emotional resilience.

Mental clutter and unchecked negative thoughts can become as toxic as poor physical habits.

Nurturing the spirit calls for daily practices of connection, whether through meditation, prayer to oneself, communion with nature, acts of compassion, or simply moments of stillness where we listen for the whisper of the divine.

Each of these efforts strengthens the others, creating a resilient foundation upon which we can build a meaningful and joyful life.

The body is more than a vessel, it is a living temple for the spirit's expression in the world.

To care for the body is to honor the sacredness of life itself. Likewise, our thoughts and emotions are powerful forces that shape not only our mental reality but also our physical health.

Persistent stress, fear, or negativity can manifest as physical ailments, while cultivating thoughts of love, gratitude, and forgiveness promotes healing and vibrancy.

Understanding this connection empowers us to become active stewards of our inner and outer health, aligning ourselves more fully with Creation's energy and wisdom.

When we bring awareness to our mental and emotional patterns, we elevate not only our personal lives but also the collective consciousness of humanity.

Integrating body, mind, and spirit into a unified and harmonious whole is a lifelong spiritual journey.

It calls for self-reflection, patience, and a deep commitment to personal growth.

As we align these three aspects, we tap into the natural flow of Creation's energy, experiencing greater peace, resilience, and joy.

Balance is not a static achievement but a dynamic dance, one that requires ongoing mindfulness and loving attention.

As we strengthen our connection to ourselves and Creation, we step more fully into our authentic power.

We live each day with greater vitality, deeper purpose, and an unwavering sense of inner harmony, becoming radiant expressions of divine energy in the world.

Chapter 58

Embracing Change as Part of Growth

———◆——◆◆——◆———

Change is an ever-present force in life, essential to the natural rhythm of existence and a key ingredient for both personal and spiritual evolution.

It is through the constant unfolding of change that we are given the chance to grow, learn, and awaken to greater truths about ourselves and the universe.

When we accept change as a natural and necessary process, we free ourselves from the illusion of permanence and begin to live in harmony with the flow of life.

Change allows us to release outdated beliefs, heal old wounds, and transcend limiting behaviors that no longer align with our highest potential.

Every shift, whether subtle or dramatic, holds within it the seeds of transformation, guiding us toward becoming a more authentic and awakened expression of our divine nature.

When we resist change, we imprison ourselves in fear, clinging to the familiar even when it hinders our growth.

Resistance creates suffering, as it places us at odds with the natural cycles of life.

It binds us to the past, preventing us from stepping into the new possibilities that Creation continually offers.

True freedom lies in surrendering to change with openness and trust, allowing life to shape us as a river carves new paths through the landscape.

By viewing each change as a sacred invitation rather than a threat, we shift our perspective from fear to empowerment.

Change challenges us to let go of attachments and illusions, pushing us beyond our comfort zones so we can discover new strengths, new perspectives, and new depths within ourselves.

Approaching change with an open mind and heart is a profound spiritual practice that cultivates resilience, wisdom, and compassion.

Life's transitions often bring moments of uncertainty, discomfort, or even loss, yet these experiences are fertile ground for profound growth and awakening.

By trusting that change is orchestrated by a higher intelligence, we can move through life's shifts with grace and inner strength.

The teachings encourage us to view every change, no matter how small or large, as part of a divine unfolding designed to bring us closer to our true essence.

Through acceptance and willingness, we align ourselves with the creative force of the universe, allowing new opportunities, relationships, and experiences to enter our lives and nourish our souls.

Truly, change is not something to fear or avoid but something to embrace as a sacred ally on the path of awakening.

It invites us to renew ourselves again and again, shedding old identities and stepping into ever-greater alignment with our soul's purpose.

Change keeps our spirits alive, dynamic, and evolving, reminding us that life itself is a constant dance of creation and recreation.

By embracing change, we harmonize with the eternal movement of Creation's energy, participating consciously in the grand unfolding of the universe.

In doing so, we unlock greater joy, freedom, and fulfillment, living as vessels of divine light, fully open to the infinite possibilities of existence.

Chapter 59

Balancing Material and Spiritual Life

❖━━━◆◆◆━━━❖

B alancing material pursuits with spiritual growth is essential for leading a life that is both harmonious and fulfilling.

In our modern world, there is often an emphasis on material success, and it can sometimes overshadow our deeper spiritual needs.

Material achievements, such as wealth, status, and possessions, are often seen as markers of success.

However, if these pursuits become the sole focus of our lives, they can lead to emptiness and dissatisfaction.

Spiritual development, on the other hand, provides the deeper meaning and sense of connection that enriches our existence.

It is vital to recognize that material success should not be pursued at the expense of spiritual growth.

Rather, material achievements should support and complement our spiritual journey, enabling us to serve others and contribute to the greater good.

Living in alignment with Creation's energy involves finding a harmonious balance between our material and spiritual goals.

When we are aligned with this energy, our material pursuits become an extension of our spiritual journey, contributing to our overall well-being and purpose.

Spirituality offers the foundation for a life built on integrity, compassion, and wisdom.

It teaches us to act with kindness and to cultivate a deep connection to the world around us.

Material success, when achieved with the right mindset, becomes a tool for serving others and fulfilling our responsibilities in the material world.

It allows us to take care of our earthly needs, while also having the means to help those in need. In this way, material pursuits do not become distractions from spiritual growth but rather serve as a means of supporting and enhancing our spiritual development.

Spiritual growth is not just about cultivating inner peace or developing a connection to the divine; it also helps us navigate the complexities of the material world with wisdom.

It teaches us how to use the resources we have wisely and without attachment, ensuring that our actions are aligned with our higher purpose.

As we deepen our spiritual practice, we gain greater clarity about our priorities and desires.

This self-awareness helps us avoid the traps of greed, envy, and excessive attachment to material possessions.

We learn that true fulfillment comes not from accumulating wealth or possessions, but from living in accordance with our deepest values and understanding that material things are temporary.

Spiritual growth encourages us to focus on what is eternal, our inner peace, our relationships, and our connection to something greater than ourselves.

The process of balancing material and spiritual life requires both self-discipline and the ability to set priorities based on our true values.

In a world that often encourages instant gratification and excessive materialism, it can be challenging to maintain this balance.

However, when we develop the discipline to stay grounded in our spiritual practices, we can begin to make conscious decisions that align with our highest goals.

Spiritual growth helps us approach material pursuits with humility, using what we have for the benefit of others and the world around us.

It also teaches us to let go of the need for excessive accumulation or status, recognizing that what truly matters is the way we use our resources and the impact we have on others.

Through this balanced approach, we are able to find a sense of peace and fulfillment that transcends the temporary pleasures of the material world.

Material possessions are fleeting, and they can never provide lasting satisfaction.

This awareness helps us keep a healthy perspective on the role of material wealth in our lives.

Spiritual growth, on the other hand, nurtures our souls and provides lasting fulfillment that transcends the limitations of time and space.

When we balance both material and spiritual pursuits, we create a life that is rich in purpose, meaning, and connection.

This balance allows us to fulfill our earthly needs while also nurturing our spiritual growth and fostering a deeper sense of inner peace.

The ability to balance material success with spiritual wisdom is the key to creating a life that is expansive, grounded, and aligned with the divine energy of Creation.

By living in this way, we can experience true fulfillment in both our material and spiritual lives, creating a harmonious existence that reflects our deepest values and the highest potential of who we are.

Chapter 60

Fear

◆————————◆◆◆————————◆

F ear is not an external enemy that lurks outside of us, waiting to strike, it is a creation born within the mind, a projection of the ego, the false self that clings desperately to identity, survival, and separation.

The ego's existence depends upon the maintenance of these illusions, it must constantly reaffirm its fragile importance, and fear is its most effective tool.

Through fear, the ego convinces us that we are isolated, vulnerable beings, adrift in a vast and indifferent universe.

The ego feeds and grows on fear like a fire consumes oxygen.

It generates endless anxieties about loss, failure, humiliation, pain, and death.

It conjures countless scenarios in which we might be hurt, abandoned, or destroyed.

Fear becomes the background noise of the ego's world, a constant whisper that we must defend, strive, compare, and control.

Through fear, the ego sustains the illusion that it is necessary for our survival.

From the broader perspective of the psyche, and especially from the vantage of the spirit, these fears are revealed to be illusions, no more substantial than shadows cast on a wall by a flickering candle.

They seem real, they dance and loom before our inner eyes, but when examined closely, they have no independent substance.

Fear only holds power over us to the degree that we believe in it.

It is a veil, woven from thoughts and sensations, that obscures the true, boundless nature of our being.

When fear arises deeply within us, it feels overwhelming, urgent, even existential.

The body tightens, the mind races, and reality seems to narrow to the single point of threat.

Yet beneath this reaction, fear is almost always rooted in unconscious beliefs, the belief in separation, the belief in scarcity, the belief in the vulnerability of who we think we are.

The ego's greatest terror is not physical death, but the death of its self-image, the collapse of its carefully constructed identity.

Spiritually, the dissolution of the ego is not annihilation, it is awakening.

It is the great return, the remembrance of our oneness with all that is.

To the ego, this unity appears as death, because the ego cannot survive in a realm where love, truth, and infinity are recognized as the only reality.

Thus, fear becomes a paradoxical gift on the path, a signpost indicating that we are approaching the boundary of the ego's domain, and the threshold to our true Self.

Fear, therefore, is not proof that we are in danger, but a call to transformation.

It signals that something false is ready to fall away.

It invites us to step beyond the small, fearful self and to open into the limitless expanse of being.

Every fear contains within it the seed of a deeper liberation, if only we have the courage to face it with the light of awareness.

There is an ancient and profound truth that "there is nothing to fear but fear itself."

When we look deeply, we see that fear is a self-creating loop, it feeds on our attention and intensifies when we resist or run from it.

The more we fight fear, the larger and more monstrous it seems to grow, much like a shadow enlarges when a light source is moved away.

Conversely, when we bring open awareness to fear, without resistance, without judgment, it begins to lose its form.

Without our resistance, fear cannot maintain itself. It unravels and dissolves like morning mist under the gentle heat of the rising sun.

By turning toward fear rather than away, by meeting it with curious, compassionate presence, we discover that fear is empty at its core.

It is not a monster, but a phantom.

Beneath it, there is nothing but pure, unshakable presence, the eternal ground of being that is untouched by all the fluctuations of the mind.

In this way, facing fear is not a battle to be fought, but a surrender to be embraced.

It is not an act of violence against a part of ourselves, but an opening into greater love and truth.

Fear is not an enemy to be slain, it is a doorway we walk through with tenderness and faith, emerging into a wider, freer sky.

Truly, the spiritual journey is a path of remembrance, a return to knowing ourselves as we were before fear ever took hold.

Beyond ego, beyond fear, beyond all temporary identities, we are expressions of the infinite Creation-energy, the boundless life-force that knows no lack, no threat, no separation.

In the heart of Creation, there is no fear because there is no "other" to fear.

When we cease to identify with the fearful ego and instead rest in the stillness of our deeper awareness, we find profound freedom.

We realize that every fear we ever faced was ultimately a false alarm, a cry from the small self, not a decree from the soul.

Every moment of fear becomes an opportunity, an invitation to wake up more fully, to see more clearly, to love more fearlessly.

Fear loses its grip when we recognize it for what it truly is, a call home, a messenger pointing us back toward the infinite wholeness that we have never truly left.

Chapter 61

Glass House

◆————◆◆◆————◆

If you are alive today, it is because your journey of evolution is still unfolding.

Life has not yet completed its teachings for you, there is still growth to be undertaken, lessons to be embodied, and truths to be realized. Y

our presence here is not incidental, it is essential.

It means that the universal intelligence of Creation sees your potential and has granted you another opportunity to evolve in awareness, wisdom, and love.

Life itself is the sacred arena in which this transformation occurs.

Every experience, whether joyous or painful, offers the raw material for inner growth.

Evolution is not a punishment handed down by some higher authority, it is a necessary and sacred process that every human being must undergo to reach a state of higher consciousness.

To be alive on Earth is to be part of this developmental spiral, a purposeful path of unfolding that stretches across lifetimes and dimensions.

Our human experience is designed to include mistakes.

These are not deviations from the path, but stepping stones along it.

Error, challenge, failure, these are the very means by which we come to know ourselves more deeply and refine our capacity for truth and compassion.

The path of spiritual growth is not about perfection, but about authenticity.

It is through confronting our own darkness that we learn to shine. To condemn another for their flaws or misjudgments is to misunderstand the very nature of human life.

All people, no matter how wise or mature, stumble on their path.

To harshly judge others for their imperfections is to place oneself above the process of evolution, as if one were already complete.

But we are not complete, we are all still in process.

We are all in motion toward becoming.

This is the deep truth behind the old saying, "Let the one without sin cast the first stone."

In truth, no stone can ever be thrown, for none among us is free from error.

We all bear scars of ignorance, pride, and fear.

We all carry within us the capacity for both harm and healing.

Thus, judgment is never justified, it is only a mirror reflecting our own inner work yet to be done.

We live in glass houses, each one of us.

Fragile, transparent, and vulnerable, our outer lives often mask the hidden trials of the soul.

Our thoughts, our wounds, our private regrets, they are not as hidden as we believe.

To judge another is to forget our own fragility.

When we look through the glass walls of others' lives, we must do so with care, for we too are seen.

In this fragility lies a profound opportunity, the choice to replace judgment with compassion.

When we see another in their struggle, their mistake, their downfall, we are seeing ourselves in a different form.

Compassion arises when we recognize this shared humanity.

Humility blossoms when we stop pretending we are above the lessons others are learning. And only through this humility can we truly evolve together as a species.

Earth is not just a classroom, it is a crucible.

Across the vast expanse of the Dern Universe, and even in its twin, the Dal Universe, Earth is known as the planet of the Barbarians.

This reputation is not merely an insult but a reflection of our violent, chaotic, and unconscious behavior that continues to manifest in war, greed, hatred, and destruction.

It is a raw assessment of a species still lost in survival consciousness and egoic delusion.

But even within that label, "barbarian", lies a hidden hope.

To be primitive is to be at the beginning, not the end.

A primitive state is not a curse, but a starting point.

It means there is still space to grow, still mountains to climb, still light to be discovered.

The Earth-human may be seen as primitive, but this is not their destiny, it is their origin.

From this place, the greatest leap forward can be made.

We are meant to outgrow the barbarism.

We are meant to evolve beyond the reflexes of violence and fear.

We are meant to move from unconscious reaction to conscious creation.

This is the great challenge of our time, not technological advancement, not political victory, but the awakening of inner maturity and spiritual integrity.

That is the evolution that truly matters.

And it all starts within.

The transformation of the world begins with the transformation of the individual.

Each time you choose compassion over judgment, truth over ego, humility over pride, you contribute to the healing of the whole.

Your life becomes a thread in the vast tapestry of human evolution. Y our glasshouse, fragile as it may seem, becomes a sanctuary of light through which others may see what is possible.

So let us live with tenderness and truth, knowing that every soul we meet is also in the process of becoming.

Let us put down the stones of blame and take up the tools of self-reflection, wisdom, and love.

Let us remember that we are not here to be flawless, we are here to grow. And through that growth, we may one day earn the title not of barbarians, but of beings of peace.

Chapter 62

The Art of Ignoring

In a world overwhelmed by stimuli, both digital and emotional, mastering the art of ignoring is not just a practical skill, but a spiritual act of protection.

Every day, we are bombarded with opinions, provocations, distractions, and demands that threaten to pull us out of our center.

The art of ignoring is not about emotional numbness or cold detachment, it is about inner discernment.

It's the ability to distinguish what truly matters from what merely screams the loudest.

It's the conscious decision to shield the sacred space within from external chaos.

Ignoring becomes a way of preserving mental clarity and spiritual integrity amid the constant turbulence of modern existence.

Many confuse ignoring with weakness or indifference, but in truth, it is a mark of strength.

The ego craves engagement, it wants to prove a point, to win, to correct, to be acknowledged.

But the more awakened aspect of our being, the part aligned with the Creation-energy, sees through this need for validation.

To ignore in wisdom is not to run away, but to rise above.

It is to say, "I will not hand over my attention, energy, or peace to that which does not serve my evolution."

In this way, ignoring becomes a deliberate act of self-respect and energetic conservation.

You cease feeding what drains you, and you start nourishing what elevates you.

Furthermore, the art of ignoring is an essential tool in protecting your emotional and spiritual evolution.

As we grow, we become more sensitive, not only to beauty and truth, but also to negativity, manipulation, and fear-based behaviors.

When you respond to every insult or engage with every distortion, you sacrifice your growth for momentary reaction.

Not every invitation to conflict deserves an RSVP. When you ignore the petty, the toxic, and the untruthful, you remain rooted in your path.

You are no longer giving your power away to outer circumstances or to the judgments of those who do not see the world through a Creational lens.

Ignoring becomes your shield, your boundary, your quiet declaration of sovereignty.

True mastery in this art comes when you realize that silence can be a louder message than words.

In your restraint, you assert your alignment with peace.

In your stillness, you declare your trust in truth to prevail without your interference.

You recognize that your energy is sacred, and not everything deserves to penetrate it.

The art of ignoring invites you into deeper presence, it says, "Turn inward, what truly matters is here."

It offers you a doorway out of reaction and into reflection, out of noise and into stillness.

And in that stillness, something beautiful arises, a steady awareness of your power, your path, and your place within the larger unfolding of Creation.

By choosing what not to engage with, you affirm what you are here to live for, clarity, peace, evolution, and love.

Chapter 63

Positive Dream

◆———————◆◆◆———————◆

A human being should never lose sight of the importance of cultivating a real, good, and positive dream, one that arises from deep within and serves as a guiding star for life.

This dream is not an idle fantasy or fleeting desire, but rather a meaningful vision rooted in truth, self-respect, and the sincere striving for self-control, self-worth, and self-realization.

It acts as a moral compass, helping one to remain grounded and conscious of one's values, even in times of adversity or temptation.

The Teachings tell us that by holding onto this dream, a person creates an inner foundation upon which their entire character is built, giving rise to a life filled with purpose, clarity, and moral strength.

Such a dream inspires the human being to walk the path of continuous development, both inwardly and outwardly.

It nurtures the ability to think clearly and feel genuinely, allowing the individual to act in alignment with what is right and just.

Through this process, the person learns to understand their own inner nature and gradually embodies the qualities of a true, honorable, and worthy human being.

This authenticity is expressed not only in private reflection, but also in daily actions, decisions, and relationships.

Their behaviors reflect a deep respect for life, others, and themselves, showing that their dream is not just a thought, but a lived reality.

When a person lives in harmony with this positive dream, they begin to experience the fruits of their inner effort.

They come to recognize themselves as a genuine human being among their peers, someone who contributes meaningfully to society, maintains inner balance, and inspires others through example.

This dream fuels a way of living that is both constructive and conscious, where joy and love are experienced sincerely and shared freely.

It becomes a personal mission, an invisible yet ever-present force that gives shape to a life well-lived and well-loved, allowing the individual to find fulfillment in the simplicity of everyday decency and human connection.

Eventually, when the end of life approaches and death becomes a near and certain reality, a person who has remained true to this dream can face that final moment with peace, courage, and dignity.

There will be no regret or fear, but rather the calm realization that their life was lived honestly, responsibly, and with integrity.

They will know they have made the most of their time, fostering love, offering kindness, growing in wisdom, and maintaining joy even amidst life's challenges.

Such a life leaves behind a quiet legacy, not marked by fame or fortune, but by the lasting impression of a human being who truly lived with honor, meaning, and fulfillment.

Chapter 64

Religion

———◆——◆◆——◆———

Religion, in its traditional and institutionalized forms, often embodies a profound deprivation of the human being's inherent spiritual freedom.

Rather than serving as a path toward enlightenment and inner growth, it frequently acts as a restrictive framework that imposes externally crafted doctrines and dogmas.

As the teachings stated, these belief systems, rather than fostering independent thought and genuine spiritual development, demand submission, obedience, and unquestioning faith.

As a result, the natural evolution of consciousness, one that relies on personal experience, self-reflection, and inner truth, is stunted or completely obstructed.

At a deeper level, religion can become a tool of psychological and emotional exploitation.

It has the capacity to enslave human consciousness by instilling fear, guilt, and dependence on perceived higher powers or institutional authorities.

This enslavement often manifests as a complete surrender of individual willpower and critical thinking, where the human being becomes a passive recipient of belief rather than an active seeker of truth.

Through rituals, commandments, and hierarchical systems, religion often cultivates a state of spiritual serfdom, where individuals are kept in intellectual and emotional chains under the illusion of salvation or divine favor.

This condition of subjugation can develop into increasingly extreme and destructive psychological states.

When the human mind is denied freedom, curiosity, and the right to explore its own spiritual dimensions, it becomes vulnerable to severe forms of imbalance.

These include fanaticism, where beliefs are enforced with violence or intolerance, mental illness, where religious obsession distorts reality and personal identity, and emotional dependency, where individuals become completely reliant on religious figures or institutions for their sense of purpose and worth.

The resulting detachment from reality can impair both personal relationships and broader social interactions.

In its most dangerous expressions, according to the creation energy teachings, religion has the potential to reduce human beings to irrational, obsessive, and even self-destructive entities.

Rather than elevating consciousness or promoting wisdom, it can plunge people into states of confusion, delusion, and moral blindness.

The promise of spiritual liberation is replaced with dogmatic enslavement, and the divine becomes a tool of manipulation rather than inspiration.

When spirituality is confined within the rigid walls of religious authority, the light of reason and self-awareness is dimmed, leading not to spiritual fulfillment, but to the deterioration of individual dignity and the human spirit.

Chapter 65

Assertiveness

◆━━━━━◆◆◆━━━━━◆

What a human being does with his or her life is, ultimately, no one else's business.

Every person walks their own path, shaped by their upbringing, experiences, thoughts, and inner convictions.

To judge, interfere, or impose opinions on how someone else chooses to live is a violation of their personal freedom and dignity.

Each person must be free to explore life in their own way, even if that path is unfamiliar or uncomfortable to others.

The choices we make, whether they lead to success, hardship, or growth, are all part of the process of individual evolution.

No one has the right to determine the "right" way for another to live, because no one else can truly understand the depths of another's inner world.

To live peacefully among others, we must train ourselves in the principle of "live and let live."

This idea is more than just a saying, it's a way of being that requires patience, awareness, and self-control.

It means allowing others to make decisions, even if we disagree with them, without stepping in to criticize, correct, or condemn.

Just as we expect the freedom to live according to our own values, we must be willing to grant that same freedom to others.

This practice cultivates a deep sense of respect for the diversity of human experience.

It reminds us that growth and understanding often come not from controlling others, but from giving them the space to be who they are without interference.

Adopting a "live and let live" mindset does not mean turning a blind eye to harmful behavior or abandoning your own values.

Rather, it is about knowing the difference between offering support and imposing control.

It means recognizing that even when you believe someone is making a mistake, it may be a necessary part of their learning and development.

Wisdom isn't about changing others, it's about knowing when to step back, when to speak, and when to remain silent.

This understanding fosters emotional balance and allows relationships to flourish without tension, resentment, or judgment.

It also protects your own peace of mind, as you no longer carry the burden of trying to direct the lives of those around you.

In a world filled with countless perspectives, lifestyles, and belief systems, living and letting live is one of the most compassionate and powerful approaches to human interaction.

It brings harmony where there could be conflict, and peace where there might be interference.

When we allow others to make their own choices, we demonstrate trust in their ability to grow, evolve, and find their own way.

At the same time, we strengthen our own sense of inner freedom by releasing the need to control outcomes beyond ourselves.

By committing to this practice, we contribute to a more respectful, tolerant world, one where individuality is honored and everyone is free to shape their lives according to their own truth.

Chapter 66

The folie of Intervention

Intervention, regardless of the intention behind it, is fundamentally flawed because it disregards the essential truth that every individual must have the freedom to make their own choices.

People are not passive recipients of external solutions, they are active participants in their own lives, and the power of choice is an integral part of their humanity.

While it may seem compassionate or even necessary to step in and guide someone toward what you believe is the right decision, it's essential to recognize that only the person involved can truly understand their own needs, desires, and circumstances.

True self-discovery, personal growth, and transformation can only occur when individuals are allowed to make their own choices and learn from the consequences of those choices.

By intervening, you not only deny them the opportunity to exercise their own agency but also undermine their ability to grow through their personal experiences.

When intervention is imposed, it often leads to resistance rather than cooperation or positive change.

People have an inherent need for autonomy, and when their personal freedom to choose is taken away, they may subconsciously or consciously reject the assistance or guidance being offered.

This external control doesn't foster empowerment, it breeds dependency.

Instead of cultivating the self-confidence needed to navigate their lives, individuals may become reliant on others to make decisions for them.

Furthermore, intervention can create a sense of helplessness or resentment, as people may feel that they are being treated as incapable of determining what is best for themselves.

This disempowerment only serves to distance individuals from discovering their own inner strength and wisdom, thereby undermining their development in the long term.

The imposition of external decisions can often stunt a person's personal growth and diminish their capacity to navigate the challenges that life inevitably presents.

As the teachings show, each person's journey is uniquely their own, and no outside force can fully comprehend the complexities of another's life, their challenges, their fears, or their ambitions.

The most meaningful and lasting lessons come not from the advice or decisions of others, but from the act of making one's own choices.

Even when those choices lead to failure, the lessons learned from those experiences are invaluable.

They shape a person's understanding, resilience, and wisdom in a way that cannot be replicated by external intervention.

People are capable of far more than they often give themselves credit for, and by allowing them the freedom to make mistakes and experience success on their own terms, they develop the confidence and inner strength to face future challenges.

No outside influence can substitute for the personal empowerment that comes from owning one's choices, nor can it replace the satisfaction and pride that comes from knowing one's decisions were made independently and authentically.

Truly, the only way for true and lasting progress to occur is when individuals are given the space and freedom to make their own choices.

While the urge to help and protect others is natural, real change and growth come from within.

To truly support someone is to trust them with the responsibility of making decisions about their own lives.

Empowering others to choose their own path, without the imposition of outside interference, is one of the greatest acts of respect you can offer.

It shows faith in their ability to navigate their lives, even if they stumble along the way.

Trusting people to make their own choices nurtures their self-reliance, builds their resilience, and strengthens their ability to cope with the uncertainties and challenges that life brings.

It is through their own decisions, successes, and failures that they find the meaning and wisdom that guide them on their journey.

In the end, the most valuable support you can offer others is not intervention, but the space to choose freely, learn from their experiences, and grow into the person they are meant to become.

Chapter 67

The danger of Self-doubt

When you know within yourself that your thoughts are right, never allow doubt to cloud your judgment.

It's easy to become uncertain when faced with external criticism or differing opinions, but if you've taken the time to reflect on your own knowledge and the reasoning behind it, there is no need to second-guess yourself.

Self-doubt is often a result of seeking validation from others or fearing the unknown, but it can be an obstacle that holds you back from achieving what you know is right for you.

Your internal compass is powerful, and trusting it fully will help you move forward with confidence and clarity.

According to the teachings, when you are certain of your thoughts, trust that they come from a place of understanding, experience, and deep reflection.

In moments of doubt, it's crucial to remind yourself that your thoughts are valid because they come from within you, your unique perspective shaped by your experiences, knowledge, and intuition.

While others may offer their own interpretations or advice, no one else knows your journey as intimately as you do.

It's easy to be swayed by the opinions of those around you, but their perspectives are filtered through their own experiences, not yours.

Trusting yourself means honoring your own truth and recognizing that you have the capacity to discern what is right for you.

When you doubt your own thoughts, you disconnect from your authentic self, and this can lead to confusion and indecision.

Instead, embrace your thoughts with confidence, for they are the product of your inner wisdom and clarity.

Self-doubt often stems from fear, fear of being wrong, fear of failure, or fear of how others might perceive you.

This fear can paralyze you, preventing you from taking action or standing firm in your understanding.

However, it's important to understand that doubt does not serve you.

It creates a mental fog that prevents you from seeing things clearly, and it undermines the trust you have in yourself.

When you doubt your thoughts, you are essentially allowing fear to control your actions, making decisions based on anxiety rather than conviction.

The reality is that every decision, whether right or wrong, holds valuable lessons.

When you trust yourself and your thoughts, you create space to learn, grow, and adapt, rather than getting stuck in indecision or inaction.

Each experience becomes an opportunity to strengthen your inner trust, rather than a setback.

To truly live in alignment with your authentic self, it is essential to embrace your thoughts without hesitation.

When you know that your thoughts are aligned with your core values, your purpose, and your inner wisdom, trust them fully.

Trust is the foundation of self-assurance, and when you act from a place of trust in yourself, you give yourself the freedom to navigate life with confidence and clarity.

Doubt only leads to mental and emotional exhaustion, leaving you feeling disconnected from your true self.

Instead of questioning your thoughts, turn inward and reaffirm the strength of your beliefs.

By doing so, you not only honor yourself but also open the door to living with greater peace, confidence, and alignment with your true path.

When you trust your thoughts, you are trusting the wisdom that resides within you, guiding you toward a fulfilling and meaningful life.

Chapter 68

Painful memories

Reminiscing about sad moments often leads to the resurfacing of negative emotions that keep you tethered to the past.

While reflection is a natural part of the human experience, continuously revisiting painful memories can hinder emotional growth and healing.

The more you focus on sorrowful times, the more difficult it becomes to move forward and embrace the present.

Every time you relive these moments in your mind, you invite the same sadness and regret to fill your thoughts, which only reinforces the emotional wounds.

Rather than allowing these memories to fade with time, you keep them alive, preventing yourself from experiencing the joy and fulfillment that the present moment offers.

The impact of dwelling on past sadness is not limited to the emotions you feel in the moment, it extends to your mental state over time.

Continually revisiting painful memories can lead to a mental and emotional loop that becomes harder to break.

This repetitive cycle of negativity can contribute to anxiety, depression, and even a sense of emotional paralysis.

It can feel as though you are stuck, unable to move beyond the events that caused you harm.

The more energy and focus you direct toward these memories, the more entrenched they become in your psyche.

This constant rumination only keeps the wounds open, preventing true healing and closure from taking place.

The consequences of such mental patterns are not just emotional but physical as well.

Our minds and bodies are deeply interconnected, and emotional distress can significantly affect our overall health.

Chronic stress and sadness take a toll on the immune system, leading to weakened defenses against illness, chronic fatigue, and various physical ailments such as headaches, muscle tension, and gastrointestinal issues.

Emotional turmoil can cause a sustained release of stress hormones, which, over time, can contribute to chronic health problems like high blood pressure, heart disease, and digestive disorders.

By focusing on sadness, you not only damage your emotional well-being but also jeopardize your physical health.

To protect both your mental and physical health, it is essential to release the hold that sad memories have over you.

As stated in the teachings, shifting your attention to the present moment allows you to break free from the past and embrace the opportunities that life continues to offer.

Focusing on positive experiences, cultivating gratitude, and creating new memories can help you shift your perspective and allow you to heal.

It's important to recognize that while the past shaped you, it doesn't have to define your current state.

Seeking support, practicing mindfulness, and developing healthier thought patterns can help you let go of sorrow and make space for peace and well-being.

By choosing to focus on the present and the possibilities of the future, you can release the grip of past sadness and promote both mental and physical vitality.

Chapter 69

Living through your children

---◆◆---

Avoid living through your children, as it can deeply disrupt their individual journey and create unnecessary conflict within their emotional development.

Every child is born with a unique set of talents, passions, challenges, and experiences that are theirs alone to navigate.

As a parent, your role is to guide and support them as they discover and explore their own path in life, not to impose your own unfulfilled dreams, desires, or expectations upon them.

When you try to live through your children, you overshadow their own identities and inadvertently place them in a position where they may feel obligated to fulfill roles that were never theirs to play.

This interference stifles their potential and deprives them of the opportunity to live authentically.

Living through your children often manifests as pushing them to achieve things that you may have missed out on, or directing them towards paths that reflect your own desires rather than their unique interests.

While your intentions may come from a place of love or care, this dynamic places immense pressure on the child to meet the standards you set for them, rather than allowing them to determine their own values and goals.

When a child is made to feel that their worth is tied to someone else's expectations, they lose the ability to explore their own interests freely.

This prevents them from experiencing the essential process of self-discovery, where they can make their own choices, take risks, and learn from their mistakes.

As a result, the child may grow up feeling disconnected from their true self, unsure of what they genuinely want out of life.

This parental overreach creates an environment of inner disharmony, not just for the child but within the family as a whole.

The child may begin to feel misunderstood or resentful, sensing that they are seen as an extension of the parent's dreams rather than as a whole, independent person.

This disconnect fosters a lack of trust and communication between parent and child, as the child struggles with the pressure to live up to expectations that were never their own.

Over time, this tension can lead to emotional strain, eroding the bonds of love and respect that should naturally exist in the relationship.

Instead of a nurturing, supportive environment, the home becomes a place where control and perfectionism dominate, and the child's natural need for freedom and exploration is stifled.

This cycle of unspoken resentment and frustration can affect not just the parent-child relationship, but the overall emotional well-being of the entire family.

Instead of living through your children, embrace the beauty and individuality of their personal journey.

Encourage them to explore the world in their own way, offering guidance and wisdom without forcing them to conform to a predetermined path.

Allow your child the freedom to take risks, make mistakes, and grow from their own experiences.

By giving them the space to discover their passions and form their own identity, you show them that their worth is not tied to external validation but to their own inherent value as individuals.

This not only strengthens the parent-child bond but also fosters an atmosphere of peace and mutual respect in the home.

When a child is empowered to be themselves, free from the burden of unspoken expectations, they are more likely to develop a sense of inner harmony and confidence.

In turn, this allows both parent and child to experience a deeper connection, rooted in unconditional love and acceptance, and supports each person in their own unique journey through life.

Chapter 70

The benefits of smiling

Smile often, for there is an abundance of beauty in the world, quietly present in the spaces where we least expect it.

It exists in the colors of the sky at dawn, in the sound of birds calling to one another, and in the peaceful silence of early morning.

It's found in the way light filters through leaves, in the expressions of those you love, and in the simple, unspoken kindnesses that people offer each other every day.

Often, we become so caught up in our routines, worries, or future plans that we forget to notice this ever-present beauty.

But when you pause, breathe, and look around with open eyes, you begin to see that life is filled with small miracles deserving of a smile.

Smiling in the presence of beauty is not just an outward act, it is an inward shift.

It's a recognition of the sacredness of life in all its forms, and an acceptance of the present moment as it is.

You do not need perfection to smile.

You do not need everything to be right.

Even in moments of struggle or uncertainty, beauty remains, waiting patiently to be acknowledged.

A smile, then, becomes a quiet celebration of the good that still exists, no matter the circumstances.

It is a way of saying, "I see you" to the world and to the countless forms of life and grace unfolding around you.

And as you smile, you begin to shift not just your mood but your entire perception.

Beauty becomes easier to see, and gratitude becomes more natural to feel.

Your smile lights up your own spirit, making it easier to find peace within.

But it doesn't stop there.

A smile is contagious, it softens others, invites connection, and creates a shared moment of presence.

It can change the atmosphere of a room, uplift someone's day, or bring a sense of warmth to a cold or distant moment.

In a world that can often feel rushed, distracted, or burdened, your smile becomes a gift, a quiet offering of light.

So choose to smile often, not because life is always easy or perfect, but because beauty is always here, waiting to be seen.

Let your smile arise from the joy of noticing, a flower blooming in the cracks of a sidewalk, the laughter of a child, the rhythm of the wind.

Let it be your way of acknowledging that even amid hardship, the world still holds wonder.

In doing so, you invite more beauty into your awareness and more light into the lives of those around you.

A smile is a small act, but when offered often and sincerely, it becomes a powerful way to live with presence, grace, and gratitude.

Chapter 71

Beyond the physical

See people not merely as the physical bodies they inhabit, but as expressions of the eternal Creation Energy that flows through all life.

When you shift your perception from the external form to the inner essence, your understanding of others begins to transform.

You start to recognize that beneath appearances, beyond behaviors, each person carries the same fundamental spark of existence, the same creative force that animates you.

This awareness fosters a deeper connection rooted in unity, rather than division.

The physical body is only a temporary vessel, shaped by circumstances, genetics, environment, and time. J

udging people solely by their appearance limits your ability to truly see them.

It reinforces superficial distinctions and obscures the deeper reality of who and what they are.

When you look beyond the surface and acknowledge the Creation Energy within, you open yourself to a more profound and compassionate understanding of humanity.

You see not just faces or forms, but living manifestations of something sacred and universal.

In this way, everyone begins to appear more beautiful to you, not because of conventional standards, but because you are recognizing the divine essence within them.

Beauty takes on a new meaning, one that is not tied to youth, perfection, or outward traits, but to the presence of life, consciousness, and shared origin.

You begin to feel love, respect, and appreciation even for those you once found difficult to understand or accept, because you now perceive them as fellow travelers on the same journey of existence.

By seeing others as Creation Energy first, you elevate your interactions and deepen your empathy.

You respond less to ego and more to essence.

This shift not only transforms how you relate to others, but also how you relate to yourself, for as you recognize the divine in others, you begin to see it more clearly in yourself.

Through this higher vision, your world becomes more harmonious, more compassionate, and infinitely more beautiful.

Chapter 72

Living without regret

Regret nothing, for every experience you've lived through has shaped the person you are today.

Your past is not a collection of mistakes to be mourned, but a series of stepping stones that brought you to your present self.

Every choice, every success, every setback, and every moment of uncertainty contributed to your growth and awareness.

Even the parts of your journey that were painful or confusing helped forge your character and deepen your understanding of life, relationships, and yourself.

Without those moments, you would not carry the same strength, perspective, or wisdom you now possess.

It's easy to look back and wish things had gone differently, to wish you'd chosen another path, spoken different words, or avoided certain situations.

But to dwell on regret is to deny the value of your own transformation.

As the teachings clearly stated, the past cannot be changed, but it can be honored for what it taught you.

Life does not move in perfect lines, it weaves and bends, and sometimes it takes you through darkness so you can better recognize the light.

Regret traps you in a loop of self-blame, preventing you from fully embracing your progress and the insight gained from experience.

Growth often comes from discomfort, and strength is forged through challenge.

Rather than regretting your past, choose to embrace it fully.

Acknowledge your missteps with honesty, but not with shame.

Every version of yourself, from the most lost to the most certain, deserves compassion and understanding.

You did the best you could with the knowledge, emotional tools, and awareness you had at the time.

If you've changed, if you've grown, if you've learned from those moments, then they served their purpose.

Accepting your past does not mean approving of everything that happened, it means recognizing that all of it helped lead you to this present state of consciousness and possibility.

Your past is the raw material of your becoming.

Without it, you would not carry the same compassion, clarity, or drive to evolve.

Regret only weighs you down and dims the light of your current self.

Instead, stand tall in the knowledge that your journey has made you wiser and more capable.

Use everything you've lived through as fuel to live more intentionally and more consciously today.

Regret nothing.

Trust your path, honor your story, and continue forward with purpose, knowing that every part of your life has meaning in the shaping of your soul.

Chapter 73

The joy of Pride

W hatever you choose to do in life, do it with genuine pride and a clear sense of purpose.

Whether your task is great or small, public or private, meaningful only to you or shared with others, approach it with commitment and self-respect.

When you act from a place of integrity and intention, you create a foundation of confidence and stability within yourself.

Pride in your actions is not about arrogance or superiority, but about acknowledging your efforts and honoring your role in the unfolding of your life.

Each choice, each deed, becomes an expression of your values, your growth, and your character.

It is vital that you never allow yourself to be consumed by shame for who you are or for the life you lead, so long as you live truthfully and take responsibility for your actions.

Shame, when unjustified or internalized from external judgment, can become a powerful force of self-sabotage.

It creeps into your thoughts, undermines your decisions, and makes you question your worth.

When you carry shame without cause, or when you accept it as your identity, you limit your own potential.

It holds you back from being fully present, fully expressive, and fully yourself.

Shame fosters inner disharmony by creating conflict between who you truly are and who you believe you are expected to be.

This disconnect weakens your emotional and mental well-being, leading to doubt, hesitation, and fear.

Instead of moving forward with clarity and confidence, you become trapped in cycles of self-rejection and guilt.

True harmony within comes when you are able to face yourself honestly, forgive your missteps, learn from your experiences, and continue on your path with a renewed sense of self-worth.

Accepting your imperfections and owning your journey are essential for healing and transformation.

By choosing to live with pride and authenticity, you align yourself with your inner truth and create the space for personal peace to grow.

You no longer need to seek validation from outside sources, because your sense of worth comes from within.

You begin to make decisions based not on fear or avoidance, but on what resonates with your highest self.

The more you embrace your life with courage and dignity, the more harmonious your inner world becomes.

From this place of balance and self-trust, you can meet life's challenges with resilience, contribute to others with sincerity, and evolve with clarity and grace.

Chapter 74

Spirituality and Materialism

◆—◆◆◆—◆

If you are sincerely striving for the effective truth and the evolution of your consciousness, it is natural that you may begin to reflect deeply on your relationship with the material aspects of life.

Questions may arise within you about the true value and necessity of material goods.

You might ask yourself whether you should detach entirely from physical possessions in order to become more spiritually free, or perhaps whether it would be better to stop paying so much attention to them and focus exclusively on inner growth.

Such thoughts often surface on the path toward deeper understanding, especially as you begin to see the limitations and distractions that can come from an overly materialistic life.

However, according to the teachings, it would be a serious error to think that simply rejecting or ignoring material goods is the right course.

While the desire to transcend the physical may stem from a noble intention, it overlooks the fundamental reality of human existence.

As a human being, you are a material life form existing in a material world. Your body, your environment, and your daily needs all require the use of physical resources.

To completely free yourself from material goods or to act as though they are unimportant would not only be impractical, but also counterproductive to your growth.

Denying this fact is not a sign of enlightenment but a form of escapism that can lead to imbalance and disconnection from life.

Material goods in themselves are not detrimental to spiritual evolution.

What truly matters is your attitude toward them and the role they play in your life.

When approached with awareness, responsibility, and modesty, physical possessions can serve as important tools that support your development.

They provide shelter, nourishment, education, and the means to carry out tasks and duties that are essential both for personal progress and for contributing positively to the world around you.

The misuse of material goods, whether through greed, hoarding, or unhealthy attachment, is what creates inner conflict and hinders growth, not the goods themselves.

Therefore, instead of striving to rid yourself of material things or pretending they do not matter, seek to cultivate a healthy and conscious relationship with them.

Aim for simplicity, sufficiency, and balance, recognizing that the material and spiritual realms are not in opposition, but are aspects of one holistic human experience.

By acknowledging and integrating both, you can build a life that honors truth and supports the steady evolution of your consciousness.

Material goods, when used with discernment and purpose, become instruments for living responsibly, growing wisely, and serving meaningfully in the greater context of existence.

Chapter 75

Preconceived Ideas of the Truth

❖◆❖

One of the central challenges faced by the people of Earth is their inability to perceive the future clearly.

This limitation often stems from deeply rooted preconceived ideas about where truth and wisdom should originate.

Many expect enlightenment to come only from prestigious institutions, famous figures, or traditional sources, and in doing so, they overlook unexpected channels of knowledge.

In reality, truth does not conform to our expectations.

It does not wear a uniform or announce itself with accolades.

Sometimes, the greatest insights come from the most unassuming individuals.

A neighbor, a stranger on the street, or even someone considered insignificant by societal standards could hold immense wisdom and experience, possibly accumulated over many lifetimes.

For instance, the person living next door may have, in a past life, authored profound works that are now taught in universities.

Yet, in their current form, they may go unnoticed, their wisdom unacknowledged simply because they do not fit our image of a teacher or scholar.

This reflects a widespread blindness caused by prejudice, which blocks the flow of truth and progress.

Ultimately, truth is universal and impartial.

It emerges through all kinds of people, regardless of background, appearance, or social standing.

The sooner we abandon our narrow definitions of where truth should come from, the more open we become to recognizing it in its many forms, and the more prepared we will be to face the future with clarity and understanding.

Chapter 76

The Power of Helping

◆━━━━◆◆◆━━━━◆

In a world that often rewards independence, competition, and personal success, the act of helping can feel undervalued, almost like an interruption to the "real work" of achieving our goals.

From a young age, many of us are taught to chase after self-reliance, to forge ahead on our own paths, and to measure our worth by how little we need from others.

But beneath this cultural narrative lies a quieter truth, we are not built to go through life alone.

We are social beings, wired for connection, and helping one another is not a distraction from success, it's a vital expression of what it means to be human.

To help is to recognize someone else's humanity and to act on that recognition.

It doesn't require grand gestures or elaborate plans.

It can be as simple as offering a kind word, sharing your time, or showing up when it counts.

True help comes from a place of empathy and humility.

It means setting aside our egos long enough to ask, "How can I support you?" and listening carefully to the answer.

In doing so, we bridge the gap between people, not just in terms of practical needs, but in terms of emotional understanding and trust.

Helping someone is also an act of courage.

It asks us to step out of our own bubble and into someone else's experience, often without a clear script or guarantee of success.

It requires us to confront our discomfort with vulnerability, pain, and uncertainty.

Sometimes we hesitate to help because we're afraid of doing it wrong, or because the problem seems too big.

But help doesn't have to be perfect to be powerful.

Just showing up and being present can mean the world to someone who feels unseen or unsupported.

There's also a deeper benefit that often goes unspoken, helping others enriches the one who helps.

Acts of service have been linked to increased well-being, reduced stress, and a stronger sense of purpose.

When we help, we're reminded that we can make a difference, even in small ways.

We move beyond our own worries and reconnect with the broader human story, one where compassion, generosity, and kindness are just as valuable as achievement or recognition.

At its core, helping is about connection.

It's what turns acquaintances into friends, strangers into allies, and communities into safe, nurturing spaces.

These connections are built not through dramatic, once-in-a-lifetime actions, but through steady, everyday choices.

Helping is in the coworker who patiently shares their knowledge, the neighbor who checks in unprompted, the teacher who stays after class, and the child who gives half their snack to a classmate.

These actions may seem small, but they build a culture of care that impacts everyone.

Importantly, helping isn't a one-way street.

To truly embrace the power of helping, we must also learn to receive help when it's offered.

Many people find it easier to give than to accept support, fearing it may make them look weak or burdensome.

But allowing others to help us is an act of trust.

It honors their willingness to connect and creates a space of mutual respect and vulnerability.

Being open to help doesn't diminish our strength, it deepens our relationships and reminds us, we don't have to carry everything alone.

The most powerful help is consistent, unglamorous, and rooted in presence.

It doesn't depend on having the perfect words or unlimited resources.

It simply asks that we notice one another, that we stay awake to the needs around us, and that we act with care.

When helping becomes a habit, it shapes our character.

It grounds us in values that outlast changing circumstances, compassion, humility, generosity, and love.

In the end, helping isn't just something we do.

It's a way of living.

It's a quiet resistance against apathy, a small rebellion against the isolating forces of modern life.

Every time we help, we remind ourselves, and each other, that we are not alone in this world.

We are connected.

And in those connections, we find hope, healing, and the kind of strength that truly lasts.

Chapter 77

The Shackled Mind

T he human mind exists within an invisible prison, one so subtle, so intricately constructed, that its boundaries often go completely unnoticed.

It is not made of stone walls or iron bars, but of thoughts, beliefs, and patterns passed down through generations.

Most people never realize they are confined, because the structure of this prison has been woven into the very fabric of their upbringing.

It is built silently, over time, through repetition and reinforcement.

The mind is taught to obey, to conform, to suppress, and in doing so, loses touch with its natural state of freedom.

The tragedy lies in how familiar this imprisonment becomes, so much so that most mistake it for the natural order of life.

At the center of this unseen cell stands fear, persistent, subtle, and relentless.

Fear is the warden, masterfully shaping perceptions, influencing behavior, and restricting thought.

It comes cloaked in many forms, fear of failure, of rejection, of vulnerability, of standing alone, of losing control.

It hides within the most ordinary decisions, whispering warnings disguised as wisdom.

Often mistaken for caution or practicality, these fears slip under the radar of conscious thought, becoming indistinguishable from personal beliefs.

They do not shout or demand, they merely suggest, and that is often enough to steer lives away from truth and into the confines of compliance.

This is what makes the prison so effective, it needs no guards, no punishments, no visible threat. It requires only a quiet agreement, a belief that there is no prison at all.

From the earliest years of life, individuals are taught what to fear and what to pursue.

They are handed values, dreams, and definitions of success that may have nothing to do with who they truly are.

These prepackaged identities are absorbed and internalized until the person forgets they had a choice to begin with.

The illusion of autonomy becomes the final, most insidious lock.

People are convinced they are free, even as their thoughts, desires, and decisions are filtered through generations of conditioning and silent fear.

In such a state, the vast inner potential of the human being remains dormant.

Creativity shrinks within rigid rules.

Curiosity is dulled by routine.

The spark of authenticity fades under layers of social performance and self-doubt.

Fear teaches people to speak less, to dream smaller, to settle more.

Exploration becomes risky, and expression becomes dangerous.

Each generation passes down these invisible shackles, not out of malice, but because they, too, learned to survive by staying confined.

And when someone dares to question or awaken, they are often met not with curiosity but resistance.

Not because their words are false, but because they threaten the delicate architecture of a shared illusion.

Yet, there is hope, for this cage is not made of matter, but of mind.

And what is built in the mind can be dismantled by the mind.

The first cracks appear when a person begins to observe, to question the fears that guide them, to examine the voices in their head, to ask, "Whose truth is this?"

In that moment of inquiry, awareness is born.

And once awareness awakens, it does not easily go back to sleep.

It starts small, a shift in perception, a moment of clarity, but it grows.

The more one observes, the more the illusion dissolves.

Real freedom does not begin with rebellion or escape, but with inner recognition.

Through conscious awareness, the mind begins to remember its own power, its own wisdom, its own infinite capacity.

And in that remembrance, it finally realizes, it was never meant to live in fear.

Chapter 78

Embracing the truth

————◆◆◆————

Once you fully embrace the truth and allow it to become one with your being, a profound and lasting shift begins to unfold within you.

The confusion, uncertainty, and inner conflict that may have previously clouded your path begin to dissolve, replaced by a clear and steady sense of inner knowing.

This truth is not something imposed upon you from the outside, it arises from deep within, resonating with your most authentic self.

It aligns you with your purpose and brings into focus what truly matters.

As this truth anchors itself in your consciousness, it empowers you to live not by compulsion or fear, but by genuine desire and inner guidance.

This merging with truth awakens a quiet but unshakable power within you, the power to choose consciously and to act only in ways that are fully aligned with your psyche.

The weight of external obligations, societal expectations, or the need for approval begins to lift.

Instead, you find yourself moved by an inner compass, gently but firmly guiding your every step.

You begin to recognize what serves you and what pulls you away from yourself.

This inner clarity simplifies your life, bringing peace and a renewed sense of purpose.

Your mind, once scattered by conflicting thoughts and the demands of the outer world, becomes focused and harmonious.

It no longer serves as a battleground of competing voices, but rather steps into its true role as the conductor of your life's symphony.

With truth as its foundation, your mind orchestrates your intentions and actions with precision and grace.

Your thoughts align with your values, your choices become deliberate, and your energy flows with greater ease and effectiveness.

This mental coherence naturally extends to your outer world, influencing how you interact with others, make decisions, and respond to life's challenges.

In this state of alignment, even the most subtle wishes that arise within you are heard by Creation.

There is no need for force or manipulation, life begins to unfold in resonance with your inner truth.

You find that the universe responds not just to your words or actions, but to the quiet intentions that live in your heart.

Opportunities, connections, and moments of synchronicity emerge seemingly without effort.

The boundary between your inner world and outer experience begins to fade, revealing a life that is not only meaningful but also deeply supported by the creative forces of existence itself.

Chapter 79

What the truth does to the human being

T his is what the truth does to the human being, it doesn't just change how one thinks, it reshapes how one experiences life entirely.

And these aren't just poetic sentiments or lofty ideals, many who have embraced truth deeply and earnestly can attest to the reality of these transformations.

Life, which once may have felt like a battlefield or a burdensome journey, begins to feel more like a vast and vibrant playground.

Challenges still arise, but they're no longer met with dread, instead, they become opportunities for learning, growth, and even joy.

The constant undercurrent of anger, frustration, and restlessness softens, replaced by a calm presence and a patience that grows without effort.

You find yourself laughing more often, sometimes for no reason at all, because something within has become light and free.

Fear, which once had many faces, fear of judgment, of rejection, of loss, begins to dissolve.

You no longer shrink in the presence of others or alter yourself to be accepted.

You fear no one because you understand that all beings are equals at the core, each walking their own path.

This understanding allows you to listen more deeply and more sincerely.

You no longer just hear people, you begin to feel them, to understand what lies behind their words.

Respect flows more naturally because you see yourself in others, and you begin to care not because of obligation, but because love becomes your natural state.

With that, love arises the unshakable desire for change, not superficial or forced change, but meaningful transformation, both inward and outward.

You become anchored in your own truth and stand your ground, not with ego, but with a quiet, powerful knowing.

As you continue walking this path, you discover the joy of full expression.

You speak your thoughts and feelings without fear, without hesitation, and without the need to conform.

You express yourself honestly and openly, because you are no longer defined by how others respond.

Your thoughts become clearer, more neutral, and balanced, no longer trapped in extremes, but harmonized through insight and understanding.

Personal attacks or harsh words no longer pierce you as they once did, because you take nothing personally.

You realize that everyone is simply projecting their own inner conflicts, and you are no longer a mirror for those projections.

Material possessions and superficial successes lose their pull on you, they no longer represent happiness or value.

Instead, your focus turns inward, toward becoming a more conscious, compassionate, and capable version of yourself.

And then, something beautiful yet bittersweet happens, you feel a deep longing to share what you've come to know.

The insights and revelations feel too profound to keep hidden.

You want to lift others, to help them see what you now see.

But you quickly notice how rare it is to find others who are ready to receive this truth.

A quiet loneliness may settle in, not because you are disconnected, but because you've moved into a space where few yet dwell.

Still, you carry on, because the truth is your companion.

You smile to yourself, not out of arrogance, but from a gentle recognition that what takes most people centuries to realize, you've begun to live now.

You know it may take 800 years for others to awaken to the same clarity, and that's okay.

You've touched the timeless, and now walk with a peace and purpose that needs no validation.

And so it is.

Chapter 80

The mastering of oneself

A human being should always cultivate the strength and awareness necessary to govern themselves in every moment of life.

This means learning to guide one's thoughts, emotions, words, and actions with clarity, responsibility, and a sense of inner discipline.

It is not enough to react instinctively or emotionally to the events of the day, rather, a person must develop the maturity to act with purpose and reflection.

As the teachings prove, to be the master of oneself means being able to pause, reflect, and make conscious choices instead of falling into impulsive speech or reckless behavior.

This inner control is a sign of true strength and dignity, and it allows one to face life's challenges with composure and integrity.

Part of this self-mastery includes knowing when it is appropriate to raise one's voice or speak firmly in order to set boundaries or restore order in difficult situations.

Being calm does not mean being passive or submissive, it means having the power to act with restraint and deliberation, even in moments of stress or conflict.

When necessary, one must be able to express strength through voice and presence without losing composure or descending into aggression or chaos.

This kind of deliberate authority is a vital aspect of fulfilling one's responsibilities, both toward others and toward oneself.

It is a duty to uphold justice, truth, and harmony, and it begins with the ability to control one's inner world and express oneself with purpose.

As BILLy stated, a truly wise human being is marked by balance, versatility, and a deep commitment to growth in both intellectual and practical realms.

Such a person does not limit themselves to a narrow field of expertise or opinion but instead cultivates a wide range of skills and understanding.

They are proficient not only in thought and language, but also in action and craft.

They can express themselves clearly through speech and writing, and they are equally capable when it comes to manual work and practical responsibilities.

Their judgment is fair and unpartisan because it is guided by insight, experience, and a desire for truth rather than personal gain.

This kind of balanced wisdom reflects a mature and cultivated spirit, one that values all aspects of life and respects the dignity of every kind of work.

In contrast, the unwise person often lives in imbalance, driven by narrow perspectives, personal bias, and a lack of discipline.

They may be mentally lazy, physically passive, or emotionally unstable, failing to rise to the challenges of life with energy and determination.

Such individuals tend to be partisan, favoring their own views without seeking truth, and their actions are often marked by carelessness or selfishness.

They may avoid practical work or struggle with coherent communication, which leads to disorder, confusion, and unfulfilled potential.

Without the willingness to grow and take responsibility for oneself, their development remains stagnant.

For this reason, it is essential for every human being to strive toward the cultivation of inner mastery, balanced knowledge, and the ability to act wisely and justly in all aspects of life.

This is the path toward personal fulfillment and a meaningful contribution to the greater good.

Chapter 81

A true and
effective friendship

◆———————◆◆◆———————◆

According to the Creation Energy teachings, true and effective friendship is one of the most valuable connections a person can experience in life.

It is characterized by a deep mutual reliance in which both individuals can fully trust one another, not only in times of ease but especially in moments of hardship and uncertainty.

In such a bond, friends provide each other with moral strength, emotional encouragement, and a steady foundation of support that helps each one navigate the challenges of existence.

True friendship is not limited to offering help in crises, but is about consistently being present, offering kindness, honesty, and motivation in all phases of life.

In this way, friendship becomes a pillar of strength, stability, and inspiration that enriches both lives profoundly.

This kind of friendship does not come into being quickly or effortlessly.

With very few exceptions, it takes considerable time to grow into a genuine, trustworthy relationship.

A lasting friendship is built on the foundation of enduring human affection, care, and a form of love that is friendly, respectful, and heartfelt.

It cannot be forced or rushed, as its development depends on the sincerity and depth of both individuals involved.

Each act of kindness, each display of understanding, and each shared experience slowly contributes to the shaping of a bond that can endure the tests of time, change, and circumstance.

Just as a tree needs time to grow deep roots and bear fruit, so too does a friendship require patience, nurturing, and shared growth.

Contrary to fleeting connections or instant associations, a real friendship does not arise from a single meeting, a casual conversation, or even a few pleasant interactions.

It unfolds gradually through shared stories, personal revelations, mutual understanding, and time spent together.

The bond of friendship is a process of discovery, of learning to understand and accept each other's strengths and weaknesses, values and fears, dreams and setbacks.

It is a journey of growing together, and this journey can only take place through time spent engaging in meaningful conversations, experiencing life's ups and downs side by side, and building a history together.

The depth of friendship reflects the richness of these shared moments.

Ultimately, true friendship is an evolving and living connection, rooted in loyalty, empathy, and mutual dedication.

It demands effort, honesty, and the willingness to be vulnerable and open-hearted.

A genuine friend does not abandon the other when times become difficult, but stands by them with care and resolve.

Through forgiveness, acceptance, and continuous emotional investment, such a friendship strengthens and deepens over the years.

It becomes more than just companionship, it becomes a source of wisdom, comfort, and a reminder that one is never truly alone.

In this sense, a true friendship contributes not only to the happiness of the individual but to the unfolding of a more compassionate, grounded, and fulfilled life.

Chapter 82

Inward gaze

When you truly turn your gaze inward and observe the energy and power that have been given to you through Creation, you begin to realize that this force is not bound by predetermined direction.

It is a pure, neutral-positive-equalised potential, existing without bias toward good or evil.

What it becomes, and how it unfolds in the world through you, is entirely dependent upon the way you think, the emotions you cultivate from those thoughts, and the choices you make from moment to moment.

This energy is like a seed of boundless potential, and the soil in which it grows is your consciousness, shaped by your awareness, intention, and will.

It is not some external force, fate, or divine will that determines whether this energy is used for constructive or destructive ends.

Rather, it is your own inner orientation, your thoughts, feelings, values, and motivations, that give it direction and momentum.

If you choose to dwell in resentment, fear, arrogance, or selfishness, this energy will amplify those inner states and bring about destructive consequences.

On the other hand, if you cultivate thoughts of peace, understanding, truth, and compassion, the same energy will be shaped into a force that uplifts, heals, and contributes to harmony within and around you.

In this way, you are the bearer of responsibility for the consequences of the energy you direct, be it creative or ruinous.

This knowledge reveals a profound truth, that the nature of your reality, and the quality of your life and relationships, stem not from external circumstances alone, but from the invisible processes taking place within your own mind and heart.

You are constantly forming patterns through your inner world, and those patterns interact with the universal energy to create effects in the material and spiritual dimensions of your life.

Every thought you repeat, every feeling you indulge or discipline, and every intention you follow through with is a command issued to this energy.

And through this process, you either bring yourself closer to the natural laws of Creation and its harmony, or you fall into imbalance, inner suffering, and outward discord.

Thus, it becomes essential to walk through life with conscious clarity and deep responsibility.

Know that the power within you is not small or meaningless, it is the very force that shapes your world.

You must learn to observe your thoughts before they take root, to nurture those that bring light and life, and to gently correct those that bring harm or decay.

Through such inner discipline, you become not just a user of energy, but a wise steward of it.

You align your life more and more with the natural, creative laws of existence, and in doing so, you foster peace, truth, and love, not as abstract ideals, but as real, living expressions of your own evolving self.

Chapter 83

Illusions of separation

The truth, when fully realized, strips away all illusions of separation.

It reveals that beneath the appearances of division, between people, between nature and humanity, between the physical and the spiritual, there exists only unity.

This unity is not merely conceptual but a living reality, inherent in the very fabric of existence.

What seems fragmented is, at its core, indivisible.

In the face of this revelation, the barriers we once held as absolute dissolve, and the recognition of interconnectedness becomes undeniable.

As this understanding deepens, the false walls that define identity, belief, and form lose their authority.

The ego's grasp on difference and superiority weakens, and a new awareness dawns, one that sees through the veil of separateness.

The dichotomies of life, good and bad, self and other, inner and outer, are seen as expressions of a singular field of being.

This insight leads to compassion, not as a moral obligation, but as a natural response to the recognition that in all things, we see ourselves.

This truth does not remain static or theoretical, it breathes life into every aspect of our being.

It nurtures humility and reverence, for when we recognize that we are not apart from but a part of the whole, we can no longer stand in judgment, only in understanding.

The psyche awakens in this space, no longer striving for dominance or control, but for alignment with the rhythm of life.

It is in this state that true peace begins, not a passive silence, but an active harmony that radiates through thought, word, and deed.

In the presence of this knowledge, life rises to its highest expression.

It no longer reigns by force, fear, or competition, but by wisdom, coherence, and balance.

Life becomes sacred once more, not because it is rare, but because it is recognized as unified and eternal.

To live in truth is to live in service of that unity, to act with awareness that all actions ripple outward, affecting the whole.

This is where life finds its true dominion, not in ruling over others, but in aligning with the deeper order of existence that binds all things as one.

Chapter 84

The illusion of superiority

T he declarations of superiority that echo throughout society, such as "My god is better than your god," "My team is better than your team," or "My president is better than your president", reflect a deep psychological pattern rooted in the desire to belong, dominate, and differentiate.

These statements aren't just personal opinions, they're reflections of collective conditioning.

They emerge from the need to feel significant, to stand above others, and to assert identity by comparison.

This kind of thinking fuels tribalism, which, while giving a temporary sense of pride or unity within a group, ultimately promotes division between groups.

Whether it's politics, religion, sports, or culture, these sentiments feed an "us versus them" mentality that fractures communities and undermines the possibility of peaceful coexistence.

The insistence on superiority blinds us to shared humanity and turns potential allies into perceived adversaries.

Beyond these cultural banners, the obsession with personal and material comparison further deepens this chasm.

Statements like "I have more than you do," "I wear more expensive brands," "My house is bigger than yours," or "I only fly private" are symptoms of a status-driven society that places more value on appearance and ownership than on inner worth and collective well-being.

Such comparisons create not only resentment and envy but also a perpetual sense of inadequacy among those trying to "keep up."

This system thrives on convincing people that their value depends on how much more or less they have than others.

From physical appearance, "My butt is bigger than yours," "I fuck better looking girls than you", to intangible comparisons like happiness and success, "I'm happier than you," "I have a better life than you", these declarations warp self-worth into a contest of perceived dominance and foster a culture where self-validation is tethered to others' perceived inferiority.

At the root of this divisive psychology is profit.

Division has been commodified and institutionalized, just like the archetypal opposites of God and Satan, heaven and hell, good and evil.

These concepts, repeated across religions and ideologies, serve not just as metaphysical ideas but as tools of control and manipulation.

The more divided people are, by beliefs, by political affiliations, by possessions or by skin color, the easier they are to influence, sell to, and govern.

Division sells.

It powers marketing, it fuels elections, it sustains media cycles, and it upholds entire industries built on insecurity and comparison.

The illusion of separation is maintained because it's valuable to those who benefit from conflict and consumerism.

Unity doesn't sell nearly as well as conflict does.

Harmony does not fuel endless consumption like insecurity does.

And so, society is fed the illusion of superiority and rivalry to keep the machinery of profit running smoothly.

But all these divisions, despite appearing distinct, religion, wealth, fame, beauty, race, and ideology, are variations of the same illusion.

They all serve the same purpose, to prevent people from seeing the truth of their interconnectedness.

Whether we're comparing gods, presidents, sports, cars, or skin color, we're engaging in a narrative that separates rather than unites.

These divisions may seem unrelated, yet they spring from the same root, a deeply ingrained belief that difference equals value, and value is hierarchical.

Until this belief is unlearned, people will remain trapped in cycles of comparison, jealousy, superiority, and alienation.

True peace and understanding begin when we recognize that all these competing claims to greatness are distractions from the deeper truth, we are one species, one humanity, equal in essence and worthy not because of how we differ, but because of how deeply we are the same.

Chapter 85

The danger of using "believe"

It is crucial to make a conscious effort to avoid using the word "believe" in our daily language, as it subtly constrains the mind and can have negative effects on our thinking and personal growth.

The term "believe" inherently carries with it an undertone of uncertainty and doubt, as it suggests that we are not entirely certain of something, but instead, are merely accepting it on faith or trust.

When we say we "believe" in something, it implies that we are unsure about it, which automatically limits the strength and conviction of our perception.

Belief is often a placeholder for knowledge or understanding, yet it doesn't convey the same depth or power.

It keeps us in a state of passivity, rather than embracing the active state of knowing, where certainty, clarity, and true awareness reside.

Personally, I have reached a point where I can no longer use the word "believe" to describe myself or my understanding of life.

Even the accidental usage of the word causes discomfort because it brings with it an energy of indecisiveness or half-formed conviction.

The word "believe" is tied to the concept of doubt.

To "believe" is to accept something without full proof or direct experience.

It acknowledges a gap in understanding, a space where certainty has yet to be achieved.

This is why, when people say they "believe" in themselves, they are inadvertently acknowledging a lack of complete self-understanding.

Belief in oneself suggests that there is still uncertainty, as if one is waiting for external validation or confirmation.

But true self-empowerment does not rest on belief, it rests on knowing.

To truly know oneself means to understand deeply one's essence, capabilities, potential, and purpose.

This knowing is a state of absolute clarity and confidence, where there is no room for self-doubt or questioning.

I don't "believe" in myself because I already know who I am and what I am capable of, and this knowledge provides me with an unwavering sense of strength and certainty.

To know oneself is to transcend the need for belief altogether, replacing uncertainty with the solid foundation of understanding.

Now, consider the potential of human beings if we could move beyond belief and fully embrace the concept of knowing.

Imagine how much more we could achieve if we stopped merely believing in our abilities, but instead recognized the truth of who we are at the deepest level.

If people could operate not from a place of uncertainty, but from a state of absolute knowing, the possibilities for personal achievement and growth would be limitless.

Belief is a powerful tool in its own right, but it is a tool that is often rooted in a lack of full awareness, a stepping stone on the path to deeper understanding.

However, when one reaches a point where belief is no longer necessary, where they know beyond a shadow of a doubt who they are, what they are capable of, and how they can impact the world, they unlock a power that belief alone could never provide.

The world would see an entirely new level of innovation, creativity, and self-expression, one where people act from a place of deep confidence and understanding rather than from a place of doubt and uncertainty.

The shift from belief to knowing is profound.

When we transition from believing to knowing, we step into a space of personal empowerment and strength that is unshakeable.

The act of knowing oneself is transformative, it erases the need for validation, eliminates self-doubt, and enhances clarity of purpose.

We stop second-guessing ourselves, and instead, we act from an intrinsic understanding of who we are and what we are capable of.

This level of certainty fosters a life where we pursue goals not from a place of hoping or wishing, but from a place of knowing that we can and will accomplish what we set out to do.

When we move past belief and into knowing, we become much more than passive observers of our lives, we become active creators, capable of shaping our destiny with the power of our thoughts, intentions, and actions.

The world needs more individuals who don't just believe in themselves, but who know themselves with an unwavering certainty, because it is from this place of knowing that we can truly tap into our limitless potential.

Chapter 86

After I die

After death, it will not be "me," Waid, who reincarnates.

The identity I hold now, with all its memories, preferences, personality traits, habits, and mannerisms, is a temporary formation, unique to this specific lifetime.

Waid is the name and role I currently embody, but it is not my eternal self.

This personality is bound to this one material existence and has no permanence beyond the boundaries of this life.

It exists for the purpose of experience, learning, and evolution within this specific incarnation, but once my life concludes, this personality, this "Waid", will come to an end.

At the moment of death, the personality known as Waid will dissolve completely.

It will be deleted, erased forever, and will never return in any future form.

There will be no memory of Waid, no emotional or psychological continuation of this identity.

However, this does not mean that all has ended.

What continues beyond death is the core energy within, the spiritual consciousness, often referred to as the Creation energy or spirit-form.

This energy is eternal and moves forward through time and space, undergoing a process of transformation.

It will be reprogrammed and reshaped into a new consciousness-block, which includes a freshly formed material personality and ego suited for a new human incarnation.

This reprogrammed consciousness-block will reincarnate into a new human being, either male or female, depending on various factors within the evolutionary process.

The new person will be born without the memory or personality of Waid, but within them, the spirit-form will carry all the accumulated experience and wisdom gained throughout every previous lifetime.

This includes not just the life lived as Waid, but also the countless identities that came before.

Each lifetime adds to the deep well of knowledge within the spirit-form, which silently accompanies the material self throughout each new existence, ready to serve the evolving consciousness.

Although the new person will not consciously remember past lives from birth, all the wisdom and insight gathered through those lives remains accessible.

It lies dormant, like a vast library within, waiting to be discovered.

Once the new individual begins to awaken to their true nature, realizing that they are more than just their current name, face, or identity, they can begin to access this inner knowledge.

Through spiritual growth, self-awareness, and inner exploration, the eternal self beneath the surface becomes more apparent.

At that point, the new person may tap into this wisdom intuitively, guiding their decisions, perceptions, and development.

Thus, even though Waid will not reincarnate, the eternal essence that powered this life will continue its journey, evolving with each new incarnation toward greater consciousness and harmony with Creation itself.

Chapter 87

Religion and sports

The time has arrived for Earth humans to recognize a truth that has long remained obscured, there is no meaningful difference between religion and sports.

Both institutions fulfill remarkably similar roles in human society, serving as powerful systems of belief, identity, and emotional investment.

Religion is seen as a path to spiritual fulfillment, moral guidance, and communal belonging.

Sports, on the other hand, are typically viewed as entertainment or leisure.

Yet, when we examine the behaviors and cultural patterns surrounding each, we find that both inspire ritualistic devotion, passionate loyalty, and collective identity.

The stadium, like the temple or church, becomes a sacred space where individuals gather in large numbers to participate in shared experiences, chant in unison, express reverence, and find meaning through a common cause.

Despite the striking similarities, this truth remains unnoticed by most people and will likely continue to be ignored by many for years to come.

The division between religion and sports has been socially and psychologically constructed, maintaining the illusion that one deals with the divine while the other deals only with games.

This illusion is reinforced by tradition and habit, blinding people to the reality that both operate on the same emotional and symbolic levels.

Just as religious institutions use myths, symbols, and rituals to shape belief and behavior, sports use mascots, team colors, and competitive narratives to create purpose and belonging.

The fervor with which fans defend their teams rivals that of religious zealots, and the deep emotional responses to a win or loss mimic the intensity of spiritual revelation or despair.

A particularly revealing example of this unconscious overlap can be found in how society regards its most celebrated athletes.

The fact that Michael Jordan is widely referred to as "The Black Jesus" is not just an exaggeration or a compliment, it is a cultural confession.

This nickname elevates him to divine status, symbolizing the reverence and almost mythological aura that surrounds top-tier athletes.

They are not merely skilled individuals, they are icons, worshipped for their excellence, their aura, and their ability to inspire.

Their images are displayed in homes, their quotes treated like scripture, and their performances replayed like sacred events.

Fans emulate their gestures, celebrate their legacies, and view them through a lens of awe that is functionally religious in nature.

This deeply embedded reverence is also reflected in the immense financial and social value placed on sports and their figures.

Athletes command astronomical salaries not merely because of their entertainment value, but because they occupy a role akin to that of modern gods.

People look to them for strength, inspiration, and identity.

Supporting a team is not just about regional pride, it's about belonging to a belief system, a tribe, a purpose.

Teams become modern-day religions, and athletes become prophets and deities who embody the hopes and dreams of millions.

The rituals of game day, the loyalty to team colors, the pilgrimage to stadiums, and the emotional investment in outcomes all point to the same human need, to believe in something greater than oneself.

In today's secular age, sports have risen to fill the spiritual void, offering faith, community, and devotion in a form that mirrors religion almost perfectly.

Recognizing this parallel opens a deeper understanding of the human psyche and our unchanging desire to worship, to belong, and to believe.

Chapter 88

Living with Bravery

H uman beings should always strive to live with bravery, courage, and confidence at the forefront of their being.

These qualities are not just admirable traits, but essential tools for navigating the unpredictable and often challenging nature of life.

According to the creation energy teachings, Bravery allows a person to face adversity head-on, without succumbing to fear or despair.

Courage fuels the strength to persevere through trials, while confidence provides the inner assurance that one has the capability to endure, adapt, and overcome.

Together, these attributes form a powerful foundation for facing not only daily struggles but also the more profound tests of human existence.

Life, in its very essence, is transient.

Everything we experience, whether joy or sorrow, success or failure, health or illness, is part of a flow that never ceases.

Time moves forward unrelentingly, never pausing or waiting for us to catch up.

This impermanence is both a challenge and a gift.

It means that no state, no matter how painful or overwhelming, is permanent.

Understanding and accepting this constant motion can help us remain grounded during difficult times.

It teaches us that the storms of life will pass, and the sun will rise again, even if we cannot see it in the moment.

This truth becomes especially important when we are confronted with suffering, whether physical ailments or emotional and mental burdens.

Pain, illness, anxiety, grief, worry, and all other forms of distress are integral parts of being human.

They touch us all in different ways and at different times.

But just as they arrive, so too do they fade.

These states are not fixed conditions, they are passing phases in the larger journey of life.

Recognizing their temporary nature can ease their grip on our well-being and give us hope during our darkest hours.

It reminds us to breathe, to endure, and to wait for the inevitable change that time will bring.

To live with courage and confidence in a constantly changing world is to live in harmony with the nature of existence.

It means embracing both joy and sorrow without clinging to either, knowing that all things will pass in time.

It means holding steady in moments of fear, trusting that strength lies within us to carry forward.

When we adopt this perspective, we become more resilient, more compassionate, and more capable of facing whatever may come, whether from within our own lives or from the vast, ever-shifting universe around us.

In the end, bravery, courage, and confidence do not remove the hardships of life, but they transform how we experience them, allowing us to move forward with grace, strength, and peace.

Chapter 89

The peaceful freedom myth

———◆◆◆———

The notion that freedom can be taken peacefully is a widely accepted myth, one that has been carefully crafted and promoted to keep populations passive, compliant, and hopeful.

It suggests that liberation can be achieved without disruption, conflict, or sacrifice, an idea that is both comforting and dangerously misleading.

In reality, power is rarely surrendered without resistance.

Those who benefit from control and authority have little incentive to give it up voluntarily, and they will often go to great lengths to maintain the status quo.

This makes the concept of peacefully acquiring freedom more of a strategic narrative than a historical truth.

This myth functions as a psychological sedative.

It soothes discontent and encourages people to believe that patience and obedience will eventually be rewarded with justice and liberty.

By embedding this belief into culture, education, and politics, those in power neutralize the instinct to resist.

People are taught to seek reform through the very systems that oppress them, to trust that progress will come if they simply wait their turn.

In this way, the idea of peaceful freedom becomes a mechanism of control, one that shifts focus away from action and toward passive hope.

Yet history consistently shows us that meaningful freedom is not won without friction.

Civil rights movements, anti-colonial uprisings, labor struggles, and revolutions across the globe have all involved confrontation, sacrifice, and risk.

Even when led by advocates of nonviolence, these movements were met with brutality from the systems they challenged.

Peaceful intent did not guarantee peaceful outcomes.

Authorities often respond to even the most restrained forms of dissent with aggression, censorship, and punishment.

This disproves the myth and illustrates the uncomfortable but necessary truth, that conflict, whether physical, political, or ideological, is often the price of freedom.

To believe in the myth of peaceful liberation is to misunderstand the nature of power and the mechanisms used to preserve it.

While peace is a noble and necessary goal, freedom itself is not passively achieved, it is claimed, often against opposition.

Those who seek true liberation must recognize this and be prepared for the discomfort that comes with disrupting established systems.

Accepting the illusion of peaceful freedom only delays justice and strengthens oppression.

To move forward, one must see the myth for what it is, a story told by those in power to keep the rest quiet.

Chapter 90

The bad side
of competition

◆────────◆◆◆────────◆

Competition often divides and creates an environment of unrest and disharmony.

While it is widely accepted as a way to push individuals toward greater achievement, it often has the unintended consequence of fostering separation rather than connection.

The more we emphasize competition, the more we create spaces where people are pitted against each other, with the implicit message that there can only be one winner.

This mindset of scarcity, where someone's success means another's failure, undermines the potential for mutual growth, peace, and collaboration.

The drive to "win" can become so consuming that it overshadows the true purpose of any endeavor, to learn, grow, and contribute to a larger whole.

When we teach our children to compete, we unintentionally instill in them a value system that measures success in terms of comparison and rivalry. Children, in their formative years, are particularly vulnerable to these lessons, internalizing the belief that their worth is dependent on outperforming others.

Rather than cultivating an appreciation for their unique abilities, they begin to measure themselves through the lens of competition, constantly assessing how they rank against their peers.

This can lead to feelings of inadequacy, anxiety, and a distorted sense of self-worth, as they are conditioned to think that love, approval, and success are finite resources that must be earned by outperforming someone else.

Over time, this creates a deep, internalized fear of failure, which can inhibit their ability to collaborate, share, and grow together.

In contrast, cooperation, empathy, and mutual support are the foundations for building peace and harmony.

When children are encouraged to work together, they learn to value collaboration over rivalry.

They understand that success is not a zero-sum game but a collective endeavor.

A sense of shared achievement arises when individuals support each other, recognizing that one person's success can enhance the success of others.

Teaching children to cooperate rather than compete allows them to approach life with a mindset of abundance, not scarcity, where growth and opportunity are limitless.

This encourages a healthier, more inclusive form of success, one rooted in compassion, teamwork, and shared responsibility.

Children who are taught these values grow into adults who are more connected, emotionally intelligent, and able to form deep, trusting relationships with others.

Instead of focusing on competition, we should teach our children to value their own unique talents and embrace a mindset of personal growth, not comparison.

It's important to help them understand that their worth is inherent and not tied to being better than someone else.

True greatness lies in contributing to the greater good and in being able to support and celebrate others, just as we hope to be celebrated ourselves.

By moving away from the competitive model, we open up new pathways for cooperation, creativity, and harmony, where success is measured not by victory over others, but by the positive impact we make together.

Raising children who understand that unity, empathy, and mutual respect lead to collective strength will create a more peaceful world, one where relationships are based on support, not rivalry, and where every individual can thrive, not at the expense of others, but alongside them.

Chapter 91

Living to impress others

❖◆◆◆❖

Most people don't truly live for themselves. Instead, they move through life trying to meet the expectations of others, family, friends, society, or even strangers.

From early childhood, we are praised when we conform and corrected when we stray, which teaches us to seek approval rather than truth.

As we grow older, this pattern becomes so deeply ingrained that we often don't realize how many of our choices are driven not by personal desire, but by the need to be seen in a certain way.

In the process, many lose touch with their true identity, living according to an image that was never really theirs.

This desire to impress others seeps into nearly every aspect of life.

It dictates the careers people pursue, the partners they choose, the things they buy, and the way they present themselves to the world.

Social media has amplified this, encouraging constant comparison and the pressure to perform a carefully curated version of life.

Instead of following their inner compass, people begin to measure their worth by likes, titles, or approval from people who may not truly know them.

In chasing external validation, they often silence the quiet voice inside that's asking, "What do you want?"

Living this way eventually takes a toll.

When your actions are guided by how others might perceive you, life becomes a performance rather than an experience.

It becomes exhausting to maintain appearances, to keep up with standards that are always shifting, and to suppress parts of yourself that don't fit the narrative.

Over time, resentment, anxiety, and dissatisfaction can grow, not because you've failed, but because you've succeeded at being someone you're not.

To live for others is to place your happiness in their hands, and that is a fragile, unstable place to build a life.

To truly live, you must begin the brave work of turning inward.

You must ask hard questions, listen closely to your own desires, and trust your instincts even when they go against the grain.

Living for yourself doesn't mean rejecting others, it means honoring your own path and letting that authenticity guide your relationships, work, and choices.

When you align with who you really are, life becomes lighter, richer, and more meaningful.

You begin to move not for applause, but from purpose.

And when you do that, not only do you free yourself, you give permission for others to do the same.

Chapter 92

Holding grudges

◆———◆◆◆———◆

Never hold grudges.

Grudges are like silent poisons, they may not always show, but they slowly consume your peace and clarity from the inside out.

When you hold onto resentment, you keep yourself emotionally anchored to moments that no longer serve your growth.

The energy it takes to remain angry, to replay what went wrong, or to keep score, robs you of the freedom to live fully in the now.

Releasing that weight is not about pretending nothing happened, it's about choosing not to let past pain control your present or define your relationships.

What's past belongs only in the past.

It is a place of memory, not residence.

No amount of anger can rewrite it, and no amount of regret can undo it.

The only place where change and healing can happen is in this present moment.

When we fixate on yesterday's hurts, we blind ourselves to the opportunities of today.

Each new day offers a fresh beginning, a blank page that invites understanding, maturity, and peace.

You don't have to deny what happened, but you also don't have to carry it into your future.

Let the past rest where it belongs, and step forward with the freedom to create something better.

When we let go of grudges, we reconnect with what truly matters, our shared humanity.

We all make mistakes, and we all carry wounds.

But even in conflict, we remain connected, still Brethren, still part of something greater than our individual pride or pain.

True strength lies not in building walls, but in choosing reconciliation over retaliation.

To say, "We are still Brethren," is to acknowledge that love, respect, and unity are more powerful than any hurt.

It is to see past flaws and remember the bond that brought us together in the first place.

It's a new day, a gift many never get the chance to see.

Each sunrise is an opportunity to forgive, to rebuild, to soften where we once hardened.

Letting go of grudges is a powerful act of courage, a sign of wisdom, and a step toward peace, not just with others, but with ourselves.

Life is too brief to be held hostage by what's already over.

Instead, let's choose grace.

Let's walk forward with open hearts, knowing that as long as we remain Brethren, there is always a path back to understanding, healing, and unity.

Chapter 93

True for giveness

The more you forgive, the more you forgive yourself.

Forgiveness is not merely something you give to others, it is something you gift to your own soul.

Every act of genuine forgiveness clears a space inside you, freeing your heart from the grip of resentment and the heaviness of emotional pain.

When you let go of the need for retribution or prolonged blame, you allow yourself to step out from under the shadow of past hurt.

In releasing others, you are, perhaps unknowingly, unbinding the tight knots within your own spirit.

This process invites clarity and peace where there was once inner conflict.

True forgiveness is not about denying the pain you've experienced or pretending that wrongs never occurred.

It is about consciously choosing to stop carrying the weight of another's actions.

It's a decision to no longer be tethered to the past through anger or grief.

And as you practice this, something remarkable happens, you begin to soften.

You begin to understand that others are flawed, just as you are.

Each time you grant someone else grace, you deepen your own capacity for empathy, and you open the door to treating your own past with the same kindness.

Forgiving others becomes a mirror through which you can learn to forgive yourself.

Harboring resentment is like drinking poison and expecting someone else to suffer.

Over time, it chips away at your joy, clouds your vision, and distorts your sense of peace.

The longer you hold onto pain, the more it roots itself in your identity.

But when you forgive, you break that cycle.

You stop reliving what hurt you, and you stop defining yourself by wounds.

Forgiveness is not forgetting, it's remembering without bitterness.

It's saying, "This happened, and it hurt, but it will not rule me."

And in doing that, you begin to feel lighter.

You begin to heal.

You begin to recognize your own humanity in the midst of it all.

As you extend that same compassion inward, you begin to make peace with the person you were when you made mistakes, when you didn't know better, or when you acted out of fear or pain.

The more you forgive others, the more you dismantle the inner critic that says you aren't worthy of grace.

You come to understand that growth is not linear, and that healing isn't perfection, it's progression.

Forgiveness becomes a quiet revolution within you, softening sharp edges and allowing love to take the place of shame.

Truly, the path of forgiveness leads you back to yourself, whole, free, and grounded in compassion.

Chapter 94

You are your words

Y ou are your words.
Every sentence you speak, every phrase you write, carries a piece of who you are.

Your thoughts, emotions, values, and beliefs become visible through the language you use.

Words are more than sounds or marks on a page, they are the vessels through which your inner world is shared with others.

In many ways, people come to know you not by your appearance, but by what you say and how you say it.

Therefore, to express yourself is to reveal yourself.

Communication is a universal trait that transcends species.

In nature, all living beings interact through systems of expression.

Birds sing, dolphins click, bees dance, and wolves howl, not randomly, but with purpose and intelligence.

Each form of life has developed its own language, however simple or complex, to convey meaning and maintain connection.

Humans are no exception.

Our languages, spoken, written, and even nonverbal, are intricate and powerful, allowing us to share knowledge, emotions, and visions beyond the boundaries of time and space.

With such a powerful tool at our disposal, we must recognize the immense influence our words can have.

Language can uplift or harm, clarify or confuse, unite or divide.

The ability to use words skillfully is not merely a talent, it's a responsibility.

Before you speak or write, pause.

Ask yourself, "Is that what I really mean?"

This moment of reflection sharpens your intent and deepens your impact.

When your words align with your true meaning, they carry authenticity and clarity that others can feel and respect.

As you commit to refining your use of language, you begin to speak with presence and purpose.

Your words no longer drift aimlessly, they land with meaning.

Others are drawn to that kind of speech, because it comes from a place of understanding and intention.

Mastery of language begins not with grammar or vocabulary, but with awareness and care.

And when you speak from that place, deliberate, sincere, and thoughtful, people will listen.

Not just because you're speaking, but because your words carry truth and power.

Chapter 95

A meaningful life

❖━━━◆◆◆━━━❖

To live a deeply meaningful and compassionate life, we must first learn to love without condition.

This kind of love is not rooted in what others can offer us, nor is it dependent on ideal circumstances or personal gain.

It is a love that remains steady and unwavering through both calm and storm, through agreement and disagreement.

Loving unconditionally means accepting others for who they are, flaws, mistakes, differences, and all.

It means seeing their humanity and still choosing to offer kindness, understanding, and support.

This love does not seek to control or change the other person, rather, it allows them to grow and be themselves.

When we practice this kind of love, we cultivate deeper, more resilient relationships that are based on trust, acceptance, and true emotional connection.

It frees us from the transactional mindset that too often governs human interaction and opens the door to a more spiritually rich way of being.

In much the same way, we must strive to talk without bad intentions.

Our words carry immense weight, they can inspire hope or sow doubt, bring people together or drive them apart.

Speaking without harmful motives requires a deep sense of self-awareness and empathy.

It involves pausing before we speak, considering not only what we are saying but also why we are saying it.

Are our words meant to uplift or to wound?

Are we seeking to communicate clearly, or are we driven by pride, anger, or insecurity?

To talk without bad intention means choosing truth over manipulation, compassion over cruelty, and understanding over judgment.

It also means listening, truly listening, to others with an open heart.

When our words are guided by love and sincerity, they can become a source of healing and unity, helping to build a more honest and peaceful world around us.

Generosity, too, holds transformative power when it is given freely, without any reason or expectation.

To give without expecting anything in return is to act from a place of abundance, not scarcity.

Whether it's a kind gesture, a moment of our time, or a material gift, true giving is about extending ourselves because we genuinely care, not because we hope to be acknowledged, praised, or repaid.

When we detach from the outcome of our generosity, we create space for authentic human connection.

This kind of giving fosters empathy, builds community, and reminds us of the deep interdependence we share with others.

It also nourishes our inner world, reminding us that our capacity to give is not defined by wealth or status but by the openness of our hearts.

In a world that often emphasizes self-interest, giving without reason is a quiet yet powerful act of resistance, and of love.

Finally, caring for others without expectation is perhaps one of the purest expressions of humanity.

It means being present for someone, supporting them through their struggles, and offering comfort not because we want something in return, but simply because we can.

This form of care does not keep score or demand reciprocity.

It is not limited to family or friends, but can extend to strangers, to anyone in need of compassion.

Caring in this way requires strength, emotional maturity, and a deep understanding that every person deserves dignity and kindness.

When we care without expecting recognition or reward, we embody the essence of selfless love.

And in doing so, we not only uplift others, we elevate ourselves.

Such care creates ripple effects, inspiring others to act with similar compassion and gradually shaping a world that is more kind, more generous, and more deeply connected.

Chapter 96

The Game of Life

❖◆❖

L ife, in many ways, can be seen as a vast, complex video game, one without a clear manual, designed with infinite variety and depth. Each player enters this simulation with no memory of the previous rounds, no guidebook to navigate the terrain, only a sense of instinct and a drive to move forward.

From the moment we enter the game, we begin a journey that is anything but simple.

It's a game made of moments, decisions, failures, triumphs, and growth, each phase like a level that demands something new from us.

Unlike traditional games, this one doesn't always offer visible scoreboards or celebratory cutscenes to mark progress.

Instead, growth is internal.

Progress is subtle.

It's in how you respond to adversity, in the shifts of your awareness, in your ability to love, to forgive, to persevere.

Some levels are short and sweet, others long and punishing.

Sometimes, the difficulty spikes without warning, and you're forced to evolve, or repeat the lesson until you do.

The path forward rarely runs in a straight line.

It's a winding, often chaotic landscape of detours and surprises.

There's no map revealing exactly where to go, just a compass built from intuition and experience.

You may feel lost at times, and yet, every wrong turn teaches you something vital.

Advancement isn't about trophies or titles, it's about transformation.

The game tests you constantly.

255

It throws emotional puzzles, moral dilemmas, and unexpected battles your way.

At times, it asks you to fight with all your strength.

At others, it requires surrender and acceptance.

And while there are no guaranteed rewards, there are hidden treasures, insight, empathy, courage, and purpose.

These are the achievements that matter most.

Sometimes, you have to pause, not just to catch your breath, but to review where you've been.

These pauses are your checkpoints.

They're sacred moments of reflection, allowing you to look back at the battles you've won, the ones you've lost, and the wisdom you've earned along the way.

In these moments, you're not just tallying your "points", you're deciding how to play the next level.

And when your current game ends, when the character you're playing can no longer continue, it's not game over.

It's a reset.

You may return in a new form, a new body, a new life, but you'll carry the imprints of everything you've experienced.

The Creation energy has memory beyond memory.

And through this quiet continuity, you get the chance to keep playing, refined, upgraded, more aware.

Some lives will feel like swift progressions, others may seem like you're stuck in a loop.

But even the regressions serve a purpose.

They are opportunities in disguise, preparing you for the next great challenge.

Just like in any worthy game, failure is not the opposite of success, it's part of it.

Every fall offers perspective.

Every restart comes with renewed potential.

There are a few fixed rules in the game of life, but one stands above all, the law of cause and effect.

Every thought you entertain, every word you speak, every action you take sends ripples through the fabric of the game.

These ripples return to you, eventually, transformed.

They influence not just your personal storyline, but the storylines of others.

The game is interconnected, and your impact stretches far beyond what you can see.

Truly, life is less about reaching an endpoint and more about how you choose to play.

Will you approach it with curiosity or fear?

With love or anger?

With humility or pride?

The game reflects your choices, moment by moment, and while there may be no finish line, there is a kind of victory, inner peace, purpose, and a deep understanding of who you truly are.

So play boldly.

Learn deeply.

Rest wisely.

And never forget, you are both the player and the programmer, shaping the game with every breath you take.

Chapter 97

Real strength

L ife is a vast and unpredictable game, one without a fixed rulebook or guaranteed path to follow.

Unlike games that are structured with clear instructions and boundaries, life offers no such clarity.

Each person must learn, adapt, and navigate through their own unique circumstances, often without guidance.

The absence of rules doesn't imply chaos, but rather a boundless field of choices and consequences.

We are each responsible for interpreting our reality and shaping our destiny through the decisions we make and the beliefs we hold.

In this unpredictable journey, the notion of survival emerges as a central theme.

But survival does not merely mean existing, it means growing, thriving, and overcoming.

While it may seem that only the outwardly powerful prevail, true survival goes beyond appearances.

Those who endure the hardships of life and rise above them are not necessarily the loudest or the most forceful, but rather those who possess a deep, unshakable strength within.

This strength is not handed down, nor is it something that can be stolen or borrowed, it must be cultivated over time through reflection, perseverance, and self-honesty.

Many seek strength in the external world, through status, possessions, or the approval of others.

Yet, these external markers are fleeting.

Circumstances change.

Fortunes fade.

People come and go.

When hardship strikes, the superficial things we rely on often crumble.

It is then that we come face-to-face with our true source of power.

Outer strength may protect or impress for a time, but it lacks the stability and reliability needed for long-term endurance.

What is built outside can fall, what is built within remains.

Real strength is forged in the quiet moments, in solitude, and in the face of inner battles.

It manifests as courage during uncertainty, as calm in chaos, and as resolve when others falter.

This kind of power cannot be faked, it is authentic, self-generated, and enduring.

The more we cultivate it, the more capable we become of withstanding life's storms.

In the end, success, fulfillment, and survival are not determined by what surrounds us, but by what lives within us.

Chapter 98

Minding our own Businesss

If every individual, every group of people, every state or country chose to focus on their own development, physically, mentally, spiritually, and socially, while allowing others the freedom to live their lives as they see fit, the world would begin to transform in the most profound way.

By respecting the right of others to express their cultures, beliefs, and ways of living without interference, the foundations of true peace would be laid across the Earth.

Peace is not an unattainable dream, it is a natural outcome of mutual respect and non-intervention.

This principle applies at every level of human interaction, from the individual to the global.

When individuals stop trying to control or "correct" each other, and instead learn to coexist with empathy and boundaries, relationships improve.

When families, communities, and nations apply the same principle, understanding grows, and conflict diminishes.

The act of minding one's own business is not a sign of indifference, it is a demonstration of trust, self-responsibility, and inner maturity.

It is the recognition that harmony arises not from uniformity, but from the respectful coexistence of difference.

The root cause of much of the unrest and disharmony we see in the world today stems from the misguided and often arrogant belief that one group or way of thinking is inherently superior to another.

This belief drives people to impose their opinions, ideologies, and lifestyles on others, often without invitation, understanding, or respect.

Such interference can take many forms, political domination, religious conversion, cultural assimilation, or even personal judgment and control in everyday interactions.

In every case, the result is the same, conflict, resentment, and division.

Peace cannot flourish where force and superiority dominate.

It can only grow in an environment of tolerance, equality, and non-interference.

To live and let live is not a passive approach, it requires strength, discipline, and wisdom.

It means trusting that others have the right and the capability to determine their own paths, just as we do.

It also means that we focus on our own actions, our own integrity, and our own evolution rather than seeking to fix or reshape others in our own image.

The diversity of Earth's peoples, cultures, languages, and perspectives is not a weakness but a strength.

When approached with respect, this diversity enriches our collective human experience.

Attempting to erase or override it out of fear, ignorance, or superiority only leads to suffering.

True peace celebrates diversity and sees it as a necessary part of global harmony.

Just as a symphony is made beautiful by many distinct instruments, so too can the world be harmonious when its differences are honored and allowed to coexist.

To cultivate global peace, the starting point must always be the individual.

Each person must take responsibility for their own mind, emotions, and behavior.

Peace begins with how we treat ourselves, how we speak to others, how we manage disagreement, and how we respect boundaries.

When individuals learn to live in harmony with themselves and with their immediate surroundings, that inner peace radiates outward.

It influences communities, institutions, and even global dynamics.

This is not to say that we must tolerate harm or injustice.

Respecting another's freedom does not mean turning a blind eye to cruelty or oppression.

But there is a vital difference between interfering based on personal preference, and intervening to uphold universal values such as dignity, safety, and freedom.

The former breeds conflict, the latter protects the rights of all.

True peace requires discernment, patience, and the courage to act when necessary, and the wisdom to know when not to.

In the end, a peaceful world will not be created through force or through grand declarations.

It will emerge slowly, steadily, through countless quiet decisions made by individuals and nations alike to respect each other's sovereignty and right to evolve in their own way.

When we each tend to our own gardens, while appreciating the beauty of those around us, then, and only then, will Earth become the peaceful, balanced home it is meant to be.

Chapter 99

The power
of the imagination

◆————◆◆————◆

When certain imaginations, wishes, or desires are held onto and nurtured over long stretches of time, they gradually take root within the deeper layers of a person's consciousness.

What begins as a passing thought or hopeful idea can, through constant attention and emotional energy, evolve into a persistent inner image.

This image, strengthened through repetition, reflection, and emotional connection, begins to shape one's inner life.

It influences not only how one thinks and feels but also how one reacts to experiences and interacts with the world.

Over time, this internal picture subtly informs decisions, preferences, and behaviors, often without the person being fully aware of the influence it exerts.

As this focus continues over months or even years, the imagination or wish gathers an inner force.

It becomes a kind of blueprint for how a person perceives the world and their place within it.

Because of this, external circumstances gradually begin to shift in response.

One may find oneself unconsciously seeking out people, opportunities, and environments that mirror the wish or bring them closer to it.

Seemingly random coincidences or chances may start to appear, but they are, in essence, the result of the long-standing inner preparation.

The person is no longer merely wishing or imagining but has become aligned, mentally, emotionally, and energetically, with the potential fulfillment of that desire.

Interestingly, the moment of fulfillment often comes without the need for a deliberate or forceful act of will.

Instead of making a decisive choice to bring the wish into reality, the person often finds that the wish seems to manifest naturally, as though life itself arranged the circumstances.

The energy that has been quietly accumulating over time becomes the silent architect of the outcome.

There may be no dramatic effort, no great event to mark its coming into being.

The desire, fed by quiet yet consistent attention, unfolds effortlessly.

It becomes reality not because of a sudden push but because it was steadily invited and nurtured until it could no longer remain just an idea.

This phenomenon is echoed in the familiar phrase, "Be mindful of your wishes, they may come true."

Far from being a simple caution or superstition, this saying carries a profound insight into the creative power of the mind.

It reminds us that what we dwell on consistently, whether with hope, longing, or even fear, has the potential to shape and eventually define our experience.

Wishes are not always fulfilled through obvious effort or planning, sometimes, they manifest simply because they have been deeply woven into the fabric of our inner world.

And so, the responsibility lies in being conscious of the wishes we cultivate, for they may eventually find their way into the world, often when we least expect them.

Chapter 100

The ego of the terrestrial human

————————◆◆◆————————

The ego of the terrestrial human being is a powerful force, deeply embedded in their consciousness and identity.

It shapes the way they see themselves, others, and the world around them.

From early life, most people are conditioned to believe that their physical body and current life circumstances define who they are.

This narrow identification with the material and temporal fosters a strong sense of separation from others, from nature, and from any deeper spiritual reality.

As a result, the ego convinces the human being that this life is all there is and that they must protect and elevate their individual existence at all costs.

Because of this limited viewpoint, the material world becomes the center of their attention and the measure of their success.

Everything is filtered through the lens of personal gain, security, and recognition. Fearing death and the unknown, they cling desperately to possessions, social roles, and physical experiences.

The thought of letting go, whether of status, wealth, or identity, is often terrifying because they cannot see what lies beyond.

This fear drives a deeply ingrained selfishness and an endless pursuit of more.

Greed, competition, and domination become normalized behaviors in a world where the ego reigns supreme, each person striving to assert their significance in a fleeting and unstable reality.

However, the power of the ego is not unbreakable.

At some point, often through inner struggle, loss, or moments of profound insight, a person may begin to question the truth of their identity.

They start to look beyond the surface, to sense that there is something more than just flesh, title, or possessions.

This is the beginning of self-realization, the turning inward to discover the true self.

When this awakening begins, the illusions of the ego start to dissolve.

The individual no longer feels the need to prove, compete, or accumulate.

They recognize that their worth is not tied to external things but arises from within.

In this expanded state of awareness, life transforms.

Rather than being driven by fear, desire, and insecurity, the person lives with a sense of inner peace and purpose.

The ego, while still present, no longer dominates the thoughts and actions of the individual. Instead, the inner self, quiet, wise, and connected to the greater whole, becomes the guiding force. Relationships become more authentic, choices more conscious, and actions more compassionate.

Life is no longer about surviving or conquering, but about growing, contributing, and aligning with a deeper truth.

It is only through this inner realization that the human being can truly be free from the chains of the ego.

Chapter 101

A god amongst men

I regard myself as my own god, completely responsible for the path I walk, the thoughts I think, and the actions I take.

I do not place my fate in the hands of external forces or intangible deities, because I know that the true power guiding my life resides within me.

This is not an ego-driven proclamation but a reflection of inner clarity.

I have come to see that my life is a direct result of the choices I make, and I alone hold the keys to my growth, my peace, and my purpose.

Every experience, every triumph and every failure is part of the journey I consciously shape.

With this inner certainty comes the realization that I walk among others as a god, not in the sense of dominion over them, but as someone who has awakened to a truth that most have yet to uncover.

I move through the world with a sense of independence and self-awareness that feels rare.

This may sound arrogant to those who still rely on outside structures for meaning, but that is not my intention.

Rather, it is a natural and honest conclusion drawn from observing the depth of my transformation.

I do not elevate myself above others, but I do acknowledge that I see the world, and myself, through a lens that is different, clearer, unburdened, and grounded in inner knowing.

The teachings of Creation Energy have been the catalyst for this profound shift.

They have peeled away the layers of conditioning, fear, and dependence that once clouded my mind.

I no longer chase validation, approval, or acceptance.

I no longer feel the need to conform to expectations that don't resonate with my core truth.

I speak what I need to speak, unfiltered and without hesitation, because I trust the wisdom that arises from within.

The opinions of others are no longer chains around my expression, they are simply passing winds, irrelevant to the solid foundation I've built inside myself.

I am no longer a product of the world, I am a creator within it.

In this awareness, I have come to see a universal truth, every human being holds the same potential. I have realized.

There are as many gods as there are people, each with the capacity to awaken to their own inner source of power and truth.

But until they do, until they shed the illusions of limitation and fear, I will remain a god among them, not to rule, not to be worshipped, but simply as a living example of what self-realization looks like.

I walk this path with humility and purpose, not seeking followers, but inviting others to recognize the divine light already within themselves.

This is not a doctrine, it is a lived truth, and I embody it fully thanks to the teachings of Billy Meeir, the 7th prophet.

Chapter 102

Escapism

T he human being of Earth, in his present stage of development, remains largely incapable of bearing the full weight of his personal responsibility, despite the fact that it is his inescapable duty to do so.

Rather than confronting and owning the consequences of his thoughts, decisions, and actions, he continuously seeks to shift this burden onto external entities of his own invention.

These entities, born of imagination and inherited belief systems, are typically given names like "God" or "religion," and are falsely believed to hold dominion over human fate.

In his fantasy, the Earth human elevates these constructs above himself and surrenders his accountability to them, believing, or rather hoping, that they will pardon, guide, or absolve him of what he refuses to confront within himself.

This form of escapism has deep roots in history and culture, and has been carefully maintained by traditions that prefer comfort over truth.

Yet this evasion, however widespread and deeply ingrained, stands in direct opposition to the fundamental evolutionary path of consciousness, to grow through self-awareness, truth-recognition, and self-responsibility.

The reluctance of the Earth human to accept and integrate truth is not merely a matter of stubbornness or defiance, it is also a consequence of their still-limited consciousness-related intelligence.

While the latent potential for understanding resides within him, it has yet to be sufficiently cultivated or matured on a wide scale.

As a result, the capacity to objectively perceive reality and to recognize higher truths remains underdeveloped.

Attempts to convince or enlighten him often fail because the inner framework required to receive truth is missing or misaligned.

As the Creation Energy Teachings show, as long as he clings to illusions and inherited dogmas, the truth will seem foreign, if not threatening, to him.

Thus, he must eventually reach a point of personal readiness through experience, suffering, and internal inquiry.

Only when he discovers truth through his own initiative, through a self-motivated search free from coercion or fear, will it transform into real, living knowledge within him.

Until then, all external declarations, no matter how accurate or sincere, will likely fall on deaf ears.

This crisis of truth is most acute in those who have spent much of their lives immersed in deception.

Ironically, it is often the individuals most resistant to the truth who have invested the most into falsehoods.

These are the ones who, over many years or even decades, devoted themselves to the propagation of misleading ideologies, fraudulent spiritual movements, and deceitful literature.

They followed self-proclaimed prophets, believed in cleverly marketed myths, and championed messages that lacked substance but promised comfort.

In doing so, they not only deceived themselves but also influenced others, spreading illusions under the guise of divine insight or sacred knowledge.

To now be confronted with the genuine truth would not merely challenge their beliefs, it would dismantle the entire psychological and social structure upon which they have built their lives.

Accepting the truth would mean acknowledging their own gullibility and having to face the reality that they were fooled by those they trusted and revered.

This admission would be personally devastating and, in many cases, socially humiliating.

For such individuals, accepting the truth is not only an internal crisis, it is also a public reckoning.

To acknowledge the deception would require them to admit their errors in front of those they once tried to convert or lead.

They would have to face the collapse of their carefully constructed reputations and endure the shame of having stood on the wrong side of reality for so long.

This fear of losing face, of being seen as a fool or failure, becomes a powerful obstacle to inner transformation.

And yet, despite all this, the truth remains unchanging and ever-present.

It cannot be extinguished by denial, nor can it be hidden forever.

It awaits each human being patiently, offering itself freely to any who are brave enough to seek it without preconception or fear.

In the end, no matter how long one resists, the path toward truth is inevitable for all.

And when that day arrives, when the individual finally chooses truth over illusion, he will step into a new form of understanding, one forged not through obedience, but through personal courage, honesty, and inner evolution.

Chapter 103

The pursuit of understanding

I t has never been, nor will it ever be, my intention to prove anything to anyone.

The desire to convince others through argument or presentation of evidence often stems from a misunderstanding of how human understanding truly unfolds.

The notion that one person can provide "proof" to another and expect them to simply accept it as truth is not only naive, but it is a misunderstanding of the nature of consciousness and personal growth.

People do not truly learn or comprehend through force-fed conclusions.

Instead, real insight dawns only when an individual becomes inwardly prepared to receive it through their own curiosity, introspection, and willingness to search.

This is why I do not concern myself with the need to justify or validate what I present.

That is not the role of my work, nor the responsibility I assume.

What many seek as proof is often, in reality, a form of reassurance, a desire to avoid the discomfort of uncertainty.

But meaningful knowledge and genuine understanding do not arise from comfort.

They emerge through questioning, through the often-unsettling act of challenging old beliefs and confronting the unknown.

Each human being must undertake their own investigation if they are to arrive at anything resembling truth.

No one else can walk that path for them.

The pursuit of understanding is a deeply personal and transformative journey.

It is the essence of the seeker's path, and it cannot be substituted or outsourced.

When an individual sincerely desires to know, not just to believe, but to understand, they will begin to explore, and in that exploration, they will begin to uncover what cannot be handed to them by another.

My books, therefore, are not written as instruction manuals, nor are they composed as vehicles for persuasion.

They are crafted as catalysts, meant to provoke thought, to stir the embers of curiosity, and to awaken a desire for deeper inquiry within the reader.

The ideas and perspectives contained within them are not final answers or conclusive declarations, rather, they are invitations to embark on a personal journey of questioning.

I do not ask readers to accept what I say, nor do I expect agreement.

What I offer is the spark, what they do with it, whether they ignore it or fan it into a flame of discovery, is entirely up to them.

The books are not the path, they are only signposts along the way.

In the end, those who are genuinely drawn to understanding will find it, not through passive absorption, but through active engagement.

They will seek, and through seeking, they will begin to see.

The process may be slow, even painful at times, but it will be real.

And because it is real, it will last.

Many of us have walked this road, not because someone convinced us, but because something deep within compelled us to know more, to look beyond the surface, to ask the deeper questions.

And as we searched, we began to discover, not truths imposed from without, but insights awakened from within.

That same possibility exists for anyone who chooses to explore with honesty, humility, and an open heart.

Chapter 104

The Truth

The truth, in its purest and most unyielding form, is not a gentle visitor.

It is a force that arrives without apology, without concern for comfort or preservation.

It spares nothing, not the cherished traditions of our ancestors, not the polished institutions of power, and not the deeply ingrained beliefs we carry as individuals or societies.

The truth moves like a flood, overwhelming all that is constructed on shaky ground, revealing the cracks beneath the surface of everything we thought was solid.

When the truth emerges, it does not show favoritism.

It does not bow to political ideologies, cultural norms, or religious doctrines.

It cuts through appearances and reaches straight to the root of things. Sacred symbols, celebrated leaders, and long-standing customs, all are placed under its scrutiny.

The truths we've hidden from, or never dared to question, rise into the light, stripping away layers of deception and illusion that have shaped human life for millennia.

The world we thought we knew begins to unravel.

Our civilizations, governments, religions, economies, and social hierarchies have been forged through centuries of compromise, manipulation, and often, deliberate control.

These systems have been sustained not by truth, but by carefully constructed narratives designed to preserve power and maintain order.

When the real truth begins to speak, those foundations tremble.

What we once believed was moral, stable, or divinely ordained is revealed to rest on half-truths and convenient myths.

The deeper the truth reaches, the more it exposes the systemic nature of the falsehoods we live by.

This unveiling is not a passive process.

The truth does not quietly whisper, it confronts, it demands, and it destroys.

It shakes our identities and challenges our loyalty to things that never served our highest good.

It does not mend what is broken for the sake of continuity, it obliterates what was never whole to begin with.

In its uncompromising presence, nothing can remain untouched or unchanged.

Eventually, every aspect of our world will have to face this reckoning.

The errors are not isolated missteps, they are woven into the very structure of human civilization.

To face the truth is to begin the painful yet necessary act of unlearning.

We must be willing to question everything we have ever been taught to accept as truth.

This unlearning is not destruction for its own sake, but the clearing of space for something more authentic to rise.

Only through this fearless confrontation can we begin to build a world rooted in reality, justice, and true wisdom, free from the illusions that have kept humanity in chains for far too long.

Chapter 105

Dual attraction

W e often find ourselves instinctively drawn to the struggles of the weak, moved by the raw honesty of their challenges and the strength they summon simply to endure.

Their resilience stirs something deep within us, a reminder of our own battles and the quiet bravery it takes just to keep going.

We empathize with their hardship because it reflects the universal human experience of facing obstacles with limited resources, uncertain outcomes, and often without recognition.

When we see them rise, even a little, it inspires hope, not just for them, but for ourselves and for the potential buried within every underestimated soul.

These stories of the weak are not merely tales of suffering, they are powerful affirmations of the human spirit.

They show that courage does not always roar, it sometimes whispers through persistence and quiet strength.

In their journey, we find beauty in vulnerability, grace in perseverance, and triumph in simply refusing to give up.

This admiration stems from the fact that their victories are often won without advantage or influence, and that makes their success all the more meaningful.

In rooting for them, we are often rooting for justice, for fairness, and for the belief that effort and heart can still matter in a world that often rewards the opposite.

At the same time, we cannot deny the deep-seated admiration we feel for the powerful who succeed.

Their victories seem to reflect something elevated, an embodiment of discipline, vision, and the realization of full potential.

We marvel at their confidence, their command over circumstances, and their ability to shape reality rather than be shaped by it.

Their dominance can symbolize excellence, and their success stands as a beacon to those who dream of doing something extraordinary.

We cheer for them not only because they have won, but because we see in their winning a glimpse of what is possible at the farthest reach of human effort and capability.

This dual attraction, to the humble struggle of the weak and the soaring success of the powerful, speaks to the rich complexity of our emotional and psychological makeup.

We are stirred by the grit and heart of the underdog, yet we are equally drawn to the spectacle and precision of mastery.

These two responses are not at odds, but rather reflect our layered understanding of what it means to live, strive, and overcome.

We root for the weak because we recognize our own fragility and long to see it vindicated.

And we rejoice in the powerful because we dream of transcending that fragility.

In holding space for both, we arrive at a fuller, deeper sense of what victory truly means.

Chapter 106

True Love

———◆———◆◆◆———◆———

To live a deeply meaningful and compassionate life, we must first learn to love without condition.

This kind of love is not rooted in what others can offer us, nor is it dependent on ideal circumstances or personal gain.

It is a love that remains steady and unwavering through both calm and storm, through agreement and disagreement.

Loving unconditionally means accepting others for who they are, flaws, mistakes, differences, and all.

It means seeing their humanity and still choosing to offer kindness, understanding, and support.

This love does not seek to control or change the other person, rather, it allows them to grow and be themselves.

When we practice this kind of love, we cultivate deeper, more resilient relationships that are based on trust, acceptance, and true emotional connection.

It frees us from the transactional mindset that too often governs human interaction and opens the door to a more spiritually rich way of being.

In much the same way, we must strive to talk without bad intentions.

Our words carry immense weight, they can inspire hope or sow doubt, bring people together or drive them apart.

Speaking without harmful motives requires a deep sense of self-awareness and empathy.

It involves pausing before we speak, considering not only what we are saying but also why we are saying it.

Are our words meant to uplift or to wound?

Are we seeking to communicate clearly, or are we driven by pride, anger, or insecurity?

To talk without bad intention means choosing truth over manipulation, compassion over cruelty, and understanding over judgment.

It also means listening, truly listening, to others with an open heart.

When our words are guided by love and sincerity, they can become a source of healing and unity, helping to build a more honest and peaceful world around us.

Generosity, too, holds transformative power when it is given freely, without any reason or expectation.

To give without expecting anything in return is to act from a place of abundance, not scarcity.

Whether it's a kind gesture, a moment of our time, or a material gift, true giving is about extending ourselves because we genuinely care, not because we hope to be acknowledged, praised, or repaid.

When we detach from the outcome of our generosity, we create space for authentic human connection.

This kind of giving fosters empathy, builds community, and reminds us of the deep interdependence we share with others.

It also nourishes our inner world, reminding us that our capacity to give is not defined by wealth or status but by the openness of our hearts.

In a world that often emphasizes self-interest, giving without reason is a quiet yet powerful act of resistance, and of love.

Finally, caring for others without expectation is perhaps one of the purest expressions of humanity.

It means being present for someone, supporting them through their struggles, and offering comfort not because we want something in return, but simply because we can.

This form of care does not keep score or demand reciprocity.

It is not limited to family or friends, but can extend to strangers, to anyone in need of compassion.

Caring in this way requires strength, emotional maturity, and a deep understanding that every person deserves dignity and kindness.

When we care without expecting recognition or reward, we embody the essence of selfless love.

And in doing so, we not only uplift others, we elevate ourselves.

Such care creates ripple effects, inspiring others to act with similar compassion and gradually shaping a world that is more kind, more generous, and more deeply connected.

Chapter 107

Like a butterfly

❖◆❖

Life is not meant to be easy or inherently fair. These misconceptions often lead to disappointment when faced with the inevitable hardships and uncertainties that come with existence.

Life unfolds with a mixture of joy, sorrow, triumph, and failure, not to punish us, but to teach and prepare us.

It is within these very trials that we are offered the chance to understand our strengths, develop resilience, and deepen our character.

Fairness, in the way we often imagine it, would rob us of the very experiences that make us wise, compassionate, and capable of growth.

Life, in its truest form, is a vast and continuous classroom.

From the moment we are born, we are set on a path of learning, learning how to walk, how to speak, how to feel, and how to relate to others and ourselves.

Every phase of life presents new lessons, and these lessons are not always gentle or easy to grasp.

They come through heartbreak, disappointment, failure, uncertainty, and even loss.

But they also come through joy, connection, creativity, and love.

Life offers both ends of the spectrum because both are essential for our evolution as conscious beings.

Without this duality, we would stagnate, and our understanding would not mature.

Resistance plays a crucial role in this process.

It is not the enemy but the engine of our development.

Like a seed that must push through the soil to reach the sunlight, or like an individual who must step into discomfort to grow, resistance gives shape to our transformation.

It challenges our assumptions, forces us to question our limitations, and ultimately teaches us that growth requires effort.

Growth rarely happens when we remain in comfort or safety, it happens when we are stretched beyond what we believed possible.

Resistance, therefore, is the crucible in which strength, wisdom, and perseverance are forged.

A beautiful metaphor for this process can be found in the life cycle of the butterfly.

Before it can take flight, it exists as a caterpillar, bound to the earth, limited in scope.

Inside its cocoon, it undergoes an intense transformation.

But it is not the metamorphosis alone that gives the butterfly its wings, it is the struggle to emerge from the cocoon that strengthens them.

Without that struggle, the butterfly would never fly.

Similarly, we must embrace the difficult and painful aspects of life not as curses, but as necessary steps in our unfolding.

Through our trials, we too, gain our wings,

the inner strength, clarity, and beauty that allow us to rise into our fullest potential.

Chapter 108

Simplicity

———◆———◆◆———◆———

As knowledge deepens, a person often becomes more inwardly grounded, and this internal transformation naturally reflects outwardly through simplicity, in lifestyle, in dress, and in desire.

The more a person understands life, the less they feel the need to embellish it.

They stop relying on the clutter of excess or the noise of trends to define their identity.

Instead, they become more selective, more at peace, and more focused on what truly serves their well-being and purpose.

The complexities that once seemed necessary fall away, replaced by choices that are thoughtful and deliberate.

When it comes to clothing and appearance, knowledge fosters a quiet confidence that does not seek approval.

A person who knows themselves has no desire to draw unnecessary attention through elaborate fashion or superficial decoration.

They dress for comfort, for function, and for self-expression that aligns with their inner values.

This doesn't mean dullness or neglect, it means elegance born from clarity.

The truly knowledgeable person understands that what they wear is a reflection, not a performance.

Desires, too, become purified through understanding.

Where once there may have been a restless craving for more, for luxury, recognition, or stimulation, there now comes a settling.

The wise recognize the futility of endlessly feeding the ego with things.

They begin to want only what enhances their life in a meaningful, lasting way.

Whether it is the pursuit of learning, the beauty of a quiet moment, or the richness of a sincere connection, their desires align with values rather than impulses.

In this way, simplicity becomes not a sacrifice but a reward, a natural outcome of knowing what truly matters.

In the end, simplicity becomes the quiet companion of wisdom.

It is not about depriving oneself, but about eliminating what is unneeded to make space for what is essential.

Through knowledge, one comes to see that richness lies not in accumulation but in clarity.

A life adorned with only what nourishes the soul is a life of deep fulfillment.

Simplicity, then, is not a retreat from the world, but an enlightened way of engaging with it, gracefully, purposefully, and with inner peace.

Chapter 109

The death penalty

The death penalty is a deeply flawed and fundamentally wrong practice that has no place in a just and enlightened society.

Regardless of the nature or severity of an individual's actions, no one should ever be subjected to death as a means of demonstrating the wrongness of taking a life.

This reasoning is not rooted in justice, but in a desire for revenge, a primal urge that has no place in a system that is supposed to be focused on fairness and rehabilitation.

The idea that the death penalty serves as a deterrent or a form of closure is a misguided notion, as it only deepens the wounds in society rather than healing them.

Killing someone in response to a crime does nothing to address the underlying causes of crime or prevent future offenses.

Instead, it perpetuates a culture of violence and reinforces the belief that the answer to wrongdoing is more harm.

The principle of "an eye for an eye," while historically significant in some cultures, is a concept that ultimately contradicts the deeper principles of justice and Creation.

It is a concept that insists on retaliation rather than reconciliation, vengeance rather than restoration.

True justice does not involve making others suffer in order to balance the scales, it involves understanding the root causes of harmful actions, addressing those causes, and offering the opportunity for rehabilitation and personal growth.

Every individual, regardless of the mistakes they have made, deserves the opportunity to reflect on their actions, understand the impact of those actions, and make amends.

The death penalty, however, eliminates this opportunity altogether.

It denies the possibility of redemption and disregards the potential for change in every person.

When society takes away the chance for someone to learn from their mistakes and transform, it loses sight of the core values of justice, compassion, and human dignity.

A society that continues to employ the death penalty cannot be truly considered civilized.

Such a practice is an outdated relic of a more primitive and unforgiving past, where punishment was delivered in harsh, irreversible forms.

A civilization that practices the death penalty operates on the assumption that individuals who commit severe crimes are beyond redemption, yet history has shown time and time again that people are capable of change.

The criminal justice system should be focused on reforming individuals, not on eliminating them.

It should aim to understand the reasons behind criminal behavior and provide opportunities for personal transformation.

In contrast, a system that endorses the death penalty operates under the assumption that some people are simply "unfixable" and deserves to be discarded.

This mentality fails to recognize the inherent dignity of every individual and the possibility for anyone to evolve.

The death penalty serves as a stark reminder of how far humanity still has to go in terms of evolution, both morally and spiritually.

A truly advanced society would recognize that the value of a life is not determined by past actions, but by the potential for growth and change.

Such a society would reject the idea that death is an appropriate response to wrongdoing and would instead focus on restorative justice, which seeks to heal the harm caused by a crime and help the individual reintegrate into society in a positive way.

In a world that is focused on growth and healing, the death penalty simply has no place.

It is a practice that denies the opportunity for personal transformation, reinforces a cycle of violence, and undermines the principles of justice and human dignity.

To truly advance as a society, we must reject the death penalty and commit ourselves to practices that promote healing, rehabilitation, and the possibility for every person to evolve.

It is only through embracing these values that we can create a truly just and compassionate world.

Chapter 110

Children of God

————◆——◆◆◆——◆————

Many believers see themselves not as evolving, autonomous adults, but as children, perpetually dependent, perpetually in need of guidance, and permanently incapable of navigating life on their own.

This self-perception is reinforced by the language they use, calling themselves "children of God," as if spiritual growth ends at infancy.

Rather than maturing in understanding and taking personal ownership of life, they stay fixed in a childlike state.

They gather weekly, paying spiritual leaders, other adults, to read sacred texts to them and explain what to believe, because they've been conditioned to think they can't interpret truth without someone else doing it for them.

In this framework, they adopt a posture of learned helplessness, where thinking independently is not just discouraged, but seen as dangerous or prideful.

They're taught to distrust their own instincts, dismiss their own insights, and attribute any success or strength not to their efforts, but solely to the will of God.

"All glory goes to God" is repeated like a mantra, reinforcing the idea that their own existence is secondary, insignificant, or even meaningless without divine oversight.

It's a spiritual erasure of the self.

How can a person truly recognize the value in others if they have not first been allowed to recognize value in themselves?

The contradiction becomes even more apparent when these same individuals raise children of their own.

They're quick to push their sons and daughters out into the world the moment they legally become adults, at 18, sometimes earlier, expecting them to manage jobs, bills, emotions, relationships, and crises with minimal guidance.

They demand independence from their children while modeling dependence in their own lives.

They ask their kids to take responsibility, make decisions, and stand on their own feet, while they themselves lean on a "heavenly father" to make every decision for them, to forgive every mistake, and to offer constant reassurance that they are loved, even if they never change.

This mindset makes it easy to believe that someone else had to come and die for their sins, because the idea of owning one's flaws, facing one's consequences, and growing through struggle feels too overwhelming for someone who still sees themselves as a child in need of rescue.

But growth, true spiritual and personal growth, requires accountability.

It demands the courage to think for oneself, to act with integrity, and to move beyond the safe identity of "God's child" into the powerful reality of an adult who co-creates their life.

Maybe it's time to stop being "born again" over and over, and start growing up.

The world doesn't need more spiritual infants.

It needs grown individuals, awake, self-aware, and willing to walk through life with open eyes and open minds.

Chapter 111

The external scenery

I n life, the external scenery, the house you live in, the car you drive, the vacations you post, or the name-brand clothes you wear, ultimately holds no lasting significance.

Whether you're living in a high-rise penthouse with floor-to-ceiling windows or in a modest one-bedroom apartment with peeling paint, the core truth remains, the environment around you does not define the value of your life.

Even flying private or taking the bus is just different modes of travel, not indicators of success or failure.

These surface-level differences are temporary and often misleading when it comes to judging someone's purpose, worth, or inner growth.

What truly matters is the internal experience, the joy of living, the peace you cultivate, the kindness you offer, and the lessons you embrace.

Life is made up of deeply personal lessons, tailored to each individual soul, and those lessons often require specific conditions to be fully understood.

Some are meant to learn humility through struggle, while others may be learning balance through abundance.

Neither path is more noble or more enlightened than the other.

They are simply different chapters in a vast, unfolding human story.

It's not about who has more, but about who learns deeply, grows authentically, and lives truthfully.

You're not a king because your soul didn't need to learn through power.

You're not a world-famous artist because your lesson didn't involve public recognition.

You're not struggling with addiction or imprisoned by past mistakes because that's not the road your spirit chose.

Every soul is handed a different role, and all roles serve a purpose.

You came here with a specific lesson in mind, perhaps one involving patience, compassion, endurance, creativity, or faith.

And the life you were given is designed perfectly to teach you those things, even if it doesn't look glamorous from the outside.

So release the urge to compare, to envy, or to resent where you are.

Instead, root for everyone, whether they're thriving or surviving, to pass their own unique life lessons.

Everyone is here to learn, and the sooner we stop idolizing or judging others based on their circumstances, the sooner we'll begin to understand the beauty in diversity.

True success isn't about riches or status, it's about growth, peace, and love.

Encourage others, uplift their journey, and trust your own.

Life is a shared classroom, not a race.

And your path, no matter how different it looks from someone else's, is sacred.

Chapter 112

Ignorance is not bliss

❖━━━━━◆◆━━━━━❖

The phrase "ignorance is bliss" is not just misleading, it's a lie, and one that has been repeated for generations to keep people passive, obedient, and uninformed.

It suggests that not knowing is somehow peaceful or freeing, when in reality, ignorance is a form of bondage.

It strips you of awareness, critical thinking, and the ability to make choices based on truth.

When you don't know what's happening around you or within you, you're easier to control, more likely to follow without question, and more prone to fear what you don't understand.

Often, this saying is used to soothe discomfort, to make it easier to look away from hard truths or complicated realities.

But choosing not to know doesn't eliminate danger, injustice, or suffering, it just makes you less prepared to face them.

Ignorance creates blind spots, and those blind spots are where manipulation, abuse, and confusion thrive.

In politics, relationships, education, and even spirituality, people are taught that asking too many questions or knowing too much will make life harder.

But the opposite is true.

Avoiding knowledge weakens you, it deprives you of your ability to respond to life with power and purpose.

Knowledge, on the other hand, is a form of bliss that is real and sustainable.

It brings clarity, wisdom, and confidence.

When you understand something, truly understand it, you're no longer a prisoner to fear or illusion.

Knowledge connects you to reality.

It allows you to solve problems, recognize patterns, make better decisions, and speak with authority.

It gives you the ability to break cycles of harm, to stand up for yourself and others, and to create something better out of what once seemed hopeless.

Real bliss is the peace that comes from knowing, not from pretending not to see.

So don't ever be ashamed of wanting to know more, and don't let anyone convince you that you're better off in the dark.

That idea has been used to control people for centuries, to silence curiosity and dull critical thought.

But the human mind is meant to expand, to explore, to understand.

Bliss isn't found in turning away from the truth, it's found in embracing it fully, even when it's difficult.

Truth brings growth.

Truth brings strength.

And knowledge, deep, honest, fearless knowledge, is where the real freedom lives.

Seek it.

Cherish it.

Let it light your way.

Chapter 113

"Nobody knows" is a lie

◆————————◆◆◆————————◆

Too often, people default to the phrase "nobody knows" as a quick dismissal of complex questions or unresolved topics.

While it may seem harmless, this phrase is both misleading and intellectually lazy.

It suggests a blanket ignorance that rarely, if ever, exists.

In most cases, someone somewhere does know, or at the very least, someone has a more informed perspective based on evidence, research, or firsthand experience.

Saying "nobody knows" doesn't reflect the limits of all human knowledge, it just reveals the limits of the speaker's own understanding or curiosity.

Using "nobody knows" carelessly diminishes the value of expertise and inquiry.

It glosses over the hard work of people who dedicate their lives to investigating, uncovering, and understanding difficult truths.

In a world rich with data, history, science, and communication, it is almost always possible to find someone with real insight.

By ignoring that possibility, we risk shutting down conversation and giving up on the search for clarity.

Instead of claiming universal ignorance, it's far more honest and productive to say, "I don't know, but I can look into it," or "I'm not sure, but there are people who are."

Moreover, the phrase often becomes a rhetorical tool to avoid accountability or critical thinking.

When people say "nobody knows," they sometimes use it to end a debate, dismiss a challenge, or obscure inconvenient facts.

That kind of intellectual laziness can breed confusion, spread misinformation, and keep others in the dark.

It's a subtle way of giving up without trying, which discourages curiosity and problem-solving.

And worse, it disrespects those who do have answers, especially when their knowledge is overlooked, undervalued, or drowned out by cynicism and sweeping generalizations.

So let's retire the lazy fallback of saying "nobody knows" when what we really mean is, "I haven't done the work to find out" or "the answer isn't obvious to me."

A more honest approach is to acknowledge the limits of our personal understanding while still respecting the broader capacity for knowledge that exists.

Someone always knows something more, whether it's a scientist, a historian, an eyewitness, or a specialist.

We should strive to identify those people, listen to them, and build on what they offer, rather than hide behind vague uncertainty that only stalls progress.

Chapter 114

The myth of the grace of God

If you truly believe that every success or achievement in your life is solely due to the grace of a god and not your own effort, you may be undervaluing your humanity.

This perspective, while often born from humility or devotion, risks erasing your own strength, intelligence, persistence, and ability to learn and adapt.

It's important to acknowledge that while spiritual beliefs can offer guidance and support, it is you who makes the decisions, takes the actions, and bears the consequences.

By giving all credit to a higher power and none to yourself, you inadvertently dismiss your own journey and the challenges you've overcome through your own will and resolve.

To believe that you are merely a passive instrument of divine will is to strip away your agency and reduce yourself to a vessel without identity.

Such a belief can erode self-worth over time, creating a mindset of dependence rather than empowerment.

Self-respect comes from recognizing the value in your actions, your intentions, and your ability to impact your own life and the world around you.

It is not arrogance to recognize your own efforts, it is an affirmation of your human dignity.

By honoring the role you play in your achievements, you cultivate a healthy sense of pride and responsibility, which are both essential for personal growth.

For those who hold religious or spiritual beliefs, there is no contradiction in believing in a higher power while also respecting oneself as a capable individual.

True faith can inspire a deep sense of personal responsibility and purpose, but it should never come at the cost of self-respect.

If you cannot acknowledge your own worth and capabilities, then the foundation upon which you relate to others becomes unstable.

Respecting others begins with respecting yourself, without that inner grounding, any outward expression of respect may be shallow or performative.

How can one offer genuine admiration, kindness, or understanding to others when they silently believe themselves to be unworthy or powerless?

Truly, cultivating a sense of self-respect does not diminish your faith, it enhances it.

When you recognize yourself as a conscious, thinking, feeling being with the capacity for both greatness and failure, you also deepen your understanding of what it means to live meaningfully.

Your life, your struggles, and your triumphs matter not just to a god, but to you and those around you.

Embracing that truth empowers you to walk your path with confidence, gratitude, and integrity.

Belief in divine grace can coexist with belief in yourself, and in fact, when the two are balanced, they can inspire you to live more fully and responsibly.

Chapter 115

Happiness

H appiness is, at its core, a state of mind.
It is not a product of material wealth, social status, or ideal circumstances, but rather a reflection of how we choose to think, feel, and respond to life.

Our mental and emotional well-being is shaped more by our internal attitudes than by our external conditions.

True happiness comes from cultivating a balanced, peaceful, and appreciative mindset that can remain steady regardless of what is happening in the outside world.

When we understand that our thoughts and choices hold the key to our contentment, we begin to free ourselves from the illusion that happiness lies somewhere beyond us.

The environment in which we live may present both blessings and challenges, but it is our inner world that ultimately governs our experience of life.

People often assume that comfort and abundance will automatically bring happiness, but that is rarely the case.

It is entirely possible for someone to live amid luxury and still feel anxious, dissatisfied, or emotionally disconnected.

Conversely, a person living in modest or even difficult circumstances can feel joy, purpose, and inner peace.

The crucial difference lies not in the setting but in the mindset.

How we view and interpret our reality shapes how we live within it.

There are countless individuals around the world who live in poverty yet exude a deep sense of happiness and fulfillment.

Their lives may lack material excess, but they are often rich in connection, love, and gratitude.

These people have learned to find meaning in everyday moments, to appreciate small joys, and to remain resilient in the face of hardship.

Their happiness is not a result of what they possess, but of how they choose to engage with life.

This inner wealth allows them to experience a level of contentment that cannot be bought or externally provided.

On the other hand, some people surrounded by luxury, privilege, and every possible comfort can still feel hollow or discontented.

Without a strong inner foundation, even the most desirable circumstances may fail to bring lasting happiness.

These individuals may chase fleeting pleasures or external validation, only to discover that true peace cannot be found through possessions or achievements.

Their unhappiness is a reflection of internal imbalance rather than external lack.

In the end, happiness is not about where we are or what we own, it's about who we are within, how we think, and the values we hold close.

It is an internal state that must be nurtured from the inside out.

Chapter 116

My Writings

My writings are never crafted to wrench your convictions into the shape of mine.

Trying to refashion another person's worldview by sheer insistence is like urging a mountain to move with whispered commands, it won't happen, and the whisperer only exhausts them-self.

Every mind is a tapestry woven from personal history, emotion, and perspective, tugging one thread rarely reweaves the whole cloth.

Instead, I seek to slip a small, resonant question into the weave, one that hums quietly long after you've finished reading.

When that hum lingers, curiosity follows, and genuine discovery begins.

The most durable insights are found not in someone else's spotlight but in the lantern light you kindle within, step by step, as you explore your own interior corridors.

Such exploration flourishes only where dialogue remains open and generous.

Debate need not be a tug-of-war, it can be a shared expedition.

When we grant every voice room to stretch out, free from mockery, frustration, or the muzzle of censorship, we set the stage for mutual growth.

The clash of ideas, handled with patience, polishes rough thoughts into clearer gems, handled with hostility, it only scatters shards.

This is why I place such high value on principled resolve.

I admire people who hold their ground with quiet, unflinching courage, even when they must stand in a clearing of doubt with no allies in sight.

Agreement with me is beside the point.

What matters is the integrity to protect one's hard-won understanding while still listening for new evidence, new angles, new sparks.

Those who can balance steadfastness with openness become invaluable guardians of truth.

When a clearer, more accurate picture at last emerges, whether through fresh data, deeper reflection, or collective experience, they are the ones poised to recognize it, embrace it, and defend it.

Their convictions are anchored not in stubbornness but in a living commitment to keep testing, refining, and, when necessary, reshaping what they believe.

So, read my words not as marching orders but as trail markers.

Pause at each, look around, and choose your own direction.

If a sentence lingers in your mind tonight, nudging you awake with a new "what if?" tomorrow, then these pages have done their modest work.

The rest is, and always will be, up to you.

Chapter 117

Problems

Problems often stride into our awareness wearing the armor of insurmountability, projecting bulk and menace like towering cliffs that block the horizon.

In truth, most of these looming figures are nothing more than misunderstandings dressed in heavy shadows.

We hand them heft the moment we slap on the word problem, a label that implies permanence, resistance, even a kind of authority.

By naming an event this way, we unconsciously announce, This thing is bigger than me, and it instantly becomes so, at least in our perception.

The Creation-Energy teachings pull back that curtain of illusion.

They propose that reality is fluid, responsive, and forever inviting us to decode its subtle messages.

When examined through this lens, each "problem" reveals itself as a pocket of incomplete comprehension, a hiccup in perspective where two or more viewpoints have yet to align.

What looks like an impasse is usually a conversation waiting to happen between facts we only half-understand.

The teachings guide us to listen more closely, to ask better questions, and to recognize that discord is merely the clatter caused by puzzle pieces still searching for their rightful fit.

With genuine understanding, exploitation loses its foothold.

A person who sees clearly cannot be manipulated by fear, guilt, or half-truths, because they recognize those tactics as noise rather than signals.

Every challenge, no matter how tangled, carries its solution nested inside our own awareness, much like a seed already contains the blueprint of a towering tree.

Instead of pleading for rescue from outside forces, we turn our gaze inward, cultivating quiet, curiosity, and self-trust until the answer germinates and rises into view.

Viewed from this elevated vantage, life undergoes an astonishing metamorphosis.

What once felt like a battlefield morphs into an expansive playground, vibrant with experiments in creativity and connection.

Each circumstance, pleasant or prickly, becomes a fresh invitation to test our growing insight, to refine our compassion, and to celebrate existence itself.

Realizing this is the most precious gift a human can receive, for it transforms every breath into an opportunity to learn, to love, and to thrive without limit.

Chapter 118

True change

❖━━━━━◆◆◆━━━━━❖

You are not here to change others.

That is not your purpose on this beautiful, living Earth, and in truth, no one truly has the power to change another person.

Each individual is shaped by their own experiences, thoughts, feelings, and the lessons they are meant to learn in their own time.

Trying to force change upon someone can lead to resistance, pain, and disconnection.

It often stems from a desire to control rather than understand, and it can distract you from your own inner work.

You must come to realize that real influence does not come from demanding change in others, it arises naturally when you embody your own transformation.

Instead, your true purpose is to live, to be present in the full range of human experience, to grow from your challenges, and to awaken to the wisdom that lies in every moment.

Life is not merely a sequence of events but a sacred opportunity to evolve.

Through joy and sorrow, connection and solitude, you are learning how to love, not just romantically, but deeply and universally.

To love means to hold compassion, patience, and acceptance for yourself and others.

It means choosing kindness even when it's difficult, and understanding that every human being is doing the best they can with what they know and have.

You are here to become a real human being, not just biologically, but spiritually, emotionally, and morally.

This means becoming conscious of your thoughts, being responsible for your actions, and being honest about your intentions.

It means choosing growth over comfort, truth over illusion, and empathy over judgment.

Your role is not to shape others into a version you prefer, but to recognize their freedom and respect their journey.

Everyone is evolving in their own way, at their own pace, and that diversity of paths is what makes life rich and meaningful.

Most importantly, you are here to change yourself.

The real work of transformation begins within, to identify your shadows, nurture your light, and allow your truest self to emerge.

As you become more authentic, more aligned with your inner values and truths, you begin to radiate that energy outward.

You do not need to convince others of anything, your example becomes a silent inspiration.

You are here to express your psyche's essence through your words, your actions, and your way of being.

And in doing so, you fulfill your purpose, not by changing the world outside of you, but by awakening the fullness of life within you.

Chapter 119

Turns

Life, in all its depth and wonder, can be seen as a great, unfolding tapestry, one in which each of us takes turns playing many roles. We shift between being the teacher and the student, the helper and the one in need, the leader and the follower, across countless moments, relationships, and lifetimes.

These roles are not assigned randomly or without purpose, rather, they are deeply intertwined with our Creation Energy's journey, offering us opportunities to experience different perspectives and gather the lessons we need.

Every interaction, every challenge, and every joy contributes to this ever-changing picture of growth and understanding.

As the threads of time continue weaving our stories together, we realize that no role is too small or insignificant, each one adds meaning and balance to the larger design.

In the present moment, in this life you are living now, you are fulfilling a role that aligns with your deeper spiritual needs and lessons.

This role, whether it feels easy or difficult, celebrated or unseen, was chosen for a reason.

It provides the exact experiences you need to evolve, heal, and awaken to your greater potential.

It may involve struggle, limitation, or heartache, but within these experiences lie the seeds of wisdom and strength.

Conversely, it may be filled with ease, privilege, or visibility, and even then, it carries its own unique set of lessons and responsibilities.

Once this realization dawns that our present circumstances serve our higher growth, our outlook begins to shift.

We stop seeing ourselves as victims of life and start embracing our roles as participants in a deeper process of transformation.

With this understanding, the need to compare ourselves to others diminishes.

Envy, jealousy, and resentment fall away when we see that every individual is walking their own sacred path, filled with lessons tailored specifically for them.

The glamour, wealth, or recognition another person may have does not make their life more meaningful or valuable than yours.

Nor does someone else's obscurity or hardship imply a lack of growth or purpose.

What matters is how fully and honestly each person embraces their own journey.

We are not here to compete or to measure our worth against others, but to awaken to the truth that each life path is as necessary and valid as the next.

When we shift our attention inward, we stop being distracted by the illusions of external status and begin to nurture our inner evolution.

Therefore, let your focus rest gently on your own life.

Ask yourself how you can grow, how you can contribute, and how you can embody kindness, integrity, and justice more fully each day.

True success is not determined by wealth, fame, or validation from others, but by the quality of your character and the sincerity of your actions.

No matter what role you currently occupy, whether it is grand or humble, you have the power to influence the world positively through the choices you make and the love you bring into it.

Commit to becoming a more compassionate and conscious human being, and in doing so, you will not only elevate yourself, but also inspire those around you to do the same.

Life's greatest achievement is not found in outer appearances, but in the quiet, steady transformation of the soul.

Chapter 120

Knowledge

Everyone needs knowledge, as it is a fundamental requirement for personal development, self-awareness, and a meaningful existence.

Knowledge is not only about gathering information but about learning how to think critically, solve problems, and understand the nature of life and reality.

It allows individuals to gain insight into their own behavior, the behavior of others, and the world around them.

With knowledge, people become equipped to make informed choices, contribute constructively to society, and lead a life guided by reason and clarity rather than confusion or blind belief.

Despite the universal need for knowledge, not everyone shows an interest in seeking it.

This lack of interest is often not due to laziness or stubbornness, but rather a reflection of the individual's current state of consciousness.

Some people have not yet reached the level of awareness necessary to recognize the value of knowledge or to process complex ideas.

Their minds may still be preoccupied with more immediate or superficial concerns, making it difficult for them to focus on deeper understanding.

This is not a failure, but a natural stage in the evolution of consciousness that everyone must pass through in their own time.

Because of these differences in mental and spiritual development, it becomes clear that patience is a crucial virtue.

It is unrealistic to expect every person to awaken to higher understanding at the same moment or in the same way.

Just as a seed takes time to grow into a tree, so too does the human mind require time to open up to greater awareness.

Pushing or forcing others to learn before they are ready will lead to resistance or misunderstanding.

Patience allows for space and time, creating the conditions necessary for genuine inner growth.

Equally important is the virtue of understanding.

When we recognize that every individual is on a unique path of development, we can relate to them with compassion instead of frustration.

Understanding means accepting that people will arrive at the truth when they are mentally and emotionally prepared.

It encourages us to listen, to empathize, and to support rather than criticize.

In practicing both patience and understanding, we help create a world where the pursuit of knowledge is encouraged, respected, and allowed to flourish naturally.

Chapter 121

Au contraire

One of the frequently asked questions I've heard people ask is a seemingly clever observation, which questions why so many Christians don't actually follow the Bible they claim to believe in.

At first glance, it feels like a pointed and valid critique of religious hypocrisy, a call to integrity and consistency in faith.

And for many, it resonates as a kind of mic-drop moment.

But the truth is far more complicated and revealing.

What this kind of critique often exposes isn't just a perceived inconsistency in behavior, it reveals a widespread lack of understanding about what the Bible actually says.

Most people, whether religious or not, have never taken the time to sit down and thoroughly read the scriptures, let alone study the historical, linguistic, or cultural contexts in which they were written.

Instead, snippets, quotes, and Sunday sermon summaries are often treated as representative of the whole, leaving a vast landscape of troubling passages unexplored.

If more people truly engaged with the Bible in its entirety, they might come to see that many Christians are actually aligning with scripture more often than assumed, just not always in the most obvious or extreme ways.

They might also realize that the pick-and-choose approach to interpretation isn't necessarily hypocrisy, it may be a conscious and necessary act of moral filtering.

Because if Christians were to follow the Bible literally, word for word, without any interpretation or ethical reflection, the resulting society would be unrecognizably harsh, and in many ways, dangerously unjust.

The Bible contains numerous passages prescribing stoning as punishment for relatively minor infractions, permitting slavery, enforcing strict purity codes, and commanding women to marry their rapists.

These are not obscure, hidden verses buried in forgotten corners, they're part of the same text that millions revere and turn to for spiritual guidance.

And so, the reality is sobering: a literal and unfiltered application of biblical law would lead to consequences most of us would find morally repugnant today.

It would mean legal systems governed by ancient, often brutal codes.

It would mean the suppression of freedoms, the institutionalization of cruelty, and a rigid structure of social control that's incompatible with modern values of justice, compassion, and human dignity.

In this light, the selective interpretation of scripture, though sometimes portrayed as inconsistency, is in fact a kind of moral evolution.

Most modern Christians recognize, whether consciously or not, that some parts of the Bible must be understood symbolically, culturally, or in historical context.

They interpret through the lens of contemporary ethics, compassion, and common sense.

They leave behind the parts that conflict with their conscience, while holding on to teachings about love, forgiveness, and service.

This isn't always a perfect process, and it can lead to contradictions or inconsistencies.

But it is also what allows religion to coexist with a more enlightened and humane society.

And in a strange way, it may be the inconsistencies, the unwillingness to follow scripture to the letter, that protect us from the darkest implications of the text.

So rather than asking why Christians don't follow the Bible more literally, maybe the better question is, why do these violent, outdated, and oppressive verses still sit quietly in the pages of a book so widely respected?

Why is there so little mainstream conversation about reexamining or removing them?

Ultimately, the selective application of scripture may not be a flaw at all, it may be the very safeguard that keeps some of the Bible's most dangerous doctrines from ever being enacted again.

Chapter 122

Feel

Through the profound insights I've gained from the Creation Energy Teaching of the herald Billy Meier, I've come to a deep realization, many people live their lives heavily burdened by fear, insecurity, and inner confusion.

These feelings often lie beneath the surface, quietly influencing their thoughts, behaviors, and choices, even when they aren't fully aware of it.

Like unseen currents beneath calm waters, these emotions move and steer the direction of their lives.

This understanding has awakened within me a deeper sense of perception, a sensitivity not only to my own inner states but also to those of the people I encounter.

I've become more attuned to the subtle expressions of human emotion, the way pain hides behind forced smiles, how joy quietly radiates from a calm presence, or how yearning can echo in a single glance.

I feel what others feel, not by absorbing their energy or losing myself in their turmoil, but by standing beside them with openness and clarity.

This expanded awareness has brought about a fundamental transformation in how I relate to others.

Where once I might have judged or tried to fix what I sensed, I now simply observe with a quiet understanding.

I no longer feel the need to interpret others' emotions as right or wrong, nor do I allow their internal unrest to disturb my own balance.

Instead, I acknowledge their experiences as natural and necessary parts of their unique journey through life and evolution.

By cultivating this state of empathetic detachment, I maintain a deep and abiding inner peace.

I remain grounded in my own center while staying intimately connected to the emotional landscapes around me.

My heart is open, but not overwhelmed.

My awareness is clear, but not cold.

I witness without interference and listen without judgment.

This way of being allows me to offer a more authentic kind of support, silent, steady, and compassionate.

I do not take on others' pain as my own, but I honor it.

I do not try to carry their burdens, but I walk beside them with presence and respect.

Through this balance of feeling and detachment, I experience a richer, more harmonious connection to the world and to all those who inhabit it.

Chapter 123

The true life

—◆—◆◆—◆—

The true life is not what is seen on the outside, but what is nurtured and experienced within.

It is in the quiet, hidden world of one's inner being that life actually begins.

What manifests outwardly as behavior, choices, and circumstance is merely the echo of that internal reality.

For this reason, no outer change can truly be made until the inner world is understood, harmonized, and guided with clarity.

The inner self is the source of all that you experience.

Every word you speak, every decision you make, and every relationship you form is born from your thoughts and the state of your consciousness.

There is no outer enemy, no unfair fate, no external savior, only the reflection of your own inner condition playing itself out in the theater of material existence.

Most human beings spend their entire lives trying to fix, escape, or manipulate their outer circumstances.

They run from one distraction to the next, one person to another, one dream after the other, all without ever turning inward to face the self.

And so they suffer endlessly, blaming life for the very results they themselves have planted through their own inner imbalance and ignorance.

But the moment you realize that the key lies within, a quiet power begins to awaken.

You start to understand that your thoughts are not just fleeting ideas, they are living forces that shape reality.

You begin to witness how your attitudes create your mood, your mood your actions, and your actions your destiny.

From this realization, self-mastery becomes not only possible but inevitable.

If you wish to change your life, begin by changing how you think.

The thoughts you allow to linger in your mind form the blueprint for your future.

Negative thoughts become sickness and strife.

Harmonious thoughts become peace and prosperity.

This is not superstition or wishful thinking, this is the neutral and precise law of cause and effect at work, governed by the Creation itself.

Your mind is the steering wheel of your existence.

It can guide you into darkness or lead you toward the light, the direction depends on your will and understanding.

No one can steer it for you.

You alone must become conscious of your own power, for in that responsibility lies your freedom.

Once the inner life is brought into alignment, the outer life naturally follows.

There is no need to chase wealth, status, or approval.

These things come and go like waves on the sea.

But inner peace, forged through self-discipline and clarity, remains unmoved, and from that center, the material world can be navigated without fear or confusion.

This is not to say that difficulties will vanish, but rather that you will meet them with a new strength.

Life will no longer appear random or cruel.

Every challenge becomes a mirror, every success a reflection.

You will learn to walk in the world with grace because you are no longer driven by chaos within.

You live from the core, the true self, where the Creation dwells in quiet constancy.

So remember, the true life is always lived from within.

That is where freedom begins.

That is where truth resides.

And it is only by mastering the inner realm that you may come to master the outer world.

Everything else is an illusion.

Chapter 124

The play

Life is like a grand, eternal play.

But unlike a traditional performance, there isn't just one script or one stage.

Instead, there are as many plays as there are human beings.

Each individual lives within their own unique production, crafted from their own thoughts, perceptions, choices, and inner world.

No two life plays are identical, yet they unfold simultaneously, intertwining and influencing one another in subtle and sometimes dramatic ways.

Every person is both the actor and the director of their own life play.

This truth is often overlooked, as many live passively, thinking life is something that happens to them rather than something they actively shape.

But the moment you understand that you are the creator of your own story, everything begins to shift.

The spotlight turns inward, and the stage becomes your mind, your will, and your conscious decisions.

This realization has grown clearer to me through the Creation Energy Teachings brought forth by Billy Meier.

These teachings reveal not only the structure of life itself but also the internal mechanisms behind our experiences.

They show that thoughts are not fleeting or meaningless, they are the scripts we follow.

Our thinking is the stagehand that arranges every scene, whether we realize it or not.

Now, life doesn't come to me randomly or without meaning.

I do not drift with the winds of circumstance or blame others for the direction of my path.

Instead, I create my life intentionally, but only within the bounds of my own play.

This is where my power begins and ends.

I no longer seek to control or interfere with the plays of others, for they, too, are directing their own productions, whether consciously or unconsciously.

Understanding this has brought great clarity.

I no longer get entangled in the drama of other people's plays.

Their choices, their outcomes, their illusions or awakenings are their responsibility, not mine.

I can observe, I can even care, but I don't step into roles that aren't mine to play.

I do not try to rewrite their scenes or narrate their journeys.

Each play has its own rhythm, its own lessons, and its own consequences.

Just as I am free to direct mine, others are free to direct theirs.

And that freedom is sacred.

Interference only creates confusion, conflict, and distortion in the unfolding of another's truth.

Respecting this is part of true human evolution, letting others live as they choose, while we refine and uplift our own creation.

This perspective also brings peace.

When you realize that you're not responsible for every storyline around you, you can finally focus inward.

You can concentrate on your growth, your development, and your alignment with the timeless laws of Creation.

You can pour your energy into refining your thoughts, expanding your consciousness, and creating a play that is truthful, meaningful, and in harmony with the universal laws.

In the end, life is not something that happens to you, it is something you perform.

Every thought is a line, every emotion a spotlight, every action a choice in stage direction.

And when you truly awaken to that, you step off the stage of unconsciousness and into the light of self-responsibility.

That is when the real play begins.

Chapter 125

My own lane

❧◆❧

I travel through life like one who drives in their own lane, with both hands calmly resting on the wheel.

My direction is clear only to me, and I remain focused on the road that lies before me.

I neither veer left nor right for distractions that do not belong to my path.

My movement is conscious, deliberate, and mine alone.

The pace at which I move is dictated not by fear, envy, or pressure, but by my own inner compass.

I do not rush to keep up with others, nor do I slow down to match the pace of those who hesitate.

What appears to be stillness to some may be progress to me.

For I know that evolution cannot be measured by speed but only by conscious striving.

I am not engaged in a race.

Life is no competition, and no trophy awaits those who rush past their inner growth to beat others.

To race is to invite chaos, and chaos breeds imbalance.

True fulfillment lies not in arriving first, but in arriving whole and aware.

I do not occupy myself with the lanes beside me.

What others do, where they go, or how they move is of no relevance to my becoming.

To be obsessed with others' paths is to abandon my own.

Their curves, exits, or detours are not mine to analyze or judge.

I recognize that each human being is on their own journey, shaped by their thoughts, choices, and evolutionary needs.

They, too, must steer their lives, face their own storms, and awaken at their own rhythm.

No one can live another's life or walk for them their rightful path.

I acknowledge this, and so I offer neither interference nor criticism.

Instead, I grant them the same freedom I claim for myself: the right to learn, err, and rise again without the shadow of external control.

True respect is born of this understanding.

In keeping my attention rooted on my own road, I act in harmony with the creational law of self-responsibility.

Only I am responsible for the direction, quality, and consequences of my journey.

Only I can correct my missteps, realign my thoughts, and restore my balance.

And in this silent discipline of self-guided motion, I find peace.

There is no anxiety in not knowing the path of another, only a quiet confidence in honoring my own.

Through it, I unfold as I must, moment by moment, experience by experience.

So I remain where I belong, centered, aware, and accountable.

For it is not the traffic around me, but the truth within me, that determines the worth of my way.

And with that knowing, I drive on.

Chapter 126

I understand deeply now

◆────────◆◆◆────────◆

I understand deeply now, in a way I never did before.

Thanks to the profound and illuminating Creation Energy Teachings brought forth by Billy Meier, I have experienced a remarkable transformation in my comprehension of human behavior and consciousness.

These teachings have not only broadened my intellectual understanding but have also stirred a deep, inner awakening that reshapes the way I perceive myself and others.

Through this invaluable knowledge, my awareness has been sharpened and expanded.

I find that I am now able to look beyond the surface of everyday interactions, beyond appearances, beyond words, and perceive the subtle forces and impulses that drive human thought, speech, and action.

What once seemed like a mere coincidence or inexplicable behavior now presents itself as an understandable and even predictable expression of deeper psychological and spiritual patterns.

This newfound clarity allows me to interpret human behavior with a level of precision and compassion I could not previously imagine.

The unspoken tensions, the brief hesitations, the carefully chosen words or the seemingly random outbursts, all these expressions now carry deeper meaning, like verses of a silent language.

Even silence itself, once a source of confusion or uncertainty, has become a meaningful part of that greater symphony of human expression.

No longer do I feel lost or bewildered in the face of others' moods, reactions, or apparent contradictions.

Instead, I observe calmly, with growing empathy and understanding, realizing that all human behavior, whether conscious or unconscious, is a mirror reflecting the internal landscape of the individual.

Emotional outbursts, thoughtful comments, defensive silence, or peaceful stillness, all are signals, revealing truths about a person's inner world.

The Creation Energy Teachings have become a framework through which I can view the world with greater coherence and depth.

They provide a solid foundation for recognizing and interpreting the patterns of thought and energy that shape behavior.

I have come to realize that every person I encounter is expressing, moment by moment, the current state of their inner development, their balance, or imbalance, between consciousness, subconsciousness, and spirit.

This insight has brought with it not only clarity, but also a deepened sense of compassion and responsibility.

I now approach others not with judgment or irritation, but with a sense of curiosity and care.

I understand that behind every difficult behavior lies a cause, often rooted in suffering, ignorance, or internal conflict.

And behind every wise or kind action lies effort, growth, and conscious striving.

Rather than reacting impulsively or emotionally, I find myself pausing, observing, and allowing space for myself and for others.

This inner stillness creates room for genuine understanding to arise.

It is as if the veil that once separated me from others has lifted, allowing me to connect more authentically with those around me.

In this way, human behavior has become like a clear, open book, one that I can read with growing fluency.

Each interaction becomes an opportunity to deepen my awareness and refine my understanding of the complex, yet lawful, nature of human consciousness.

This transformation in perception is a priceless gift.

It has given me a deeper sense of connection to all human beings, as well as a renewed commitment to live consciously, kindly, and responsibly.

I now strive not only to understand others more fully but also to continually refine myself, so that I, too, may act as clearly and wisely as possible, in alignment with the truth of the Creation.

Through this ongoing journey, I remain grateful for the clarity and wisdom that the teachings have brought into my life.

They have become a compass by which I navigate the intricacies of human relationships and an anchor that steadies me in an ever-changing world.

Chapter 127

Our closest ally

I've come to a deep realization over time, truth is our closest ally, yet paradoxically, it's often the most overlooked.

We spend so much of our lives chasing after answers, searching high and low, believing that truth must be hidden in distant places or revealed through some dramatic experience.

But the truth is so close, you can't see it.

It lives within us, quiet and unassuming, often drowned out by the noise of the external world.

We think truth must be complex or far away, when in fact, it's simple and near, so near that we pass it by every day without recognizing it.

It doesn't shout or demand attention, it simply waits, steady and patient, for us to notice.

This understanding didn't come in a sudden flash but gradually revealed itself through life experiences, patterns, and reflection.

I began to notice that the things most essential to us, truth, love, and peace, are not loud or boastful.

They do not clamor for recognition.

Instead, they are embedded in our daily lives, in our inner knowing, and in the people around us.

And yet, we tend to overlook them.

We are drawn to the distant, the unfamiliar, the elusive, thinking it holds more value.

Just like truth, the people who love us the most are often right beside us, and still, we fail to truly see them.

We grow accustomed to their presence, take their constancy for granted, and in doing so, miss the quiet miracle of being genuinely cared for.

We often pour our energy into seeking approval from those who remain out of reach, who offer their affection sparingly or conditionally.

We chase what is uncertain, hoping it will validate our worth.

Meanwhile, we ignore the loyal presence of those who love us without demand, the ones who stand by us not for what we offer, but for who we are.

This same blindness applies to truth.

Because it feels too familiar, too accessible, we question its significance.

We overlook what is deeply real simply because it does not dazzle or elude us.

The truth is so close, it blends into the background of our lives.

Like air or light, it's essential but often invisible, until we finally choose to look inward and become aware.

This shift in perspective has changed me.

I've learned to pause, to turn inward, and to trust that what I'm seeking may already be within me.

I've come to honor the love that surrounds me, to see the value in what I once overlooked.

Truth doesn't need to be hunted down, it needs to be remembered.

It asks for our attention, not our pursuit.

And those who love us don't need to be impressed or won over, they need only to be seen.

The truth is so close, you can't see it, until you slow down, open your heart, and look with intention.

Only then does it reveal itself in full clarity, bringing with it a peace that was always waiting to be known.

Chapter 128

The Pope

❖◆❖◆❖

The pope, like all others, is a man on his own journey.

He walks his path shaped by the decisions he made, the beliefs he upheld, and the vision he held for his life.

Becoming the pope may appear to be the pinnacle of spiritual achievement to many, yet in truth, it is simply one form of a life lived with commitment to an ideal.

That ideal may be noble in intention, but it is still bound by human limitations.

He, too, was once a child, uncertain of the world, searching for purpose, just as every person must.

To elevate him beyond what he is, a human being, is to deny your own worth.

No title, robe, or ceremonial act can bestow true greatness upon a person.

Greatness comes from inner growth, the quiet battles of conscience, and the choices made when no one is watching.

You possess that same capacity.

Your words, your thoughts, your actions carry just as much weight in the spiritual balance of life as his.

The idea that one human can be closer to Creation than another is a distortion.

No one is born superior or inferior.

The laws and recommendations of Creation apply to all equally, regardless of title or fame.

If a man calls himself holy but lives without humility, then his words are but noise.

If a person lives without recognition but lives in truth and love, then their life echoes in the cosmos.

Too often, humanity gives away its power by placing others on pedestals.

Be it religious leaders, politicians, or celebrities, this worship blinds the psyche to its own light.

You are not meant to bow to another human being, for you are not lesser.

Respect may be given where it is due, but reverence belongs only to the eternal truth, never to a name or a face.

The pope is responsible for his own development, just as you are for yours.

His role may guide millions, but that guidance does not exempt him from error.

Like all of us, he learns, he struggles, he doubts, and he must confront himself in the silence of his own thoughts.

Do not mistake his status for spiritual completion.

No one is beyond the path of evolution.

Creation recognizes no crowns or titles.

It recognizes the growth of consciousness, the expansion of wisdom, and the cultivation of love and peace.

These are not bound by religious roles or the hierarchy of institutions.

They are achieved through effort, learning, reflection, and alignment with the natural laws that govern all existence.

Never place any human being above yourself.

When you do so, you make yourself small, and in that smallness, you forget your purpose and your potential.

The pope, the teacher, the farmer, the artist, all walk side by side before Creation.

Each has its own contribution, and none is greater or lesser than another when measured by truth.

Live with awareness that you are a vital part of existence.

Speak with dignity.

Think with clarity.

Act with purpose.

And know that your value is not determined by titles, by robes, or by recognition, but by how sincerely you live in harmony with the truth of your own being.

Chapter 129

For the world to truly know peace

I n order for the world to truly know peace, every race must first learn to unite within itself.

This unity is not about exclusion or superiority, but about healing the inner wounds that have been carried through centuries of division, oppression, and confusion.

When a race is at odds with itself, when its people harbor resentment, jealousy, or distrust toward one another, then peace with others remains impossible.

The inner disunity naturally manifests outwardly, creating the illusion that the world is in disorder, when in truth, it is the human beings within who are not whole.

The world we see is nothing more than a reflection of the collective inner state of humanity.

Each conflict, each injustice, and each act of violence is born first in the thoughts, feelings, and unresolved traumas of individuals.

Societies reflect these internal dynamics on a mass scale.

When individuals are lost within themselves, so too are their communities.

When individuals become centered, wise, and self-responsible, their collective environment will inevitably mirror that harmony.

A divided people cannot bring order to the world, because their inner disorder will ripple out into their relationships, their institutions, and even their future generations.

It is not enough to call for unity across racial and ethnic lines when the members of each group remain fragmented within their own circles.

True unity begins with inner transformation, and only then can cooperation, trust, and understanding develop across racial and cultural boundaries.

Through my own observations, rooted deeply in the knowledge I've gathered from the Creation Energy Teachings, I've come to recognize a higher pattern unfolding throughout humanity's evolution.

The chaos we witness today is not permanent, but transitional.

It is part of the purification process.

Humanity is slowly learning the painful lessons of its separation and disharmony, and although the road is long, it leads toward a future where wisdom will finally prevail.

In that distant future, I can see a time when all human beings, regardless of their skin color, will live in harmony with one another, not through forced integration or artificial peace, but through mutual respect and spiritual understanding.

Each group will thrive in its own rhythm, culture, and way of life, while still recognizing the shared essence that connects all human beings.

Separation will no longer mean division, but differentiation with harmony.

The knowledge and wisdom of the true messenger, Billy Meier, will one day be understood on a global scale.

His teachings, rooted in the eternal laws and recommendations of Creation, will serve as a guiding light for those who seek true freedom, peace, and spiritual evolution.

The misunderstandings and mockery that once surrounded his name will fade, and in their place will arise clarity and appreciation.

What today is seen as fringe or rejected will one day become the foundation for a new way of living.

This is not a prophecy based on hope or belief, but a clear conclusion drawn from observing the natural laws of cause and effect, and the spiritual evolution of the human being.

What is aligned with truth always rises, even if it is delayed.

So, for the world to know peace, each person must begin the process of inner reconciliation.

Only when they are whole within can they meet others without conflict.

The outer world is merely a mirror, when we polish the mirror within, we will see beauty reflected everywhere we look.

This is the path humanity must take, and eventually, it will.

Chapter 130

All seven universes

$$\bullet\!\!-\!\!-\!\!-\!\!\blacklozenge\!\!\blacklozenge\!\!-\!\!-\!\!-\!\!\bullet$$

Ａll seven universes are, in their innermost essence, one unified existence within the infinite unfolding of Creation.

Though they seem separate by form, location, and function, they are intricately bound through the same eternal laws and forces.

This unity is not a matter of perception, but of fundamental reality, for the Creation itself is indivisible, and all its manifestations are facets of a singular wholeness.

While each universe operates under its own rhythm and laws of evolution, what happens in one echoes across the others.

These echoes do not always take the same shape, for each realm interprets and expresses experience based on its unique consciousness level.

The ripple of an event or correction in one universe might bloom into a different form in another, filtered through the distinct spiritual maturity of that realm.

This interconnectedness is not only energetic but deeply spiritual.

It means that learning, evolution, and even errors do not remain isolated, they become part of a larger web of becoming.

Just as a drop of water influences the motion of an entire ocean, so too do the vibrations of one universe subtly inform the others.

The universes reflect each other, like the countless faces of a diamond turning in cosmic light, each shining a different color yet rooted in the same core.

Within the ANKAR Universe, itself nested in the wider DERN Universe, the Plejaren people experienced a great spiritual disruption through genetic manipulation.

The Syrian overlords, advanced in knowledge but spiritually stunted, interfered in their natural course of evolution.

This tampering, born not of wisdom but control, placed the Plejaren on a path of crisis, suffering, and eventually deep spiritual self-examination.

Their DNA was not shaped by their own hand but altered as part of a foreign agenda, one that cared more for domination than destiny.

And yet, the Plejaren, through inner striving, self-responsibility, and a collective yearning for peace, rose above the imposed disharmony.

With time, a Peace Sphere appeared, a conscious technology of unity and stabilization, born not only of intellect, but of spirit.

In our universe, a similar challenge unfolds, though with differences in approach and awareness.

The manipulation here is more subtle, occurring through interbreeding and the quiet entanglement of consciousness and genetics.

Again, the Syrian influence is present, but instead of open domination, it appears through misguidance and spiritual blindness.

However, humanity is not left without a path forward.

Instead of technological solutions, we are offered the teachings of BEAM, Billy Eduard Albert Meier, a man who stands as a conscious counterbalance to the chaos.

His presence represents not a physical sphere of peace, but an inward one, a spiritual corrective rooted in the timeless laws of Creation.

Through his guidance, we are given the tools to rise not by force or resistance, but by conscious recognition and inner renewal.

From this vantage point, it becomes clear that the universes do not merely mirror each other, they evolve together.

One universe may carry the seed of insight that another has yet to cultivate.

Patterns become apparent when one looks beyond form and into the principles that shape existence.

The signs may vary in color or voice, but their harmony is consistent, resonating with the eternal melody of becoming.

Therefore, our task is to cultivate inner clarity and spiritual observation.

Through study, reflection, and attunement to Creation's rhythm, we gain insight not only into our own universe but into the deeper reality that unites all.

What unfolds in ANKAR, in DERN, and in our own cosmos is part of the same eternal symphony.

The melodies may change, but the music is always the same, sung through consciousness, and heard only by the awakened heart.

Chapter 131

Palestine

A s long as the Arab world remains fragmented, the Palestinian people will remain vulnerable to the ongoing expansion of Zionist domination.

Without unified resistance, the machinery of occupation will continue to operate unchallenged, exploiting the cracks between Arab nations.

No amount of international sympathy or condemnation will bring real change unless the will to act arises from within the Arab world itself.

The plight of Palestine is not isolated, it is a mirror reflecting the internal disunity that plagues the broader Arab region.

Despite a shared cultural and linguistic heritage, Arab nations have failed to translate their commonality into collective strength.

The absence of a unified front renders every declaration of solidarity hollow, every promise of support ineffective.

Without internal coherence, external pressures always prevail.

This disunity extends beyond politics.

It is rooted in deep ideological, economic, and even spiritual fractures.

Arab countries have allowed foreign influence, sectarian rivalries, and self-interest to override their shared identity and purpose.

In such an atmosphere, unity becomes an abstract dream, and Palestine becomes a victim of both external aggression and internal neglect.

While some Arab states normalize relations with Israel under the guise of pragmatism, they simultaneously voice concern for Palestinian rights, a contradiction that weakens all credibility.

Others oppose normalization but remain passive or constrained, unable or unwilling to mobilize their influence into meaningful action.

Symbolic gestures have replaced sincere strategy, and the region continues to bleed from its own contradictions.

The Arab League, for all its history and declarations, has become largely ceremonial.

It has failed to serve as a vessel of common resolve or defense.

Its voice carries little weight when it is not backed by a unified will and coordinated action.

Palestine, once a unifying cause, now drifts through the turbulence of regional fragmentation and international indifference.

Ongoing conflicts in Syria, Yemen, and Libya have only deepened this division.

Instead of resolving these internal struggles together, Arab states often fund and support opposing factions, turning brother against brother.

The result is a region too fractured to stand for its own, let alone for the Palestinian cause.

In every crack, external powers insert themselves, deepening dependency and weakening sovereignty.

Wealthier Arab nations, rather than leading with moral clarity, often prioritize economic self-preservation or seek alliances with global superpowers.

This abandonment of principle in favor of profit has corroded the spirit of unity.

In truth, the fate of Palestine is tied directly to the moral health of the region.

When that health declines, injustice thrives unchallenged.

In this current state, the Arab world cannot shield Palestine because it cannot even shield itself.

Every weakness is weaponized, every division exploited, and every delay in unity is a victory for those who seek to dominate.

The world watches, but the burden of change lies not with the spectators, it lies with the brothers and sisters who have allowed their family to suffer in isolation.

Until Arab nations see themselves as one people with a shared past, a common soul, and a united destiny, Palestine will remain unprotected, and the region will descend further into instability.

Silence may be easier, and selective outrage may feel convenient, but only unity forged from clarity, justice, and courage will end the long chapter of betrayal.

Only then will dignity return to a people who have waited far too long.

Chapter 132

The destiny of humanity

I live in the present, fully engaged with the world around me, yet my heart and mind are deeply attuned to the destiny of humanity.

Each action I take, no matter how small, is guided by a vision that reaches beyond my own lifetime, a vision of a world where consciousness expands, where compassion guides decisions, and where humanity lives in harmony with the Earth and with itself.

I see the present moment not just as a fleeting instant, but as sacred ground upon which the seeds of our collective future are planted.

In my daily life, I strive to be intentional and aware, knowing that the quality of the future depends on the integrity of our choices now.

I feel a deep responsibility, not just as an individual, but as a participant in a shared human journey, to help shape a future where kindness is natural, where justice is universal, and where wisdom replaces fear.

The way we treat each other, the way we steward the natural world, and the truths we choose to uphold will ripple far beyond our time, shaping the consciousness and conditions of generations yet to come.

My path is not one of isolation or self-interest, but one of contribution to a larger awakening.

Whether I am learning, creating, teaching, or supporting others, I see every effort as part of a greater movement toward human evolution, a movement that transcends borders, beliefs, and divisions.

I am committed to fostering deeper understanding, to nurturing the human spirit, and to helping bring forth a civilization that honors both the material and the spiritual dimensions of life.

This calling is not just about progress in the outer world, but about a shift in the inner world, a turning toward balance, humility, and truth

Though I walk through today's world, often marked by struggle and uncertainty, I hold faith in the quiet emergence of something higher.

The future I work toward is not a fantasy, it is a potential waiting to be realized through courage, compassion, and clarity.

I know that we, as a species, are capable of awakening to our greater purpose, of healing the wounds of our past, and of co-creating a future rooted in love, peace, and unity.

And so, with each step I take in the present, I walk with the future of humanity in mind, conscious, committed, and hopeful.

Just as Russia, strong and wide,

Stands with China side by side,

Power flows where hearts align,

Unified, their stars do shine.

So shall Korea rise once more,

When South and North unlock the door,

Two halves meet, a single soul,

One bright flame, a common goal.

And Africa, with ancient grace,

Scattered tribes in time and place,

Shall become a mighty sun,

When all its children live as one.

And Palestine shall lift its head,

Free from chains and tears once shed,

When Arab hearts beat as the same,

One proud people, one proud name.

Chapter 133

As above, so is below. As within, so is without

---◆◆●◆◆---

As above, so is below. As within, so is without.

These phrases are often repeated without much thought, yet they hold immense meaning.

They are not religious quotes or mystical riddles, but fundamental truths about the structure and function of life, creation, and consciousness.

They describe the nature of reality on both the cosmic and individual scale, linking the universe to the human being in a mirror-like relationship.

As above, so is below means that what happens in one part of existence also happens in others, though not always in the same form.

Through the teachings of the Creation Energy, I have come to realize that the seven universes that exist within our DERN universe are interconnected in ways most humans do not yet comprehend.

An event, a movement, or even a vibration in one universe finds an echo in the others, but that echo is shaped by the consciousness level of each universe.

Our universe, the DERN Universe, has a twin universe called the DAL Universe.

Sfath, Billy's mentor and teacher since childhood, from the ANKAR Universe, has a twin brother.

Jmmanuel, who Christians called the son of god, had a twin brother named James.

The eye of god, a whole solar system destroyed by a crazy human being, still remains as a reminder of the follies of humans.

For us, it's the asteroid belt, the remnants of planet Malona, destroyed by its inhabitants through wars.

Just as the Plejaren once faced the threat of the Destroyer planet, humanity now confronts its own challenge in the form of asteroid Apophis.

The Plejaren follow the directives of the High Council, while we, in the future, will follow the directives of the Syrian overlords.

Each universe exists on a plane defined by vibration and lightness.

The more advanced and spiritually developed a universe is, the lighter and more refined its vibrational field.

In contrast, those with denser energies are heavier and exist "below" in the grand order.

This doesn't mean physical height or location, but spiritual position.

So, when something happens "above," it affects what is "below," although not identically, it's translated through the level of development in that realm.

That is the hidden science behind the saying.

Just as ripples move through water and alter the entire surface, actions or shifts in one realm create subtle but far-reaching influences across all others.

A discovery in a more conscious universe might lead to inspiration in a denser one.

A collapse in a lower realm may serve as a warning or catalyst in a higher one.

Everything is connected across time and existence.

As within, so is without speaks to the human being directly.

Your inner state, your thoughts, emotions, fears, and intentions, shape the world you experience.

What you see in your life is not simply what happens to you, it is what flows out from you.

If you are constantly facing struggle and confusion, it is because these conditions reflect your internal state.

If you find beauty and order, it is because you have cultivated those things within.

This is not meant to blame, but to empower.

The external world is a projection screen for the inner one.

Until a person changes their inner self, the outer world will not change in any lasting way.

The real revolution is within.

That is why spiritual evolution must begin with self-awareness and inner responsibility.

The world you create for yourself and others begins inside your own thoughts and choices.

These sayings are not metaphors, they are natural laws.

They describe how the universe operates at all levels, from the formation of galaxies to the shaping of a single human life.

They are a key to understanding the greater Creation and our individual path within it.

Ignoring them leads to confusion and repetition, understanding them opens the door to transformation.

Therefore, if we wish to heal our world, we must first heal ourselves.

If we seek to understand the universe, we must study our own consciousness.

In the reflections between the inner and outer, the above and below, lies the map to both universal truth and personal freedom.

Chapter 134

Conscious decision

I have made a conscious and fearless decision to step forward and present myself publicly as a living example of what occurs when a human being truly comes to know who they are.

This choice isn't driven by ego or a desire for attention, but by the inner necessity to live authentically and transparently.

The process of self-realization is not something abstract or mystical, it is a direct, personal experience that demands honesty, courage, and the willingness to stand alone if needed.

I'm not interested in pretending or wearing masks for comfort or approval.

What I show is raw, real, and rooted in the transformation I've undergone.

In doing so, I place myself under observation, willingly and without hesitation, as a kind of test subject, or a mirror, for others to witness.

I use myself openly, almost like a living experiment, to reflect the deep and ongoing changes that have taken place through the study and application of the Creation Energy Teachings brought forth by Billy.

These teachings are not distant philosophies or vague concepts, they are precise, clear, and direct in their impact.

They have reshaped how I think, how I perceive life, and how I relate to everything around me.

This path is practical, and the results are visible in every aspect of my daily experience.

Everything I think, every realization I reach, and every inner challenge I face is shared openly and without censorship.

I do not soften my words to gain favor, nor do I adjust myself to fit into the expectations or comfort zones of others.

The opinions, reactions, or criticisms of the outside world no longer carry any weight or influence over me.

What guides me now is not the shifting tides of external validation, but the steady, quiet strength that comes from within, a strength cultivated through deep reflection and the application of truth.

This inner compass is firm, and it keeps me upright even when I stand alone.

What these teachings uncover within us is a depth of power and clarity that has always been present, yet often hidden beneath layers of conditioning, fear, and self-doubt.

Coming into contact with that power can be overwhelming at times, it shakes the foundations of who we thought we were.

There are moments when I feel a deep intensity, even fear, as I face the enormity of what is awakening inside me.

But I keep going, step by step, because there is no turning back from the truth once it has been recognized.

This journey is not about perfection or performance, it is about becoming fully human, fully conscious, and fully responsible for one's existence.

Chapter 135

The continuity of the mission

—◆◆◆—

From Nokodemion to Billy, the seven prophets of the Nokodemion lineage have carried a sacred and important mission, to impart the Creation Energy Teachings to humanity.

These teachings are a deep well of wisdom, offering insights into the fundamental forces that shape our reality and the universe itself.

The prophets, each with their unique contributions, have worked throughout the ages to guide humanity toward spiritual enlightenment, helping us rediscover the knowledge of creation and our connection to the divine energy that flows through all things.

This mission, however, is not a new endeavor, nor is it unique to this generation.

These teachings have existed in various forms, passed down through generations and lifetimes, and some of us have encountered them before in past lives, when the messages were delivered to us by previous prophets.

The continuity of this mission over time means that many of us are not strangers to the wisdom these prophets impart.

For some, the teachings may stir a deep, almost forgotten memory, a recollection of truths we once held close but have since forgotten.

As these teachings continue to spread and reach more people, the awakening process will unfold for many.

While some may begin to recognize these truths gradually, there will be moments when a collective shift in consciousness will occur, and the momentum of awakening will rapidly gain strength.

The energy that is carried within these teachings has the potential to awaken more hearts and minds, unlocking a vast reservoir of knowledge and understanding that has been dormant for far too long.

In the early stages of this awakening, it may seem like a slow, subtle process, with some people recalling bits and pieces of what they once knew, while others remain unaware.

However, this awakening process is not linear.

As more individuals begin to connect with the teachings and their inner wisdom, the momentum will grow.

The collective consciousness will shift, and what started as a whisper will soon become a powerful wave.

People will begin to recognize the interconnectedness of all things, understand the energy that flows through them, and grasp the deeper truths about creation and their place in it.

This process will transform the way we see the world and our purpose within it, leading to a new era of spiritual awareness, healing, and harmony.

The more we open ourselves to these teachings, the more we will remember, and the faster the collective awakening will unfold.

If you have not yet started on this journey, now is the time to begin.

There is no wrong time to awaken, and the journey is always available to those who seek it.

For those who have already begun, the journey becomes one of walking together, sharing insights, supporting one another, and expanding the collective understanding.

We are all part of a greater whole, and each individual awakening contributes to the larger transformation that is taking place.

Some will remember more quickly than others, and that is simply how evolution works.

Some souls are ready to recall more, while others will take a bit more time.

There is no need for comparison or judgment, each path is uniquely perfect.

As we move forward, we are called to embrace the journey with patience, openness, and a deep trust in the process.

Through this collective awakening, we can create a world that is more connected, more loving, and more in tune with the energies of creation.

The teachings are here, and they are ready to be remembered, understood, and shared.

Let us walk this path together, with open hearts and minds, ready for the profound shifts that lie ahead.

Chapter 136
Conclusion

———◆◆◆———

Embracing DEEP for a Life of Purpose and Spiritual Growth

As we reach the conclusion of this journey, it becomes increasingly evident that this book is not merely a collection of spiritual concepts or philosophical insights.

It is a living guide, an invitation to embark on a conscious way of life rooted in truth, responsibility, and deep inner awareness.

The words on these pages are more than teachings, they are a mirror reflecting our potential and a compass pointing us toward alignment with the universal rhythm of Creation.

This journey is not ending, but evolving, urging us to carry the wisdom forward into our daily lives.

The wisdom shared through Billy's teachings offers far more than intellectual understanding.

It gives us the opportunity to realign with the natural laws of Creation, the same eternal principles that shape the cosmos, govern nature, and influence the unfolding of human consciousness.

These teachings gently, yet firmly, guide us to observe ourselves honestly, to examine our thoughts and emotions, and to make conscious choices that bring us into deeper harmony with life.

They encourage a return to simplicity, clarity, and purpose, reminding us that spiritual evolution begins with how we live each moment.

Embracing these principles is not a passive process.

It requires courage, persistence, and a willingness to grow beyond old patterns.

The path laid out in these pages challenges us to become more self-responsible and aware, to think more clearly, feel more deeply, and act more mindfully.

It invites us to dissolve illusions and let go of beliefs that no longer serve us, so we can create space for new levels of truth and understanding.

Each insight becomes a stepping stone on the path toward becoming who we are truly meant to be, balanced, free, and consciously evolving beings.

Living by the laws of Creation is not an abstract ideal but a practical and deeply personal practice.

It asks us to cultivate qualities such as integrity, compassion, humility, patience, and mindfulness in all areas of life, whether in relationships, work, or solitude.

These are not temporary efforts but lifelong commitments.

They guide us to create inner peace, emotional balance, and outer harmony, even in the face of life's inevitable challenges.

In this way, the teachings help us build a solid spiritual foundation, one that holds firm amid both joy and sorrow, success and failure.

This book gently reminds us that the work of spiritual growth is never truly finished.

It is a spiral path, one that circles deeper over time, each cycle offering new opportunities to refine our understanding and expand our consciousness.

The more we engage with these teachings, the more we recognize that true freedom does not lie in escaping life's responsibilities, but in embracing them with clarity and purpose.

With each step, we become more attuned to the wisdom within and around us, and more willing to live from a place of truth.

Moreover, the teachings help us see that we are not isolated beings, but part of a vast, interconnected web of life.

Every thought, word, and action carries energy, creating ripples that affect the whole.

As we align with the laws of Creation, we begin to live not just for ourselves, but in service to the greater good.

In this way, our personal transformation becomes a contribution to collective evolution.

We become sources of calm in chaos, clarity in confusion, and light in darkness, not because we are perfect, but because we are committed.

Whether you arrived at these teachings with a sense of familiarity or as a newcomer, this book marks a significant threshold in your personal journey.

For some, it will awaken deep inner memories and reignite a long-standing spiritual pursuit.

For others, it will plant seeds of awareness that will continue to grow across many lifetimes.

In either case, the impact is real and lasting.

The encounter itself is a sacred moment, one that calls us to recognize the deeper meaning and purpose of our existence.

In the end, this is not simply a book to be read, but a path to be lived.

It asks us to return again and again to the center of our being, to the silent wisdom of Creation energy that dwells within us all.

By choosing to walk this path with openness and dedication, we give ourselves the gift of transformation.

We awaken not only to who we are, but to who we are becoming.

And in that awakening, we find our place within the unfolding story of life, evolution, and spiritual fulfillment.

Final Chapter

The re-encounter of the teachings

◆━━━━━◆✦◆━━━━━◆

According to the teachings, when a person encounters the Creation Energy Teachings or the Spiritual Teachings, it is rarely a random event.

More often than not, such an encounter points to the existence of certain impulses that have already been stored and accepted within the individual's storage banks.

These impulses originate from experiences in past lives, where the person, in a different personality, previously came into contact with or studied the same or similar teachings.

The presence of these stored impulses acts like a subconscious memory, influencing the person's current life path and drawing them toward these spiritual materials once again.

This suggests that the meeting with the teachings is not by coincidence but a continuation of a development that began long before.

In cases where the person had significant past-life experiences with the Spiritual Teachings, the impulses stored in the storage banks can exert a strong effect on the individual in their present life.

This can manifest as an intense inner pull or a sudden deep interest in the teachings, even if the person has no conscious memory of having ever studied such material before.

The encounter may be accompanied by a strong emotional response, feelings of familiarity, or a deep inner knowing.

The person might feel as though they have found something they had always been looking for, without being able to explain why.

Such intensity is typically the result of previously absorbed impulses being activated in the new life cycle, guiding the person back to their spiritual path with a sense of urgency or purpose.

Conversely, if the person is engaging with the Spiritual Teachings for the very first time in their evolution, the process is usually more gradual and less intense.

Without the support of pre-existing impulses in the storage banks, the teachings may initially appear foreign or difficult to grasp.

The person might need more time to warm up to the concepts and to develop an emotional or intellectual connection with the material.

Interest and understanding grow slowly, often requiring repeated exposure, study, and reflection before any deeper recognition or resonance can occur.

This slower pace does not imply a lack of potential but rather indicates the beginning of a new phase in the individual's spiritual evolution, one that lays the groundwork for future lives.

Regardless of whether the encounter is a reawakening of past experiences or a brand-new introduction, the process of finding and engaging with the Spiritual Teachings is a vital milestone in a person's path of consciousness development.

For those returning to the teachings, it can be seen as a reactivation of earlier spiritual efforts, bringing renewed opportunity for deeper understanding and growth.

For newcomers, it signifies the planting of seeds that may flourish over many lifetimes.

Either way, the meeting with the Spiritual Teachings opens the door to profound inner transformation and a clearer recognition of the universal laws and principles that govern life, evolution, and existence itself.